Demanding Choices

Demanding Choices

Opinion, Voting, and Direct Democracy

Shaun Bowler

and

Todd Donovan

Ann Arbor

THE UNIVERSITY OF MICHIGAN PRESS

First paperback edition 2000
Copyright © by the University of Michigan 1998
All rights reserved
Published in the United States of America by
The University of Michigan Press
Manufactured in the United States of America
⊖ Printed on acid-free paper

2003   2002   2001   2000   5   4   3   2

A CIP catalog record for this book is available from the British Library.

Library of Congress Cataloging-in-Publication Data

Bowler, Shaun, 1958–
    Demanding choices : opinion, voting, and direct democracy /
Shaun Bowler and Todd Donovan.
        p.   cm.
    Includes bibliographical references and index.
    ISBN 0-472-10942-1 (cloth : acid-free paper)
    1. Representative government and representation.   2. Elections.
3. Democracy.   4. Referendum.   I. Donovan, Todd.   II. Title.
JF1051 .B54   1998
321.8—dc21   98-19714
                                                                    CIP

ISBN 0-472-08715-0 (pbk. : alk. paper)

Contents

Figures

Tables

Preface

Contemporary scholars of politics often find direct democracy invidious and are pessimistic about prospects for voter competence in this arena. There may be good reasons for this pessimism, not the least of which are that academics know of initiatives that target minorities, while many also work in institutions that have suffered from citizen-initiated tax policies. Initiatives also limit the careers of legislators, a vocation with which some political scientists have close working relations. That could explain why our colleagues often state emphatically that voters cannot understand what they are doing when deciding on complex issues that have far-reaching consequences. Yet it is difficult to for us, or for our colleagues, to come up with many examples of approved initiatives that participating voters really did not want, or of successful initiatives voters would otherwise reject with the benefit of hindsight. How is it then, that voters come to figure out what they are doing?

This book is about voting in direct democracy. We do not attempt to provide a wide-ranging overview here—others have done so already. Readers who want more background on the process should consult Magleby 1984 and Cronin 1989. We present an analysis of how citizens might sensibly figure out what they are for or against when voting on ballot issues. Our study is motivated by some of the most enduring normative questions of politics: How democratic can a society be? Are citizens up to the task of making direct decisions on policy issues? Do democratic citizens mistakenly approve things in elections that they really did not want?

We approach these questions in fairly practical terms by asking if voters have minimal amounts of easily accessible information at their disposal and if they make choices that "make sense" given their interests and given the information they have. We assess these questions from several angles and find that there are numerous ways that voters get information and navigate the demanding context of direct democracy. Rather than positing a uniform model of choice that applies to all voters for all issues, we start with the assumption that different voters use different cues and information to decide on different types of issues. We also assume that a voter's cognitive abilities affect how she or he might go about reasoning on any given issue.

By starting with these assumptions, we can build models that reflect how well-educated voters think about initiatives as well as how voters with limited cognitive abilities can reason instrumentally about the choices presented to them. In the end, we present a more optimistic view of voter competence in direct democracy than have many previous studies. This does not mean that the citizen lawmaking necessarily produces good or bad outcomes. We suggest, however, that while direct democracy has its failings, the flaws do not necessarily lie with citizens being "duped," nor with voters approving things they do not want or do not understand at some basic level.

Throughout this book, we look at the direct-democracy decision context as one that forces voters to make choices with limited information. This perspective is consistent with that of recent works by Ferejohn and Kuklinski (1990), Popkin (1991), Sniderman, Brody, and Tetlock (1991), and Page and Shapiro (1992), among others, and it draws from a range of voting studies. In this complex decision context, voters can be expected to use shortcuts, to be risk averse, and to respond to external cues. For some voters, existing attitudes, values, and outlooks on politics—wrapped up in their political ideology—can help them evaluate various ballot measures. A simple way for many voters to manage the information demands is to use decision shortcuts and to approach choices with a default behavior that predisposes them to simply vote *no*. As we see in chapter 2, a *no* vote need not be a reflection of blanket confusion if it is systematically associated with the uncertainty and information demands that are part of ballot proposition choices.

In chapter 2, we see that the perspectives of early, prebehavioral-era critics of American state-level direct democracy were largely adopted later by behavioral-era political scientists using quantitative methods. We address this central and long-standing concern by examining microlevel behavior in direct-democracy elections. We test how voters might deal with the demands of frequent, statewide direct-democracy elections. Chapter 2 also includes a brief discussion of academic voting literature, with a demonstration of how much of the contemporary voting literature is consistent with the historical critiques of direct democracy. There are traditions in the academic literature, however, that bring us some way toward understanding how voters might sort through the demands created by voting in a direct democracy.

In chapter 3, we examine how abstention and *no* votes are a response to the information demands presented by direct democracy. But voters do not always vote *no*. How is it that they come to make the choices that they do? Why should we expect that their votes represent any sort of policy-related thinking? Because different ballot choices contain different content and cover different issues, we cannot propose a single, universally applicable model of voting behavior. Rather, we argue that each choice creates its own information demands as well as its own opportunities for voters to find the information they need and to apply shortcuts to the process of evaluating policies.

Theories of reasoning under limited information also suggest that voters who have different cognitive abilities might use different cues and modes of reasoning or that different shortcuts might apply to different issues. Chapter 2 presents a theory of voting in direct democracy. Drawing on existing literature, we suggest that well-educated voters frequently take advantage of their ability to think about politics in terms of a coherent ideology or partisanship, while other voters use different modes of evaluation. In chapter 3, we examine some of the readily available information sources that voters use, and we identify how a complex information source (the ballot pamphlet) can still provide easy-to-use cues for most voters. In later chapters we demonstrate how initiative voting is also aided by the systematic use of external cues, such as evaluations of state economic conditions (chapter 4).

Furthermore, some ballot issues might lead to voting on the basis of instrumental evaluations of policy that might be of a personal nature (chapter 5), or they might be based on local interests (chapter 6). Depending on the nature of the ballot choice, voters could employ a variety of information sources through which they respond to cues such as positions by elites or campaign contacting by political parties. In chapter 7, we examine this process during the course of a term-limit initiative campaign. In chapter 8, we examine how general levels of campaign spending might affect opinions on a number of ballot propositions. We suggest that, rather than corrupting the process, costly campaigns can increase the number of voters who are able to think of ballot choices in partisan or ideological terms. In the end, we conclude that most voters display an ability to reason at some basic level about the ballot measures they decide upon.

Can this study prove that direct-democracy voters govern wisely or that the mass electorate is as competent as a legislature to make decisions about policies? Certainly not, but that is not our purpose. We avoid evaluating the process in terms of its outcomes, and we focus instead on how voters manage the demands imposed on them by the process. In the end, we believe that a case can be made that the voter is not necessarily the weak link in the process of direct democracy. By employing a fairly conservative voting strategy and by voting on the basis of limited but readily available information, voters sort through the choices presented by direct democracy. This behavior, we argue, makes it unlikely that well-organized interests can regularly use highly funded campaigns and the initiative process to pass legislation inconsistent with voter interests.

This book has benefited from the labor and generosity of scholars who read drafts of chapters presented at conferences and from others who generously read chapters at our request. Jeff Karp, Caroline Tolbert, Susan Banducci, David Magleby, and Jack Citrin all provided useful comments. Bruce Cain, Liz Gerber, Dave Brockington, Daniel Lowenstein, and anonymous reviewers each read early versions of the entire book—often suffering through some poorly edited work. The present version benefits greatly from their invaluable comments and from Rick Roerich's careful reading. Gene Lee, Malcolm Litchfield, and Chuck Myers offered needed encouragement and insight.

Joe Snipp coauthored the original version of chapter 7, and Trudi Happ was coauthor of the article in which table 5 originally appeared. Some of their work is still in these revised presentations, and they made larger contributions in dialogues about direct democracy at the Barn. Other parts of chapter 3, now revised, come from an article that benefited from comments by Richard Brody and anonymous reviewers. We owe an intellectual debt to David Magleby and to Skip Lupia.

We are also grateful for opportunities to present part of this work at the Field Institute Workshop, department colloquia, and several conferences. Participants at those events helped us in refining our ideas. Numerous graduate and undergraduate students and several colleagues at Western and at UCR have provided encouragement and skeptical questions along the way. Ken Hoover, Deborah Salazar, Gene Hogan, David Ziegler, Jim Davis, Max Neiman, and David Lanoue all contributed ideas—sometimes indirectly—about the prospects for democratic citizens.

Mohib Ghali and Jerri Walker of the Bureau for Faculty Research at Western Washington University were helpful in locating partial funding for manuscript preparation and some funds for the research in chapter 4. Donovan is also grateful for a Summer Research Grant provided by Western. Bowler is grateful for funding from the UCR Academic Senate.

Iona Einowski at UC Data was most helpful in providing California Poll data. Our research would not be possible without the resources of UC Data; we owe them and Henry Brady, and Mark DiCamilio and Mervyn Field's organization, a huge debt. We are extremely grateful for Susan Brumbaugh's frequent assistance with data and computing crises. UC Riverside's Academic Computing Services provided each author with mainframe resources, and the Government Documents staff at the UC Riverside Rivera Library were most helpful. We also benefited from UCR Political Science/Sociology computing resources made possible by NSF Grant SBR-9413939 and thank Jim Wenzel for his assistance with this.

Of course, none of this would be possible without Jadie Lee and Deborah Donovan.

CHAPTER 1

The History of Direct Democracy:
A Critique of Voter Competence

Can voters make sense of direct democracy? Are they capable of making choices that are consistent with their interests and desires, or is the act of voting on initiatives and referenda haphazard—or, worse, is it the subject of confusion and manipulation? Do decisions reflect some underlying ability to respond to information that is relevant to a policy decision, or are the choices that citizens make on ballot measures capricious, reflecting nothing but whim? Do the choices made at the end of an initiative campaign reflect an ability to reason? These questions are the focus of this book. Indeed, questions such as these have motivated decades of criticism and analysis of direct democracy as it is used in the United States. As we shall illustrate, the conventional answer to these questions has not been flattering to voters, at least in the view of academic political scientists.

In this book, we demonstrate that voters in a direct democracy engage in a substantial amount of reasoning. We assume that different ballot propositions create different settings for voter choice—and these propositions provide voters with a variety of information cues and heuristics that guide the choices they make. Some of these choices are more informed, or more "self-interested," than others. Working from the perspective that views voters as responsive to minimal levels of information (Lupia 1992; 1994a), we provide evidence that the choices that voters in a direct democracy make are reasonably informed. In addition, these choices often appear consistent with the interests and values of the voters, and they reflect a responsiveness to the available information sources.

Before we discuss the capacity to reason that voters in a direct democracy must possess, we briefly consider the context in which their decisions are made. This context, some suggest, is simply too demanding for voters. We begin with an examination of some of the interpretations that have been put forth to explain the behavior of voters in direct democracy.

Contending Views of Direct Democracy in the United States

The American experience with the direct citizen's initiative began nearly a century ago in South Dakota. Since then, more than seventeen hundred initiative measures have been placed on statewide ballots (Magleby 1994a:231; Neal 1993). California is perhaps the most visible, if not the most discussed, example of direct democracy on a mass scale. Given its visibility, California's well-known Proposition 13 serves as a good point of departure for our examination of contending views of the prospects for voter reasoning in direct democracy at the state level.

By launching what many viewed as a national "tax revolt" in 1978, Proposition 13 produced profound changes in California and in American politics in general (for a discussion of Proposition 13, see Sears and Citrin 1982). Proposition 13 rolled back California local property taxes and reduced local government revenues. Paul Gann, the initiative's coauthor, attempted to alter his state's revenue structure further by qualifying another initiative, Proposition 4, which placed constitutional restrictions on state appropriations, for a special election in 1979. Seventy-four percent of California's voters approved Proposition 4, the so-called Gann Amendment. Because direct democracy altered California's political economy, antitax activists in other states worked successfully to qualify and to pass similar legislation.

The most common interpretation of the tax revolt in California and elsewhere views these events as an example of direct democracy at its worst. After years of struggling to write budgets under the constraints on property tax revenue imposed by Proposition 13, a major recession in the 1990s left California with its bond rating downgraded and its public services deteriorating. It seemed as if voters, shortsighted or angry or perhaps in response to elites who promised "something for nothing," stumbled into passing a policy that they were unable to comprehend at the time. When seen in this light, the budget shortfall in the 1990s that was subsequently attributed to Proposition 13 created constraints on public policy. That allowed a new crop of political entrepreneurs to propose (and pass) a new initiative, Proposition 187, which attempted to bar illegal immigrants from receiving basic public services, including education and health care. Given this interpretation, one conclusion drawn from California's experience stresses that confused and ignorant voters breed crisis and conflict when they are allowed to have a direct hand in major policy decisions (see, e.g., Schrag 1994; also "Government in California," *Economist,* 13 Feb. 1993).

A less common interpretation of the tax revolt is that it stands as an example of voters who reason—at least in a limited form—when they make choices about a serious policy crisis. From this perspective, Californians, facing significant property tax increases in the mid-1970s, acted to select a policy option that reduced the rate at which taxes increased. Each time their homes were reassessed and their tax bills were increased, California's taxpayers were made painfully aware that their residential property values were inflating rapidly. The legislature, while running a budget surplus that ran into the billions, failed to remedy the situation; the voters took it upon themselves to do so (Sears and Citrin 1982).

Yet another interpretation of the tax revolt grants more credence to the ability of the electorate to act via direct democracy. In this view, a *yes* vote on Proposition 13 reflects careful reasoning, particularly among homeowners. A defender of the ability of the electorate to comprehend the choices it faces under direct democracy might point out that the budget shortfall a decade and a half later could have resulted from factors that had nothing to do with Proposition 13. For instance, the massive restructuring of the state's economy associated with the end of the cold war was certainly a factor. Furthermore, in 1982, two years after Ronald Reagan used antitax and antigovernment themes in his defeat of Jimmy Carter, California voters showed that they could discriminate among various antitax propositions by soundly rejecting another initiative that would have reshaped the state's income tax system. From this perspective, reasoning voters got the outcome they wanted: lower property taxes. In the end, the state's tax policies reflect the will of the voters. From the perspective of supporters of direct democracy, the occasional antiminority initiative such as Proposition 187 should not be used to damn the voter's right to act directly on legislation.

In this book we attempt to determine which of these characterizations, in whole or in part, represents an accurate portrait of how the mass electorate functions in direct democracy. Direct democracy, specifically the use of the initiative and referendum, is endemic to politics in most western and in several nonwestern U.S. states. It shapes policy in nearly all states that allow the initiative, and by virtue of policy diffusion, it often affects policy in states that do not. The institutions of direct democracy rest upon the basic assumption that voters have the capacity to reason when making decisions about ballot propositions. At a minimum, a simple definition of reasoning must assume that a voter is capable of responding to information about a proposition when casting his or her vote. At the very least, a voter will make some evaluation of the proposed policy on the basis of his or her own self-interest or political ideology.

Early advocates of the direct-democracy process placed great faith in the capacity of common voters to make decisions on legislation. They anticipated that direct citizen participation would "enable the people to assume control of affairs, to insure responsible as well as responsive government" (Howe [1904] 1967, 171). If public policies emanating from the process of direct democracy are even indirectly representative of popular will, these assumptions must find some support in empirical studies. Yet such assumptions about a voter's capability for reasoning have been dismissed by antidemocratic theorists from Plato to Pareto (Ferejohn 1990).

In the following sections, we present a brief discussion of the institutions of direct democracy, we discuss the historical use of initiatives and referenda in the United States, and then we illustrate how assumptions about reasoning voters were often dismissed by scholars who examined the contemporary American electorate at the time of the introduction of the initiative process.

Direct Democracy Institutions in the United States

The contemporary American experience with direct democracy was born in the complex environment of the Populist and Progressive eras. As Thomas Cronin (1989, 43–46) notes, disaffected groups and social movements, located primarily in the West—including Farmers' Alliance groups, Grange organizations, single-taxers, socialists, labor groups, and socialist evangelists—meshed into what became the People's party and the Populist party of the early 1890s. In addition to their desire for progressive taxation and the regulation of business, these groups sought instruments of direct democracy. The advocates of direct legislation viewed the legislatures of the period as corrupted by well-financed interests, and they anticipated that the initiative and the referendum would grant access to those groups that had been excluded from the legislative process. Such devices were expected to be "a means of temporarily bypassing their legislatures and enacting needed laws on behalf of the downtrodden" (Cronin 1989, 45). These groups held that the highly unprofessional state legislatures (as well as the major parties) were beholden to "trusts" and "moneyed interests." Direct, participatory democracy, it was said, would break this grip, producing better government (Howe [1904] 1967).

Cronin explains that distinct coalitions that promoted greater popular democracy formed in different states. Populists, pro-labor Democrats, and (perhaps most critically) middle-class Progressive movements finally came together to amend many state constitutions after 1910. Although Populists had been agitating since the 1880s for more direct democracy, American political institutions were not redesigned in significant form until decades later when Populist and Progressive elements merged. In California, "[t]he Progressives were responsible for the movement of direct democracy against the Southern Pacific Railroad and other strong interests" (Sutro 1994, 945, quoted in Warner 1995, 53). Mason writes that "Oregon's adoption of direct democracy was the result of Henry George's battle between aristocratic privilege and democratic freedom" (Mason 1994, 29). A coalition of labor, farmers, and urban progressives fought for direct democracy against the "machine-controlled legislature" in the state of Washington (Warner 1995, 54; Benedict 1975).

Within a relatively short period in American politics, there were dramatic extensions of direct democracy. Between 1905 and 1916, half the states adopted presidential primaries (Beck and Sorauf 1992, 254). In 1913, voters began electing their U.S. senators directly. In 1920, the U.S. Constitution extended the right to vote to women. Between 1904 and 1918, twenty states adopted the use

of the initiative or the referendum or both, with fifteen making this decision between 1910 and 1918. Following this period, however, the expansion of direct
democracy ended abruptly. Apart from Alaska, only four more existing states
adopted the initiative or the referendum, and all these did so after 1968 (D. B.
Magleby 1984, 38–39).

The Use of the Initiative and the Referendum in the United States

In those states that had adopted the procedures, the use of the initiative and the
referendum blossomed quickly after 1910. For each of the three decades following this period, state ballots contained more than two hundred initiatives.
After a period of declining use from the 1940s through the 1960s, the final
decades of the twentieth century witnessed a return of statewide initiative use
on a scale that had not been seen since the Progressive era (Magleby 1984, 33).
Since being adopted, more than seventeen hundred initiatives and hundreds of
additional referenda have appeared on state ballots (Tolbert 1998).

Twenty-three state constitutions now provide for the direct or indirect citizen's initiative. This allows a citizen (or a group) to draft legislation independent of the legislature and then to petition voters to have the measure placed on
the state ballot. Most of these states allow both statutory and constitutional measures to be placed on the ballot, although a few allow only one form (for a discussion of content restriction in various states, see Lowenstein 1995, chap. 6).
Highly salient, divisive issues that might never emerge from a legislature, such
as prohibition, term limits, tort reform, and language laws, can reach the ballot
by initiative.

Twenty-five states (including most, but not all, of those that allow initiatives) also grant citizens the right to circulate petitions to require that laws
passed by the legislature be made subject to voter approval. More states have
rules requiring that certain types of legislation (typically bond issues) receive
voter approval. Although these procedures can result in dozens of new propositions for each statewide election, their use varies significantly among the
states that have constitutional provisions for the initiative and the referendum
(Magleby 1984). Since adoption, Oregon, California, North Dakota, Colorado,
and Arizona, in order, have used the initiative most frequently, with each having more than 140 statewide initiatives in the twentieth century. Fourteen other
states have had more than fifty initiatives on their ballots during the same period (Tolbert n.d.). Many state ballots now include several ballot measures (initiatives and referenda) during each election cycle. As we shall see, some of the
criticism of voter competence in direct democracy concerns the information
demands that are created when voters must make so many policy choices simultaneously.

It is likely that election-day decisions on these measures involve greater information demands in some states than in others, because some states use the initiative more frequently. Several factors contribute to the variation in use. One obvious reason is the level of difficulty in qualifying an initiative or a referendum for the ballot. Signature-gathering requirements, both numerical and geographical, increase the costs and the difficulty of collecting the requisite number within a fixed time period; such obstacles can lead to less usage (Magleby 1994a, 225). Other reasons for variations in usage might be less obvious. Banducci (1997) finds that states with more professional legislatures see greater use of the initiative.

There are two distinct forces at play here. First, as professional legislatures become more attractive to prospective office seekers, elections become more costly and the candidates require more money from ever larger numbers of competing interest groups. Legislators who find themselves in debt to various interest groups simultaneously (such as trial lawyers and insurance interests) may not be willing to act on key issues. This situation might lead—or even force—competing groups to resort to the initiative process, which might explain why California had five insurance initiatives on the 1988 ballot and three tort-reform initiatives on the 1996 ballot. Second, a professional legislature can also reflect the social complexity of a more populous state that has a much larger public agenda than does a less populous state (Squire 1993). A larger agenda can increase the potential level of dissatisfaction that results from legislative policy failure (Jewell 1982). This higher level of dissatisfaction, in turn, has the potential to cause greater use of the initiative (Banducci 1997).

Frequent use of the initiative might make the process by which voters make their decisions more complex. Voters are asked to make decisions on a range of public policy issues, some concerning topics with which they are unfamiliar. The range of subjects addressed by ballot propositions is large: Some of the more costly and better-known initiative campaigns have focused on tax issues (cigarettes, oil, inheritance, income, property, and so on), smoking regulations, automobile insurance, right-to-work laws, bottle (recycling) bills, reapportionment, gun control, gay rights, and school choice (Magleby 1984, 209–10; Price 1988). In an analysis of more than twelve hundred initiatives that have appeared on state ballots, David Magleby found that their focus was distributed across the areas of health, welfare, housing, business regulation, revenue and taxes, and public morality. The issues that appeared most frequently concerned government organization and revenue and taxation questions (Magleby 1984, 74). Between 1978 and 1992, 45 percent of all qualifying (state) initiatives concerned political organization (reforms) and revenue/tax issues (Magleby 1994a, 238).

In this book we examine voting patterns and public opinion on a wide variety of these issues, including tax measures (sales taxes, cigarette taxes, property tax, and tax exemptions), term limits, park bonds, school bonds, environmental regulations, school vouchers, and insurance. We capture the effects of a demanding decision context by testing many of our hypotheses with data drawn from a state where voters are confronted with numerous ballot propositions in every statewide election: California. Additional data are drawn from other states where initiative use is frequent.

Because politics and policy might appear fundamentally different in states where initiatives are used frequently than in states where they are not used, we must look closely at the decisions made on initiatives (Bowler, Donovan, and Tolbert 1998). Models of policy diffusion demonstrate that the use of the initiative is a primary, direct determinant in issues such as the adoption of legislative term limits, tax and expenditure limitations (TELs), and supermajority vote requirements for taxation. Direct-democracy states are more likely to adopt these rules (Tolbert 1994). Thus, for many states, polices selected directly by citizens create a distinct climate for governing in which legislatures can operate differently (supermajority vote requirements), rules for elections are different (term limits), and revenue structures can be different (due to TELs; see Bowler and Donovan 1994b; Clingermayer and Wood 1995, 116).

Direct democracy can also alter the incentive structures that legislators face. As a result, these structures can have an indirect effect on policies. Formal and empirical models demonstrate that legislatures in states that allow initiatives are constrained by the threat of the initiative device, which ensures that legislative policy outcomes more closely reflect the ideological composition of the mass electorate (Gerber 1996; Gerber 1998). Zax (1989) and Blair (1967) argue that an indirect link exists between legislative policy outcomes and direct democracy, because the initiative threat promises to punish legislatures for any "sins of omission."

In the remainder of this chapter, we review some of the historical critiques of direct democracy in the United States. These early scholars wrote at a time when the apparatus of direct democracy was newly constructed. Some scholars were advocates (or opponents) of institutional changes, rather than dispassionate evaluators of voter competence. Yet much of the critique they advanced was adopted by later scholars, and their arguments shaped the intellectual prism through which voting in direct democracy has been studied. The writings of early critics and defenders of direct democracy also illustrate the quandary about how we should view the use of the initiative and referendum as a policy-making process.

Assessing Direct Democracy in the States: Outcomes or Process?

A contemporary textbook on California politics discusses what its writer calls "the initiative mess," and it refers to "misplaced confidence in the voters as

competent legislators" (Lawrence 1995, 72). Other recent commentaries on direct democracy reflect similar concerns. The process of direct citizen legislation has been called the destruction of government and "elected anarchy"
(Schrag 1994), "lousy lawmaking" (Fountaine 1988), "democracy's barrier to
racial equality" (D. Bell 1978), and "the right of the people to make fools of
themselves" (Warner 1995). What is striking about these statements is how
closely they echo opinions voiced since the introduction of direct democracy
prior to the World War I. At that time the issue of initiatives and referenda generated a great deal of excited debate within the fledgling political science community. *The Annals,* for example, devoted a special issue to the topic in September 1912, and a roundtable discussion on the matter was held a year earlier
at the Eighth American Political Science Association Meeting.

The palatability of policy outcomes was an early focus for both attacks
upon and defenses of the initiative process. For example, in the debate concerning rival Oregon fishing initiatives in 1908, there was extensive discussion
of both the virtues and the vices of direct democracy, with conclusions about
the desirability of the process often resting on the observer's opinions about
particular policy outcomes. In 1908, after several years of unsuccessfully lob-
bying the Oregon state legislature to regulate the Columbia River salmon fishery, two rival groups of Oregon fishermen resorted to the initiative process in
what was called a "spectacular legislative duel":

> The lower river fishermen (qualified an initiative) to abolish all the gear
> of upper-river fishermen. It was adopted by a vote of 58,130 for, to 30,280
> against. The upper-river fishermen proposed a law limiting the length of
> seines and abolishing fishing in the navigable channels of the lower river
> and stopping fishing at night in all other portions of the river. The law was
> adopted by a vote of 46,582 for, to 40,720 against [by an electorate com-
> posed of white males twenty-one years of age and older]. (Thatcher 1908,
> 604)

Eaton (1912) noted that many of the concerns about the initiative process were
clearly illustrated in this contest. The two fish initiatives were also used to support arguments both by the staunch advocates of direct legislation and by its
dedicated opponents. Supporters contended that the action of the people of Oregon represented sound policy-making. They maintained that the legislature had
failed to act for many years, and this neglect threatened the valuable Columbia
River salmon industry with annihilation. As a result, the people approved both
measures, and as a result, they refused to let either the upper-river or the lower-
river fishermen fish. This situation forced the legislature—which had been neg-
ligent on the subject—to enact measures that were designed to protect the industry (Eaton 1912).

As Eaton (1912, 67–68) noted, opponents of the initiative viewed things differently:

> [W]hen opponents of the system of direct legislation take hold of the fish bill argument they make an entirely different story out of it, to this effect: that merely for spite one class of fishermen endeavored to put the other class out of business, and as a measure of retaliation the other class endeavored to put the first class out of business, and the people in their ignorance of the whole situation carried both bills, thus crippling the great fishing industry of the state . . .

One of the red herrings introduced here, and repeated in contemporary debate over the usefulness of a system that produced California's tax-slashing Proposition 13 and its anti-immigrant Proposition 187, is that we might judge the proposition process as good or ill according to the policy that is produced at the end. Because that is likely to tell us as much about our own beliefs and opinions as it tells us about the policies that result from direct democracy, it seems difficult to sustain an argument either for or against the process on this basis. Charles Beard and Birl Schultz reflected on the problems of evaluating the process on the basis of normative opinions about policy outputs. They viewed the approval of both Oregon fish measures as what was essentially a conservation move that provided evidence of the virtues of popular democracy by initiative (Beard and Schultz 1912, 51). Others disagreed, labeling the outcome foolish and citing it as evidence that the process is flawed (Eaton 1912, 68).

Evaluating the initiative process on the basis of its results might be easy if direct democracy politics were clearly and consistently more repugnant than are legislative policies, but, as Cronin (1989, 92–95) shows, such is not necessarily the case. Direct democracy obviously has produced its share of policies that are abusive of minorities: Oklahomans banned African-Americans from voting in 1910. Californians banned land ownership by Japanese-Americans in 1920, and they repealed fair-housing legislation in the 1960s. Voters in Colorado and Washington struck down school desegregation proposals, and Arizona voters moved to prevent noncitizens from working in their state. Conversely, at the close of the twentieth century, voters in California, Idaho, Washington, and Oregon rejected (sometimes repeatedly) measures that targeted homosexuals, while Utah voters refused censorship of cable television.

Cronin (1989, 91) also demonstrates that "the record of representative government is an imperfect one." Early in this century, state legislatures passed policies that, by many normative standards, match the abuses promoted by direct-democracy voters (anticommunist laws, antievolution laws, flag-salute laws, segregationist laws, anti-Catholic policies; laws that outlawed the teaching of the German language). It can be argued that this trend continues. In a brief period in 1996 alone, state legislative chambers approved extensions to anti-sodomy bills (Idaho and Georgia, *New York Times,* 25 February 1996), they passed legislation that would fire instructors who teach evolution as "fact" (Tennessee, *New York Times,* 29 February 1996), and they resolved that the Ten Commandments could be displayed in public places (Tennessee, *New York Times,* 29 February 1996). During the same period, state legislators passed bills of dubious constitutionality that would ban the recognition of same-sex marriages from other states, even though at the time no state recognized such unions (Utah and Washington, *New York Times,* 6 March 1996). After viewing an interest group's film in a closed session, the Utah legislature moved to dissolve all school clubs for fear that gays would use them for "recruiting" because they are unable to reproduce their own "members" (*New York Times,* 29 February 1996).

Do we damn both representative and direct democracy on the basis that each produces outcomes that many find repugnant? Clearly, an assessment of either process in terms of its results is something of an analytical cul-de-sac. An assessment of outcomes produced directly by citizens or indirectly by legislators is inevitably colored by one's own political prejudices and predispositions.

Comparing the relative virtues of outcomes produced by either process presents the same problems. It seems neither reasonable nor likely that evaluations about the worth of direct democracy can be easily resolved by an argument about particular outcomes. If it can be established, however, that choices on ballot propositions somehow reflect informed decisions by voters, then we can move a long way toward evaluating this process according to other classic standards of democracy. By establishing that, we can begin to argue that direct democracy can produce policies that emanate from decisions that reflect popular preferences.

Some of the early writers recognized the problem with debating outcomes and turned their attention to the decision process by which outcomes were reached. On the one side were those who argued that the initiative process was inherently flawed because it relied on the judgment of the great unwashed; on the other side were those who discussed the electorate's ability to master the issues at hand. The opponents of direct democracy seem to have the better line in rhetoric, noting that "The initiative smacked of Populism and found its supporters chiefly among certain faddists who sought by this means to secure, at least in a limited degree, the adoption of their political nostrums" (Lowrie 1911, 566–72). Other opponents of the system of direct government

> class it as political heresy. . . . It is condemned as revolutionary in its meaning and effect. It is supposed to undermine the very foundations of American constitutional democracy, and to violate all that is soundest and safest in the American political tradition. The system of direct government is expected to have its period of efflorescence, like Know-Nothingism,

Grangerism and Populism and then gradually sink into utter and deserved oblivion. (Croly 1912, 122)

A nicely volcanic example of the opposition to the initiative is seen in a *Los Angeles Times* editorial of 31 August 1911, in which the paper complains that an initiated law would be enacted and "nobody would be responsible for it" and that, furthermore, the "ignorance and caprice and irresponsibility of the multitude" would be substituted "for the learning and judgment of the legislature" (quoted in Key and Crouch 1939, 437).

One argument of those opposed to direct democracy was that representative democracy was necessarily better because legislators, with committees and debates, are better informed and can make more knowledgeable decisions. Letting the masses vote on "direct legislation would rob the state legislator of his dignity and destroy his sense of responsibility to the people" (Cushman 1916, 537; see also Lowrie 1911, 568; Haynes 1907, 486; or the platform of the Oregon Republicans in *1908 Oregonian,* 15 May 1908, 12).

Yet two of the most prominent social scientists of that era—V. O. Key and Charles Beard—both took issue with the idea that representative democracy in general, and legislatures in particular, were necessarily better than direct democracy. Key and Crouch, for example, note that real legislators are often far from ideal decision makers because they may "deliberate up measures which are drafted outside the legislature [and] listen to irrelevant and uninformed debate . . ." (1939, 443). Considering that, why should their policy output necessarily reflect popular will, let alone a higher level of knowledge than that exhibited by the mass electorate? As Beard stated, "the fact is that there has been growing up the notion that the legislature is inherently unfitted for some of its most important work" (in Beard and Schultz 1912, 7). Elsewhere, Beard expanded his critique of the irresponsibility of legislatures by analyzing their inability to be fiscally responsible:

> Legislatures cannot be given a free hand in laying taxes, incurring debts and making appropriations. This nearly all of our states have learned by bitter experience; and they have now written in their constitutions limitations on the extent of the taxing power and on the amount of debt which may be incurred. (Beard and Schultz 1912, 6).

Early criticism of the process of direct democracy also began to focus upon microlevels of voter behavior. Increasing notice was taken of the difficulties that voters faced in reaching a decision and of the possibility that existed for confusion and misrepresentation. But here the critics had to walk a fine line. If society trusted voters to choose representatives in elections, then why not trust them to vote on issues placed on the same ballots? One danger for these critics lay in insulting the voters' ability to make any sort of decision, although doing so could be avoided by careful word choice. For example, arguing against popular democratic procedures in 1908, Oregon Republicans thought the voters "too busy" to grasp initiative issues. Thus, in addition to concerns about policy outcomes, the competence of voters and their ability to tap information with which to reason when making decisions became a key issue in the debate over the value of the initiative process itself. Critics have identified as one of the central problems the inherent complexity of the decisions that confront voters.

The Demanding Context of Decisions

George Haynes (1907, 485) seems to be one of the earliest writers to have gained a clear sense of the information demands that voters faced in state-level direct democracy:

> [S]hall we deny that the great majority of us, when we go to the polls, have altogether inadequate information for forming a just opinion upon the men and measures there presented for our suffrage?

Others were similarly skeptical of the ability of voters to make sensible decisions concerning direct legislation. Voicing a criticism that would recur often in later academic writing (e.g., Wolfinger and Greenstein 1968, 767; J. Mueller 1969, 1211; Magleby 1984, 142; conversely, see Cronin 1989, chap. 4), Barnett (1915, 111) claimed that "the difficulty of the subject matter of measures submitted has doubtless often caused voters to vote contrary to their real intentions." Or, as Cushman (1916, 538) wrote, "to submit these matters to popular vote is to strain the interest and intelligence of the citizen and invite the most haphazard results in the way of legislation."

From the outset, there were also advocates of the process who attested to the capacity voters had for reasoning. One of the most noteworthy of these academics, Charles Beard, evaluated the low turnout (and roll-off) associated with proposition voting by noting that:

> the smallness of the vote in many instances indicates not a lack of interest, but a high degree of intelligence on the part of the voters. It often shows that the voters are aware of the fact that they do not know enough about some particular or local matter to warrant their expressing an opinion one way or another. (Beard and Schultz 1912, 39)

Advancing a similar line of logic, Waldo Schumacher concluded that "the simpler the question submitted the larger the vote polled" (1932, 247). Others make the argument more directly:

[O]n matters of immediate and local interest voters will take the trouble to express themselves at the polls, but upon more general propositions they feel less interest and so usually less personal responsibility . . . [there is a] tendency to vote upon questions which are familiar to the voters and to slight or neglect problems which need thought or study. (Peabody 1905, 443–55)

Peabody thus acknowledged that voters had limited information on some measures and that they might decline to participate where information demands were greatest. He also noted that voters should seek out those measures that they are interested in. Responding to claims that direct democracy was plagued by the problem of uninformed voters, Crouch presented a version of John Stuart Mill's classical argument that participation via the initiative educated voters and that placing issues on the ballot could stimulate the interest of voters. According to Crouch, when more than two million voters go to the polls and express their choices on the measures presented, one of two conditions must exist: either the topics represented by the initiatives must be of inherent interest to the voters, or discussion and publicity must have aroused their interest (Crouch 1943, 12). Decades later, "strong democracy" advocate Benjamin R. Barber (1984) made similar claims about the role of direct democracy in stimulating voter interest (see also Everson 1981; Dolbare and Hubbell 1996). Greater popular democracy (such as a national initiative), this thesis suggests, can increase citizen interest, or at least it can encourage voters to seek information about the measures that are placed on the ballot.

One of the most striking problems associated with the voter's ability to cope with the demands of direct democracy was the rapid emergence of highly crowded ballots. Problems associated with the complexity of substantive policy decisions were seen as being accentuated by the frequency with which these issues were brought to the ballot. Haynes quotes a Portland police officer who noted of the 1910 Oregon ballot after leaving the booth, "It's like voting a bed quilt." The Oregon state ballot that year was particularly long, yet it was not unlike recent ballots in Oregon and in other states. Thirty-two statewide referenda and initiatives were listed, with topics that included the establishment of the direct presidential primary, several tax items, term limitations and proportional representation for the legislature, liquor regulation, annexation and county boundary issues, and the prohibition of certain fishing practices. Voters rejected all but ten of these measures (Mason 1994, 200).

Two years later the Oregon ballot was another "bed quilt," measuring $34\frac{1}{2}$ inches long and $18\frac{1}{4}$ inches wide (Haynes 1913, 18–33). It contained thirty-seven statewide propositions and seven additional county-level measures. Voters rejected thirty-one of the items (Mason 1994, 200). Not only did direct democracy raise complicated policy issues, but in some states it generated (and continues to generate) dozens of such choices in each election. Critics of the process of citizen lawmaking feared that minimally informed voters were sure to be overwhelmed.

If all of this were not enough to thoroughly damn the voter's ability to cope with direct democracy, the rapid emergence of professional campaign techniques soon stimulated another distinct line of attack on the prospects for competent, informed (or even self-interested) voting on the part of the mass electorate in direct democracy. We now turn our attention to the initiative campaign industry and how it can affect the decision context by influencing the flow of campaign information and the number of choices on some state ballots.

Campaigns and Confusion

Contrary to the positions advocated by Crouch (and later by Barber), citizen choices on initiatives often were not seen as the product of a Mill-like educational process in which campaigns stimulate interest, disseminate information, and produce informed choices and policies that represent popular preferences. Instead, they were seen as something far less noble. This perception was particularly evident when attention became focused on campaigning efforts and techniques that are associated specifically with direct democracy. Here, the overlapping critique of direct democracy between this original literature and modern-day debates becomes quite striking.

The importance of money and the media in transmitting information was apparent to early observers who were less than sanguine about the quality of the information that voters would receive from these campaigns. In 1910, Hiram Johnson, one of the Progressives who had introduced the initiative process, recognized the value of a skilled newspaper writer in running initiative campaigns (Pritchell 1959, 278). Furthermore, the first initiative contests involved substantial amounts of spending. Gilbert (1916) estimated that one group, the Fels Fund, pumped $51,956 (in 1916 dollars) into Oregon in the years from 1910 through 1912 in support of the single-tax initiative campaign. From the beginning, mass mailings were also part of the process. Gardner claims that the campaign for a 1904 amendment to provide special legislation for the city of Chicago mailed out more than three million pieces of literature, including fifty thousand pamphlets in a single day. The Publicity Committee fund amounted to around $30,000, and it used eight thousand poll workers (five thousand of whom were paid), who, among their other duties, helped issue "how-to-vote" cards (Gardner 1911, 409–10). As an indication of the size of the effort, 1,089,458 votes were cast in this election.

It is also the case that simplistic slogans and negative advertising were a part of early initiative campaigns. In California in the early 1920s, the notorious lobbyist Artie Samish helped place a proposal on the ballot that favored trucking interests. Samish, describing one of his campaign techniques, stated how he attempted to get voters to think of the issue as a decision about "road hogs," because "nobody likes a road hog":

> I hired a well-known cartoonist named Johnny Argens to draw a picture of a big, fat, ugly pig. Then I splashed that picture on billboards throughout the state with the slogan
>
> DRIVE THE HOG FROM THE ROAD
> VOTE YES ON PROPOSITION NUMBER 2
>
> I also had millions of handbills printed with the same picture and message. During the last weeks of the campaign they were placed on automobiles in every city and town. You'll note that I always spelled out "Number"; I never used "No." 2 because the voter might get confused and think he should vote "No." (Samish and Thomas 1971, 37–38; see also Lowenstein 1982)

Even early campaign efforts such as these involved huge sums of money. The Jones Committee of the California State Senate reported that in the 1922 election, seven proposition campaigns spent, according to a conservative estimate, $1,081,784 (in 1922 dollars). Pacific Gas and Electric's spending against the Water and Power Act accounted for fully half of that amount (California Assembly *Senate Journal* 1923, 1782)

With such "startlingly large expenditures" (California Assembly *Senate Journal* 1923, 1782) made in support of ballot initiatives, it should come as little surprise that one of the first professional campaign firms in the world, Campaigns, Inc., was founded in California in 1930. One of the firm's earliest projects was a 1933 referendum on a Central Valley water project. Thereafter, the firm handled five or six initiatives in each election (McWilliams 1951, 348; Kelley 1956, chap. 2). V. O. Key described the firm as a specialist in handling all phases of campaigns for candidates and for organizations that were interested in constitutional amendments or other issues.

> The establishment of such a concern, operating successfully on a commercial basis, is extremely significant as an indication of the trend away from personal politics of the precinct variety and toward the use of modern propaganda techniques. (Key 1936, 719 n. 15).

By 1936, the campaign around a chain-store tax in California saw two well-organized rival groups vying for and against the tax. Campaign techniques appeared quite similar to those used with high-profile initiatives today. As Cottrell observed,

Both spent huge sums on advertising in newspapers, on billboards, over the radio, from sound trucks, on motion picture screens, on automobile stickers, by airplane or dirigible trailers and sky-writing, and by premiums to customers in the various stores. Programs were broadcast with such headliners as Conrad Nagel as master of ceremonies (Cottrell 1939, 44; see also McWilliams 1951).

Such campaigning does not seem to have been unusual. Similar methods were used in 1938 both for and against the "$30 Every Thursday" plan, the repeal of the sales tax and the adoption of a form of single tax, the revenue bond act, the labor control initiative, and the highway and traffic safety commissions. Expenditures on these 1938 propositions were estimated at more than $2 million (Cottrell 1939, 44; see also McWilliams 1951).

Just as money and media advertising characterized initiative and referendum politics from the start, so too did the practice of using paid signature gatherers to ensure qualification of measures promoted by well-financed groups. As early as 1911, B. J. Hendrick observed the situation in Oregon:

They are found in practically every part of the State. They invade the office buildings, the apartment houses and the homes of Portland, and tramp from farmhouse to farmhouse. Young women, ex-book canvassers, broken-down clergymen, people who in other communities would find their natural level as sandwich men, dapper hustling youths, perhaps earning their way through college—all find useful employment in soliciting signatures at five or ten cents a name. (Hendrick 1911)

Hoping to protect the initiative process from the narrow "interests" it was designed to counter, and in an effort to contain the number of measures reaching the ballot, some states began to prohibit paid signature gathering. South Dakota banned the practice in 1913, as did Washington in 1915. The U.S. Supreme Court, however, nullified such state laws in 1988 (for a discussion of the decision, see Lowenstein and Stern 1989). The use of modern campaign techniques and paid signature gathering led some early observers to conclude that direct-democracy campaigns would result in straightforward deception of voters. The California Senate's Jones Committee of 1923, for example, noted that large campaign expenditures corresponded with the "use of questionable, misleading and deceptive campaign methods" such as the "use of high sounding, patriotic names under which the real identity of the interested parties . . . is disguised." Further, it raised the possibility of the direct bribery of influential group leaders in exchange for their support (California Assembly *Senate Journal* 1923, 1785–86).

Fifty years later, hearings held by the California Assembly provided further documentation of the concerns surrounding campaign subterfuges, especially those regarding paid signature gatherers. The 1971 hearings echoed the 1923 Jones Committee and resonated into the 1990s. For example:

> It seems to me we are witnessing in proposition after proposition a repeated and deliberate misleading of the public and a debasement of the very [process]. (Charles O'Brien in California Assembly 1972, 24)

In the same hearings, California Assembly member Henry Waxman presented a statement that neatly contrasts the critique of advertising in direct democracy with the virtues of representative democracy:

> PR firms and advertising agencies are packing these highly complex constitutional amendments and statues with jingles challenging the creative witticisms of Alka-Seltzer commercials. Any legislator would be embarrassed to utter on the floor of the Legislature the simplistic slogans we find on television, radio and billboards. (California Assembly 1972, 2)

We have seen that voters can be confused by the complexity of policy issues associated with the ballot measure. This confusion can be amplified by the noise of the campaign that surrounds the issue. To fully complicate the matter, a final wrench is thrown into the process (or at the voter). In addition to the corrupting possibilities introduced by special-interest money, deceptive advertising, lengthy ballots, and complicated policy issues, voters in some states are faced with the prospect of sorting through competing propositions that deal with the same topic. In some cases, voters must decide on individual initiatives that address multiple policy issues.

Competing Proposals and Multiple Issues

Early critics were also concerned with the possibility that special interests might use counterinitiatives to further confuse or to take away from the public the process of direct democracy (Cushman 1916, 532–39). As noted during our discussion of the Oregon fishing initiatives, from the earliest experiences with state-level direct democracy, contending groups have made a practice of fighting one initiative by qualifying their own counterproposal. In the 1928 election alone, Oregon voters were asked to decide on four separate bills to regulate river fishing (Mason 1994, 206). Furthermore, legislatures also place referenda on ballots as alternatives to initiative proposals. The problem has not gone unnoticed. By the 1930s, Cottrell was able to state that "conflicting measures often appear on the same ballot" (Cottrell 1939, 40).

Haynes raised a fundamental concern that applied to voters' decisions on competing measures. He noted that rather than simply voting for or against a policy issue, competing measures could require voters to select their preferred option from several seemingly similar initiatives that were "framed and phrased—and every step in the procedure is of consequence—for them by someone else. By whom? For what?" (Haynes 1913, 61).

Although the use of counterinitiatives is not new, in recent years the practice has become more common. One of the most notorious contemporary examples occurred in the 1988 California election when five distinct initiatives regarding automobile insurance appeared on the same ballot (Banducci 1992; Lupia 1994a). Banducci (1992; 1998) noted that after 1988, a greater proportion of ballots from around the country contained competing choices for the same policy issue. Magleby (1994a) and Bowler, Donovan, and Tolbert (1998) note that the growth in the number of counterinitiatives is the result of the capability of the modern initiative industry to use numerous paid signature gatherers to rapidly qualify countermeasures on behalf of organized interests that may feel threatened by the original initiative. Part of the strategy "is to confuse voters so they will vote No on both measures, and making the ballot so long that voters out of frustration and fatigue vote No on all measures" (Banducci 1992, 7; Magleby 1994a:234).

Combining multiple issues in a single proposition also adds to the confusion by creating multiple beneficiary groups, which further complicates (if it does not simply lengthen) ballot questions. Voter confusion can thus be enhanced by having several complex elements contained in a single proposal. Other measures can be designed to broaden support by proposing to target benefits at highly specific areas, a practice known as the *distributive logroll*. This strategy has historical roots. For example, a 1926 California proposition that pushed for pari-mutuel betting would have split revenues between the State Board of Agriculture and the Veterans Welfare Board in a clear attempt to expand its list of potential beneficiaries (Crouch 1943, 12). In a more creative (if not more egregious) multiple-issue logroll, a group of citizens attempted unsuccessfully to place on the ballot a measure that contained an astonishing potpourri of different items that included pensions, taxes, voting rights for Indians, gambling, oleomargarine, health, reapportionment of the state senate, fish and game, the repeal of cross-filing for primary elections, and surface mining (California Assembly 1992, 312). As a result of efforts such as that, California's constitution was changed to include a single-subject rule. Seventeen other states have adopted similar measures. Nevertheless, legal scholars note that contemporary state courts allow substantial latitude in their definition of what constitutes a "single subject" (Lowenstein 1983).

Is Too Much Expected of Voters?

Several themes emerge from our discussion of the context of choice that is presented by state-level direct democracy. The process itself, or even its abuse by well-organized groups, can confuse the voters. Their confusion might be great enough to subvert the original intention of the Progressive-era reformers who introduced the initiative and referendum processes. In some cases, complex issues that compete against each other are placed on the same lengthy ballot. The typical voter might lack the capacity or the patience, or might not have access to the information sources needed, to make a competent decision. As a result, policies can be approved because of voter ignorance rather than voter preference. From the critics' perspective, voters in such a situation might approve an unwise policy at the expense of the public good or even contrary to their own personal best interests. As one early critic commented,

> the system [of direct democracy] is vicious and dangerous, affording an opportunity, as it does, of forcing a vote upon crude, ill-advised and possibly dishonest laws, which, through the ignorance or indifference of the voters, may become effective. (H. Campbell 1911, 431)

It is worth noting that this critique emerges from and is specific to the process of voter choice in American state-level direct democracy. We might assume that when voters in other countries are asked to make a rare decision on a highly visible national issue (such as Canada's 1992 referendum on constitutional concessions to Quebec, or the various European national referenda on participation in the European Community), they have fewer demands placed upon them, and far more information is available. With these high-visibility referenda, there are few, if any, other issues on the ballot that compete for the voter's attention. Debates, moreover, will be on a national scale, political parties are likely to take positions on issues, and voters might find it relatively easy to become familiar with an issue and its supporters. In this context, voters might respond to easily available information on how policies will affect them, to party cues, and to elite positions (see, e.g., Butler and Ranney 1994; Butler and Kitzinger 1976; Clarke and Kornberg 1994; LeDuc 1993; Boix and Alt 1991; Levine and Roberts 1994; Granberg and Holmberg 1986). Implicit in the criticism of voting behavior in American direct democracy at the state level is the idea that the context is so radically different from these highly charged national referenda that we should not expect to find much evidence that voters can comprehend what they are doing.

All of these issues rest on micromodels of choice that make assumptions about the ability of voters to make decisions in complex settings. The earliest observers of American state-level direct democracy could raise questions about the process of voter decision making, but lacking survey data, they could not answer them. One of the earliest writers acknowledged:

> Statistical studies as to the relative intelligence of the voters and non voters upon referendum measures are unfortunately lacking. Perhaps in the

future some investigation of this question may be undertaken. (Sanborn 1908, 595)

The central question to be resolved by such studies concerns what has ultimately become the chief argument against the statewide initiative:

It seems to demand too much, to consider the people as a body able to (use) initiatives, having the constant energy to watch their details, as well as to make themselves masters of the legislative situation. (Renisch 1912, 156)

It is this argument—that voters are incapable of meeting minimal requirements for decision making in direct-democracy elections—that forms the central component of concern about the process. As we have seen, this objection was heard in the earliest days of the initiative, and it is very common in today's debates. Some contemporary scholars do note that the charge that voters lack the competence to decide on ballot issues "is usually exaggerated" (Cronin 1989, 89). Eugene Lee, on observing direct-democracy voters in California, wrote that "although they are occasionally confused as to the meaning of an initiative and vote contrary to their intentions, they generally vote in accordance with their underlying beliefs and attitudes" (1978, 117). In this book, we seek an answer to the question, If they do that, how do they come to do it? As we shall see, findings from the most comprehensive empirical examination of direct-democracy voting thus far (Magleby 1984) offer conclusions that are much less enthusiastic about the prospects for voter competence than those suggested by scholars such as Lee or Cronin.

CHAPTER 2

Reasoning Voters: Sorting through the Demands of Direct Democracy

Many contemporary political scientists have not been sympathetic to the idea that voters have the interest, sophistication, or information required to make policy-oriented decisions in highly visible, partisan elections. It is hardly surprising, then, to find that there has been little support for the idea that voters are competent enough to make informed decisions on policy issues that are placed directly on the ballot. Our argument, grounded in more recent approaches to voting behavior, is that voters are quite capable of making decisions on ballot propositions. A central plank in this argument is that voters are able to reason and therefore are able to decide which side of an issue they support based on readily available information. The sources and types of information may, however, be quite different from those used in candidate elections.

The American Voter and Voter Competence: Early Behavioral Studies and Mass Behavior

Normative theorists of democracy have implied or assumed a microlevel model of voting behavior in which voters possess a number of attributes, with interest in and knowledge of politics of primary importance (e.g., Berelson 1952). Yet from the outset, empirical studies of voters have found an American electorate lacking the ability to evaluate issues and policies involved in the relatively straightforward choice between two presidential candidates. In studies of general elections from the post–World War II era, levels of voter information on, awareness of, and interest in politics were found to be extremely low. The dominant statement of this minimalist view of candidate races is found in the famed Michigan study *The American Voter* (A. Campbell et al. 1960). One of the more notable conclusions from this study is that voters have low levels of conceptualization and consequently are unable to think in abstract terms about politics and policy. According to the paradigm, few voters are sufficiently sophisticated to think about politics on the basis of issues and ideology. Voters were said to lack sophistication in two key ways: (1) they have limited abilities to think in the abstract about candidates and issues, and (2) they lack factual knowledge

(Smith 1989; see also Luskin 1987). This early research found that most voters lacked any ideological constraint that might allow them to make sense out of the array of issues presented during high-profile presidential elections (Converse 1964).

Moreover, the Michigan study found that voters simply did not know much about politics in general, or issues in particular, when making choices about candidates. Many postwar surveys, for example, asked voters to name a set of politicians (Cabinet members or Supreme Court justices) or asked them to place named candidates on policy scales that related to specific issues of the day. Voters tended not to know who the Supreme Court justices were, and they could not say with any great degree of precision what unemployment levels were. Where "issue voting" was identified (e.g., racist or segregationist voting associated with the 1968 Wallace candidacy), these authors noted that observed issue-based voting was distinctly different from, and inferior to, "sophisticated" voting (Converse et al. 1969). It was necessary for issues to be "easy" matters that touched on gut reactions to such topics as race relations in order for voters to respond to them (see also Carmines and Stimson 1980).

Since then, some amendments have been made to the bleak picture of voter competence revealed by the earliest studies. The Michigan-inspired portrait of a nonideological electorate composed of voters with a limited ability to conceptualize politics has, for example, been challenged as a product of the time period (the 1950s) during which it was conducted (Page and Brody 1972; Nie, Verba, and Petrocik 1976). Some other conclusions were challenged on the grounds of measurement error. When some of the earlier studies were replicated to account for measurement error, the attitudes of Americans appear more consistent and stable than Converse's work (1964) would suggest (Achen 1975; Jackson 1979). Another line of criticism of *The American Voter* emerged in the form of evidence that voters systematically use policy-specific information when evaluating candidates. Although the initial impression of the electorate was that of a minimally informed and minimally alert group, some subsequent literature made the picture less bleak. Although the evidence often appears stronger at the aggregate (Kramer 1971; Tufte 1978; Kramer 1983; Lewis-Beck 1988) than at the individual level, opinion studies from the 1980s and 1990s demonstrate that voters often respond to information concerning (their perceptions of) economic conditions (Kinder and Kiewiet 1981; Fiorina 1981; Markus 1988).

V. O. Key (1966) was one of the first to campaign against the minimalist portrait of the electorate with the cry that the "voters are not fools." Voters, he argued, consider issues when they evaluate politicians on the basis of (past) economic performance. Empirical studies illustrate that retrospective evaluations of economic conditions, perception of social group well-being, "sociotropic" concerns about the health of the national economy, and personal "pocketbook" issues all motivate vote choices (Kiewiet 1981; Kiewiet and Rivers 1984; Kinder, Adams and Gronke 1989). Further research demonstrated that voters evaluate economic conditions even when making decisions on state gubernatorial and legislative races—although some debate exists about whether voters respond to state or national economic conditions (on reactions to national conditions, see Stein 1990 and Chubb 1988; for evidence of response to state conditions, see also Chubb 1988; Howell and Vanderleeuw 1990; Partin 1995).

Still, even with these substantial amendments to the basic model, Harrop and Miller summarize the findings of this literature as a whole in the following terms:

> Most people think about politics *some* of the time and most people know a *little* about it. But relatively few think *very much* about politics or have *extensive* knowledge about parties, policies, or personalities. (1987, 102; emphasis in original)

This evidence buttressed the normative perspective of some earlier observers who saw the lack of informedness of voters as a reason for limiting popular governance. Walter Lipmann (1922, 1925) and Joseph Schumpeter (1942) both wrote critically of the public's ability to use facts to assess political reality. Page and Shapiro note that John Stuart Mill, although often seen as a champion of democracy, advocated a limited suffrage, limited constituent control over representatives, and extra votes for the educated—on the grounds that the average (common) person was not sufficiently competent to rule (Page and Shapiro 1992, 386; Mill [1859] 1947). Dahl (1956) noted that reliance on the whims of "populistic democracy" could force trade-offs between popular sovereignty and "leisure, privacy, consensus, stability, income, security, progress, and probably many other goals" (1956, 51).

Page and Shapiro claim that the reaction to the minimalist view of voters found by Converse (1964) was "a wholesale revision of [classic] democratic theory," to the point that "most of the leaders of the political science and sociology professions rejected majoritarian democracy . . . embracing [instead] some form of a . . . system in which . . . participation . . . by the general public is limited" (Page and Shapiro 1992, 387).

Mass Behavior under Direct Democracy

Empirical findings about voters from the early behavioral era came as a great disappointment when compared with expectations set by classical normative democratic theorists (Berelson et al. 1954). Given these findings from the literature on *representative* democracy, it is no surprise that political scientists have had limited sympathy for the idea of voter competence under *direct* democracy (Wolfinger and Greenstein 1968, 767).

In presidential contests, voters typically know—or quickly learn—that there are two candidates who stake out positions more-or-less consistent with the history of their respective parties, histories that developed over several previous elections. Voters possess a preexisting stock of knowledge when participating in elections at the national level, and they may acquire even more knowledge from a media barrage of news and advertisements lasting several months. With ballot measures, however, it is quite conceivable that many, if not most, voters face entirely new issues and, moreover, are not exposed to any great degree to information on the issues from news items or campaign ads. If most American voters lack factual information, a constraining ideology, and an ability to deal with issues in highly publicized candidate races, how can they be expected to sort through the complex policy choices they face in the low-information setting of direct democracy?

For much of political science, the answer is "not very well." Behavioral studies of voting in direct-democracy contests seemed only to underscore these arguments and those of the early critics of the direct-democracy process. Research in the 1960s and 1970s that was directed at initiative and referenda voting often focused on individual policy issues, allowing for little generalization beyond each study. When generalizations were made, they were not encouraging for prospects of voter competence, and they seemed to bear out the fears and warnings of the earliest critics. Early studies of the local politics of fluoridation, for example, demonstrated that rather than providing an opportunity for rational deliberation by voters, referenda were an outlet for protest voting by less-affluent and less-educated residents. This conclusion seems to have been arrived at in part because of high levels of negative voting found on some local referenda. In rejecting elite proposals, negative-voting nonelites were seen to be protesting their sense of powerlessness (Gamson 1961; Horton and Thompson 1962; McDill and Ridley 1962; conversely, see Stone 1965). Similar explanations were offered for the rejection of school bond proposals (Gold 1962; Boskof and Zeigler 1964; Agger and Goldstein 1971).

As Magleby (1984) indicates, a major problem with these studies is the lack of opinion data and the consequent measurement of alienation by aggregate indicators of low education and social status. These early scholars attempted to explain negativism in voting by focusing on how alienation affected voters' choices and their decisions to participate. Because the data were inappropriate, these studies created a tautology: a precinct was assumed to hold "alienated" voters if it had lower-than-average levels of education or status. If *no* voting was higher in these precincts, alienated voters living there were assumed to be protesting.

In addition to poor data and measures, the early behavioral-era research on referenda was dominated by the attempt to explain how voters could possibly reject the eminently sensible ballot proposals (fluoridation, school taxes, etc.) introduced by well-meaning elites. Scholars placed some positive normative value on the referenda proposal and then seemed unable to accept the fact that voters would have any sensible reason for rejecting it (Horton and Thompson 1962; McDill and Ridley 1962).

One striking element in these studies—echoing some of the critics discussed in the previous chapter—is that virtually no credence is given to the idea that there might be some reasonable basis for rejection. The idea that voters might vote *no* because they were uncertain about a proposal, because they thought the proposal too costly, or because it worked counter to their own interests was rejected out of hand.

The advent of studies based on opinion data, however, did not establish that voters act on their interests, let alone that they comprehend the choice they face. Assessing the literature on tax-revolt referenda, Lowery and Sigelman noted that "previous studies have produced little evidence supporting the self-interest explanation" (1981, 964). Lowery and Sigelman's study of support for California's Proposition 13 using NES data illustrated that standard measures of self-interest such as home ownership failed to explain individual-level support.

Moreover, many studies tended to focus on the determinants of opinions on a single referendum or initiative. In a study of nuclear power referenda, for example, we learn voters' opinions on the issue and some correlates of opinion (Benedict et al. 1980), or that few voters have enough factual knowledge to make educated decisions on nuclear power issues (Hensler and Hensler 1979). Likewise, studies of fair-housing legislation (Hamilton 1970a, 1970b; Hahn 1968), suffrage referenda (Stanley 1969), race (Hahn and Almy 1971), nuclear freeze initiatives, antigrowth measures (Gottinder and Neiman 1981; Neiman and Loveridge 1981; Baldassare 1985; Bollens 1990), referenda on the Vietnam War (Hahn 1970), environmental initiatives (Lutrin and Settle 1975) and county-city consolidation plans (Marando 1972; Bollens 1990) tell us much about opinions and support on individual issues, but not a lot about how voters might reason across large numbers and types of ballot measures.

In some of the rare instances in which earlier empirical studies acknowledged that voting might translate interest-based preferences into policy, conclusions about the results of such voting were pessimistic at least in part because the election outcomes seemed unpalatable to scholars (e.g., the repeal of fair-housing legislation, Wolfinger and Greenstein 1968; also see Hamilton 1970). As Wolfinger and Greenstein noted, "among contemporary political scientists, it is more common to assume that asking voters to pass judgment on substantive policy questions strains their information and interest, leading them to decisions that may be inconsistent with their desires" (Wolfinger and Greenstein 1968, 767). Individual voting decisions in direct democracy were characterized as "strikingly idiosyncratic" and the subject of an undefined "mood," whim, or caprice (J. Mueller 1965; 1969, 1211).

Given this point of view, explanations of voting behavior on propositions grounded in self-interest or ideology seemed unconvincing, to say the least. One of the earliest and most influential empirical political science assessments of referenda voting (again relying on aggregate data) explained behavior in terms of an "ethos" that was rooted in ethnicity (Wilson and Banfield 1963; 1964). These researchers claimed that local referenda voting at that time was structured by two "orientations," one Anglo-Saxon (e.g., British, Scandinavian) in origin, the other originating with more recent immigrants (e.g., Irish, Polish). The former ethos instilled a "public-regarding" concern for community, efficiency, and administration that led to approval of tax and expenditure referenda. The latter "private-regarding ethos" created expectations of favoritism and a selfish disregard for community. Despite the potential for ecological fallacy and the difficulty of using such value-laden conceptions of voter preferences, the work was widely accepted (e.g., Durand 1972; Ippolito and Levin 1970). A large body of literature based on the idea that the "public-regarding" ethos was dominant and that referenda voters frequently did not act on the basis of self-interest developed (see Hahn and Kamieniecki 1987, 115 n. 21, for a lengthy but partial summary).

Prior to Magleby's comprehensive study (1984), there simply was no systematic assessment of this disparate literature on referenda voting. Magleby's exhaustive analysis of opinion data greatly advanced our understanding of the individual-level correlates of voting on propositions. As we note in the chapters that follow, his conclusions about the prospects for a direct-democracy electorate composed largely of competent, reasoning voters were still relatively pessimistic. In part, the information that voters need to make informed decisions might be accessible only to those voters who have a graduate-level education (138–44; 198). He suggests further that direct democracy often is unlikely to produce instrumental voting because many voters are unable to translate their policy preferences into votes (142; conversely, see also Cronin 1989, chap. 4).

The point here is not to fault these studies. Their authors sought to make the best sense possible of voting and opinion under direct democracy, often while having very limited access to appropriate data and measures. Given this limitation, and given that the dominant contemporary theoretical explanation of voting assumed that voters had minimal competence, their conclusions are not surprising. We begin our reassessment of the conclusions and arguments of this literature by presenting in the simplest terms the decision voters face under direct democracy.

Figure 1 provides a very simple spatial representation of this decision. Assuming that the voter has a preference, her or his preferred point (I) may be

Fig. 1. A representation of the decision that voters face under direct democracy

placed on a hypothetical policy continuum. In this example, the continuum represents a possible range of policies from more liberal (Left) to more conservative (Right). The option associated with a ballot proposition and the status quo (*SQ*) are also located somewhere along this continuum. From the perspective of an uncertain voter with limited information, the location of a given proposition may be at either x_1 or x_2 (or anywhere along the continuum if the voter is completely uninformed about the measure). In order to make a minimally informed choice, the voter must decide if the ballot measure is located at x_1, at x_2, or somewhere else. If information is available, the voter might determine that the proposition is closer to or farther away from her or his ideal point. Knowing something about that, and knowing the status quo and her or his ideal point, the voter might then decide whether she or he is in favor of the proposal.

The literature we have reviewed thus far on mass behavior and on direct democracy might view this continuum as a way of representing everything that is wrong with direct democracy. It might suggest strongly that the continuum is little more than a caricature of voter behavior. From this perspective, each point on the figure 1 continuum can be said to represent some potential opportunity for failure on the part of voters. As we saw earlier, a considerable body of literature would support the argument that at the outset, voters do not know whether any given proposition is actually at x_1 or at x_2. The issues are too complex, the language contained in the ballot pamphlets is too complicated, and too little is known about the actual policies. Furthermore, even if voters know where the status quo stands, they may not know where they themselves stand. Voters might not have explicit preferences about policy issues, particularly if the first time they see them is in the form of a ballot initiative. Thus, it may be unlikely that voters could actually express what constitutes the "status quo" at any given moment, nor could they articulate a preference that resembles self-interested behavior.

In light of the literature we have reviewed thus far, we might expect that figure 1 can be said to represent what happens in direct-democracy elections only for a very small segment of the population, and then only in quite restricted circumstances. The problem is that direct democracy presents circumstances that are quite different than those presented by candidate contests in which informed voting is possible. The primary cues that voters use to make choices in candidate races are missing. There are no party labels on ballots to simplify matters and to aid evaluations, nor are there incumbents to serve as a benchmark for comparison. The use of retrospective evaluations is also difficult. Much of the criticism outlined earlier leads us to conclude that there is simply too little information available to voters for them to be able to meet the demands of direct democracy adequately.

Rather than treating this lack of information as a point of arrival, however, we treat it as a point of departure, and we ask how it is that voters are able to make decisions, given the low information setting. We suggest that figure 1 represents, in fact, a fairly plausible way of thinking about how many voters behave under conditions of direct democracy. Although we accept the premise that voters are quite ignorant of basic factual information, we argue that they are capable of understanding ballot issues and they are able to draw inferences from very modest pieces of information. These inferences allow voters to decide whether a new proposal is to their tastes or not. Further, with rather limited information, voters can and often do make decisions based on ideological or instrumental criteria. In short, we claim to illustrate that voters are able to identify and act on their preferences in ballot proposition elections. In other words, they appear to understand where propositions are located in ideological terms relative to their own interests and preferences.

Dealing with Limited Information: Voter Competence in a New Light

Recent work has begun to alter the view espoused in *The American Voter* in a far more sustained way than did the amendments made by the literature of the 1970s and 1980s. This newer literature has revised our view of voters to the point where the voter's ability to understand issues and the positions taken by candidates is not quickly dismissed. It is a body of literature that stems from Simon's insights on "satisficing" (Simon 1959; Selten 1990; Tietz 1990; Wall 1993), but since then has been developed, largely by social psychologists. As we see, it can provide some basis for optimism when we consider the relationship between information and informedness at a microlevel. One of the keys to the revision of the minimalist view of voters is that low levels of information need not translate into an absence of reasonableness or coherence in their thinking (Sniderman 1993).

Berelson, Lazarsfeld, and McPhee (1954) noted that voters fall far short of the model of classical democratic citizens but that by the use of cues and shortcuts, they can compensate for this lack of information. Cues from "like-minded citizens and groups (including cues related to demographic characteristics and party labels) may be sufficient . . . to permit voters to act as if they had all the available information" (Page and Shapiro 1992, 387–88; see also McKelvey and Ordeshook 1985). The means through which voter competence may be achieved, at least as far as representative democracy is concerned, is the use of rules of thumb, or heuristics, by voters in making decisions.

Rather than focusing on simple levels of knowledge about politics (i.e., voters' ability to offer factual responses about candidates and issues), works by Sniderman, Brody, and Tetlock (1991), Popkin (1991), Page and Shapiro (1992), and Zaller (1992) stress the reasoning capacity of voters in national elections and the conditions under which voters are motivated to begin to think about politics and politicians. For example, drawing upon Anthony Downs's (1957) ideas of voting on the basis of information shortcuts, Popkin (1991) argues that voting decisions are grounded in substantial uncertainty. Information that might reduce this uncertainty is costly to acquire and process and is of uncertain value. Thus, voters rely on information shortcuts such as party identification to make decisions. From this interpretation, party identification is not so much the product of socialized, habituated, issueless behavior, but rather a standing (or default) decision. It reflects a stock of information about government and policies that can be updated, at some cost, as voters go about their daily lives.

As a standing decision, it could be updated by information on benefits the voter might receive from some government action (Popkin 1991, 14). In addition to campaigns, voters can rely on the opinions of others as a shortcut for evaluating the information they have (Popkin 1991, 44; Lazarsfeld, Berelson, and Gaudet 1948). This argument has also been found useful in legislative studies. Notwithstanding the early claims made on behalf of the wisdom of legislators, recent studies of legislative behavior suggest that legislators cannot be fully informed when they cast their votes. They are expected to vote on bills they may not have read; yet our understanding of their behavior suggests that they can do so while making choices that are consistent with their interests (for a review see Schneier and Gross 1993, 292–98). In the main, their decisions might be anchored in an overriding default interest in reelection (Mayhew 1974) or in concerns for party and policy (Fenno 1973).

While at times legislators are asked to make decisions on matters with which they are familiar, they are often faced with choices for which they have very little information. To function in this demanding environment where information is limited and decisions are plentiful, they must use cues and shortcuts. Legislators might defer to other members who are regarded as experts in a given policy area. They make decisions based on *incrementalism* (where previous modes of operation determine future outcomes). Legislators can take their cues from the voting intentions of other members, from pressure from constituents, or from committee chairs and party leaders (see, e.g., Kingdom 1989; Maisel 1981; Kozak 1987; Mathews and Stimson 1975; Lindblom 1959).

As for legislators, so too for voters, who are thus assumed to use decision shortcuts that enable them to reason about fairly complex phenomena. Citizens, in Sniderman's words, "manage to compensate for informational shortfalls by taking advantage of heuristics" (1993, 221). Heuristics are "judgmental short-cuts, efficient ways to organize and simplify political choices." They require relatively little information to use, and they yield dependable answers (Snider-man, Brody, and Tetlock 1991, 19). Heuristics can be used to simplify the choices voters face, and they allow voters to make choices that are consistent with their ideology, their self-interest, or, to the extent that these overlap, both.

From this perspective, voters are competent to handle the demands of de-cision making in standard elections of representatives and when making choices among candidates or parties. To borrow Lindblom's (1959) term, they "muddle through," yet they muddle through by some fairly systematic methods that appear to reflect some amount of reasoning about politics. They might de-termine who benefits from a policy, they can reflect on whether or not they like the group that benefits, and they can then draw conclusions about the pol-icy. Sniderman and colleagues call this judgment shortcut the "desert heuristic" (Sniderman, Brody, and Tetlock 1991). Other heuristics might be associ-ated with feelings toward the group, or an *affective heuristic*. Sniderman and colleagues demonstrate that different people use different heuristics, accord-ing to their level of political information, interest, education, or awareness. Whichever heuristic voters choose, the end result is that voters can exhibit sub-stantial internal consistency in decision making.

One of the most interesting contributions made by this body of work is that it demonstrates that conventional ways of characterizing mass belief systems and political reasoning processes might be flawed. By concentrating on factual knowledge rather than on the ability to reason given a limited number of facts, these previous models unnecessarily emphasized inconsistency and confusion in voters. Furthermore, these previous approaches, including applications of the Michigan model, assessed reasoning with uniform models that were applied to all categories of voters. However, the processes of reasoning that each voter uses—not simply the ability to reason—are likely to be shaped by the infor-mation (or schooling) the voter has available. From this premise it follows that not all voters will necessarily use the same cues and shortcuts. When assessing the same policy, the less-educated voters might use affect as a heuristic short-cut to decide where they stand on the issues, while the more-educated voters might use a desert heuristic. Each group, then, may be able to organize what they think about politics, albeit in somewhat different ways and quite possibly in different ways over different issues.

What emerges from this newer literature is a broad-based view that voters are able to make political choices even when they have limited information. Voters, to use an analogy, may know very little about the workings of the in-ternal combustion engine, but they do know how to drive. And while we might say that early voting studies focused on voter ignorance of the engine, these newer studies pay more attention to the ability to drive. At least in some quarters, this shift of focus has led to a fundamental reassessment not just of how well we think that voters cope with democracy, but also with the kinds of questions we ask about voters. The newer literature establishes that people either use information shortcuts or have some sort of reference point on which to ground their behavior. Some of these models posit a standing decision that might simplify decision making. For example, a default selection might be to support incumbents when the economy is good, but hold them accountable and punish them when the economy slows. In other electoral settings, better-known candidates are selected over lesser-known candidates; in this case, the known candidates serve as a default basis for evaluating other primary candidates (Bartels 1988).

Of course, the trouble is that in the setting of direct democracy, the types of cues and shortcuts that may be of use in candidate elections are missing. Retrospective voting on the basis of a politician's performance is typically useless. Proposition ballots also lack party labels, which seemingly limits the ability of party or ideology to be used as a store of information or as a vote cue.

With ballot propositions, then, information is sparser, the demands made on voters are even greater, and the familiar cues and road markers are either absent or inappropriate. Thus, even the literature noting that there are microlevel models where voter behavior reflects some amount of reasoning in representative democracy offers limited room for optimism when it comes to judging citizen competence under direct democracy.

Taken without modification, these theories of reasoning voters do provide a fairly poor fit for the noncandidate context of direct democracy. And although the decision context is somewhat analogous to the situation in which legislators make multiple policy choices with limited information, voters are not legislators. Like legislators, they need to rely on cues and shortcuts, but they do so in an environment where information and interest in the substance of politics are far more limited. Moreover, it is unlikely that the shortcuts voters employ to make choices in candidate races will always apply to choices about propositions. The absence of familiar candidate-centered cues and shortcuts, however, does not necessarily mean that voters are cast completely adrift when making decisions in direct democracy. Although voters may not be able to rely on the familiar standby sources of information, we can suppose that reasoning voters should turn to other cues or rely on different rules of thumb.

A decision (vote choice) in direct democracy simply imposes different demands on voters than does a decision in a candidate election. As people reasoning about politics on the basis of limited information, voters appear to cope with decisions about candidates in a coherent fashion. We suggest that these same reasoning voters devise ways to cope with the unique information demands associated with direct democracy. The absence of familiar cues in proposition elections serves as our point of departure for analysis, rather than a conclusion about the difficulty of deciding on ballot propositions.

Assessing Voter Competence in Direct Democracy

To say that voters may or may not be "competent" presents a serious problem of definition. What does it mean to say that voters might reason under direct democracy, or that they can handle the demands of direct democracy in a competent way? There are several ways to answer this question. In the end, we select a rather broad definition of competence. An obvious concern, as stated by Bartels (1996, 200), is "the extent to which [information shortcuts, cues and various heuristics] actually facilitate informed choices by real electorates." One way to assess voter competence and reasoning from this perspective would be to compare the behavior of poorly informed voters using cues, shortcuts, and heuristics with the behavior of those voting with full information. Bartels uses NES data to discover a 10 percent average deviation of actual vote probabilities from hypothetical fully informed vote probabilities in presidential elections. He concludes that ill-informed voters using information cues reduce their errors in voting from a hypothetical base of "fully informed voting" by 50 percent. "The fact of the matter, it seems, is that they do significantly better than they would by chance, but significantly less well than they would do with complete information" (217).

In a study of voting on several insurance initiatives, Lupia (1994a, 71) demonstrates that ill-informed voters who had knowledge of the insurance industry's preferences about insurance regulation initiatives had opinions that were nearly identical to those of well-informed voters (within 3 percent or less). In this case, having a cue about who is backing the initiative caused badly informed voters to emulate the behavior of well-informed voters. From this perspective, the behavior of well-informed voters again serves as a benchmark for evaluating competence. If well-informed or well-educated voters are assumed to represent competence and are thought to have the ability to reason on the basis of relevant information, then the behavior of less-informed voters might appear to be more competent as it comes to resemble that of well-educated voters. In the analysis that follows, we will use this method to assess voter competence.

An alternative research strategy, and one that we also pursue here, is to examine if and how voters respond to the changed decision setting that direct democracy presents. Thus, one of our primary goals is to explain how voters make their decisions when faced with a large number of ballot propositions. Any attempt to quantify and define a priori "well-informed" or "fully informed" behavior across a large number of propositions is inherently problematic. To do so we would need to make assumptions about what constitutes perfectly informed behavior on all sorts of issues. One of our goals, and one of our criteria for assessing reasoning and competence under direct democracy, is thus quite modest. We seek to determine if behavior under direct democracy responds to information and information demands, if voters seek shortcuts to deal with demands, and if the use of information, ideology, or shortcuts "makes sense."

In a study of mass opinion, Page and Shapiro (1992) look at aggregated opinions and illustrate that the public can be seen as rational because its policy preferences "are real—not meaningless random 'non attitudes' . . . [and they] make sense in terms of underlying values and available information." The public can be seen as rational because "changes [in opinions] constitute sensible adjustments to new conditions and new information" (Page and Shapiro 1992, xi). Gerber and Lupia (1995) also illustrate that voter competence in direct democracy is wrapped up in information. If adequate information is available, voter choices might be competent and elections might be responsive because informed choices produce election outcomes that reflect voters' interests and preferences. It is important, then, to look at what information is available to direct-democracy voters and how the information is used.

We think that these strategies are the base for a fair evaluation of competence and reasoning in direct-democracy voters, and for framing the questions that will be posed in the chapters that follow. Do direct-democracy voters get information that allows them to use workable decision shortcuts that "make sense"? Do they respond to information demands? Do opinions about propositions make sense in terms of a voter's interests and the information that might be available? If so, we could say that these voters are competent and that they reason.

In general, we argue that voters will approach proposition elections in a way that is similar to how they approach candidate races in which information is limited. They utilize information shortcuts and they search for default points of reference. As with the use of heuristics in political reasoning, different cues might be relevant for different voters. Given the variety of choices, different cues might also be of use for different types of choices. At this point, however, we must say more about the content of the references and cues that voters are likely to use when facing direct-democracy elections where uncertainty is even more endemic, even more chronic, than in candidate races. We consider three possible decision cues in turn: avoiding uncertainty by voting *no*, using instrumental evaluations of propositions, and taking cues from political elites.

Decision Cues in Direct-Democracy Voting

Saying "No"

One theme that emerges from the psychological literature is a sense that, rather than being risk-neutral utility maximizers, people are generally risk averse.

They are found to be less sensitive to increases in income, or risk associated with increases, than to decreases in income, or risk associated with decreases (Kahneman and Tversky 1984). This asymmetry associated with evaluations of risk can also cause voters to have a negativity bias in their evaluations of politicians. They might be inclined to punish politicians as a result of economic downturns, but they might be less sensitive to improvements in the economy (Ansolabehere and Iyengar 1993, 325; Key 1966; Lau 1982). In short, it is the risk of loss that voters are most sensitive to.

In complex situations such as presidential primaries, voters choose from among several competing options. They require information shortcuts (or search aids) in order to handle the different types of information they receive. "The way they make use of shortcuts in searching among complex choices results in a Drunkard's Search, a search among obvious differences" (Popkin 1991, 92). Voters must arrive at a low-cost method of comparing several candidates about whom they know relatively little, and they are likely to focus on a single attribute or dimension as a default frame of reference. The use of such a default cue as a reference point reduces the need for additional information and it also "avoids mental strain" (93; see also Tversky, Sattah, and Slovic 1988, 372). In presidential primary races, Popkin suggests that front-runner status serves as such a reference point. Competing candidates might provide information about themselves with reference to the front-runner, and voters can make evaluations of these candidates based on comparisons with the front-runner.

In the context of primary elections, uncertainty about candidates will keep them from being considered by voters. Familiarity allows voters to make judgments about candidates (Bartels 1988, 82). If there is great uncertainty about a candidate, then she or he cannot be evaluated by most voters. In the end, voters appear to have a default strategy of preferring better-known to lesser-known candidates when other factors are equal (Bartels 1988; Bowler, Donovan, and Snipp 1993). The preference for certainty corresponds to the avoidance of uncertain options. An alternative phrasing of this idea is found in the social-psychological literature. Within this literature, people are said to conserve cognitive resources by using simple decision cues (or default reference points); they may be less receptive to complicating factors, and they may have preferences for absolute certainties over conditional or probabilistic outcomes (Dawes 1966; Jervis 1993, 341).

Compared to voting in candidate primaries with limited information, direct democracy does not offer a front-runner as a point of reference, nor is there a best-known candidate. If we assume, however, that people behave in a similar way when voting on propositions as they do when voting in primaries, we can expect that they find and use a default point of reference for evaluating the choices they face. This reference point allows voters to conserve cognitive resources and avoid "mental strain" while providing a basis for making evaluations of any proposition on the ballot. Moreover, it is sensitive to risk associated with uncertainty.

We suggest that this reference is the *no* vote. Using *no* as a reference point in direct democracy is analogous to the use of incumbency in candidate races as it preserves the status quo when the alternative—a shift away from the status quo—is uncertain. One early supporter of the process, Schumacher, identified this rule, and others have suggested it since: "[T]he elector, when in doubt, votes 'no' more often than 'yes'" (Schumacher 1932, 251; see also Barnett 1915, 121; Magleby 1984, 167–68). If voters approach a choice about a proposition with limited information, and they are uncertain about how the proposition might actually change the status quo, they can compare what they know about any *yes* vote with the potential certainty of preserving the status quo with a *no* vote. On many occasions, they will respond to cues, shortcuts, and available information and defect from the status quo (*no*) to a *yes* vote on some measures. Over the long haul, however, when the information demands created by direct democracy are greatest, negative voting should increase. In chapter 3 we examine how abstention and *no* voting vary systematically with information demands associated with different proposition choices.

These expectations about *no* voting follow from "conventional wisdom" and previous research, but also from a large body of political science and psychology research that demonstrates a "negativity bias" in decision making (for a review, see Ansolabehere and Iyengar 1993; Kahneman and Tversky 1984). In many situations, people are found to be averse to risk and worried more about potential losses than potential gains. In candidate races, risk-averse voters are found to punish incumbents more heavily in bad times than they reward them in good times (e.g., Lau 1982). Voters are consistently found to be risk averse in primary and general elections (Enelow and Hinich 1984; Brady and Ansolabehere 1989).

Some voters might also be particularly risk averse in the domain of losses, rather than gains. That is, when choices are framed so that opportunities for loss are maximized, risk aversion is more evident (Ansolabehere and Iyengar 1993). Consider, for example, minimally informed voters who are asked to make decisions on statewide ballot propositions that propose new polices, spending plans, or borrowing. Many of these choices involve clearly identifiable fiscal costs. If we assume that perceptions of the risks of adopting new policies are embedded in concerns about the state's economy, we can expect that negative voting might increase when economic conditions deteriorate. In situations of economic stagnation or decline, more voters might be making decisions in the context of the domain of loss, where risks of new spending policies appear greater. In times of economic decline, then, we might expect that the default *no* vote is more prevalent.

Using Instrumental Evaluations

Of course, if this were the extent of a theory of direct-democracy voting, we would have quite a simple model. Because uncertainty may be a chronic problem in initiative elections, we would be led to predict that all measures would fail as uncertain voters voted *no* every time. Clearly, such is not the case. Theories of choice under limited information allow voters in candidate races to be deflected from their default reference points: front-runners and best-known candidates do not get all the votes and they do not always win. Voters can also utilize instrumental evaluations and employ other cues when making decisions.

Consider that each proposition involves a potential shift away from some current status quo: some shifts can make the voter worse off, some better off. In any theory that argues that voters may be motivated by self-interest, we should see voters supporting propositions that make them personally better off and opposing those that do not. Of course, the question remains as to how voters know where their self-interest lies on some propositions. It is not enough to recognize that voters may have some self-interest at stake in a given proposition election; they also have to act upon that self-interest.

For example, voters might find out that a proposition will cost them something without providing much in return. Alternatively, they might decide that a proposition will benefit them while presenting minimal personal costs. Such determinations assume that voters have and can recognize a set of interests. These instrumental calculations may be especially relevant for tax and spending measures. For example, school voucher proposals target benefits to those who decide to send their children to private schools by promising a cash payment to voters with children and especially to those with children in private school. These propositions include details about expenditure rules that determine who can actually receive money. The rules affect how much personal money (in addition to the public voucher) is needed to send a child to a private school and what sort of private schools can receive vouchers, and they determine whether parents with children already in private schools will receive public money for keeping their children where they are.

If campaigns provide even minimal information about such issues—and voters reason on the basis of instrumental concerns—we might see that voting on school issues is structured by parental status (Hamilton and Cohen 1974), if not by simple self-interest. We presume that the voter knows her or his own interests (or preferences) to at least this degree. This scenario provides an interpretation that is somewhat different than that provided by some of the studies of the early 1960s (e.g., Gamson 1961; Horton and Thompson 1962; McDill and Ridley 1962; Boskof and Zeigler 1964) or the studies of Proposition 13 that we noted earlier.

Finding and Using Elite Cues

We must recognize that not all issues are based solely on self-interest. At times, voters do not necessarily require access to the kinds of information needed to make instrumental evaluations. It is here that cue taking can have the greatest usefulness. As noted earlier, the familiar cues and decision rules that voters use in candidate elections are not immediately applicable. The idea that voters can adapt their behavior and respond to the demands of direct democracy by using information shortcuts is best articulated in recent scholarship by Arthur Lupia (1994a; 1992). Lupia's formal work (1992) focuses on how elections produce outcomes that are consistent with an individual's preferences when there are huge disparities in information between voters and initiative proponents. He assumes that voters know more about the status quo and are uncertain about the proponent's alteration of the status quo. Lacking detailed knowledge of a proposal, voters draw information for their decisions from beliefs about the proponent's intentions and from credible cues (signals) sent by the proponents and opponents (such as an elite's endorsement). Proponents have incentives to provide credible cues, or at least to incorporate the provision of cues into their electoral strategies (Lupia 1992, 398). In another formal model, Gerber and Lupia (1995) demonstrate that rather than reforming initiative elections by limiting spending, election outcomes in direct democracy can be made more responsive to voter interests when the information cues available to voters (i.e., competition among political elites) are increased. Active campaigns and campaign spending thus provide one possible source of information.

That raises the question of which information cues direct-democracy voters might actually use, as well as whether they use them effectively. As Lupia notes,

> As an alternative to the costly acquisition of encyclopedic information, voters may choose to employ information shortcuts. For example, voters can acquire information about the preferences or opinions of friends, coworkers, political parties or other groups, which they may then use to infer how a proposition will affect them. (1994a, 63)

In a study of the competing automobile insurance initiatives on the 1988 California ballot, Lupia (1994a) examined the use of cues about elite endorsements. He demonstrates that ill-informed voters who knew the insurance industry's positions on the competing propositions made decisions that appeared very similar to those made by survey respondents who had high levels of factual knowledge about the propositions. Voters take cues from those who are in favor of (or against) a proposition. Knowing who is behind a proposition allows them to infer something about how it might affect them. Knowing who is for or against a proposition might be particularly useful for making a decision on a ballot issue when the subject is highly complex (i.e., nuclear power regulations) or largely invisible or banal (i.e., restructuring the jurisdiction of state courts).

On such issues, it might be very difficult for the average voter to obtain much factual information relevant to the decision. Learning what type of fuel a nuclear plant uses or the procedures for disposing of waste, for example, may or may not help some voters decide what an antinuclear proposition means.

Knowing which side of an issue parties, groups, and elites are promoting might allow far more voters to decide where they stand on the proposition. We might think of this as the "Who's for it?" (or "Who's against it?") cue. This is but one simple question voters might ask when evaluating an initiative deci-sion. Voters can take cues from information about who supports a measure, who drafted the measure, and who is behind the opposition to a measure. If propo-sition campaigns operate with the assumption that voters think this way, they have an incentive to contact voters and present them with information about credible, visible groups and/or individuals who have lined up in favor of (or in opposition to) the initiative. As W. S. U'ren—one of the leaders who helped put the initiative into practice in Oregon—is quoted as saying (in Pease 1907, 563),

> In all our work we have found the great value of well known names at-tached to our measures as officers or members of committees. . . . You see the average voter is too indolent, too busy or too distrustful of his own judgment to study or decide for himself upon the details of a law. . . . People always ask . . . "who is the back of it?"

Many Oregon voters, for example, could have asked "Who is the back of it?" in 1908 when forced to make a choice between competing fishing regulations. Upon learning that one initiative was backed by downstream fishers, upstream folks probably needed little additional information when casting their votes. Details about the regulations or gear allowances might be trivial to the upstream people if they know the initiative is backed by groups that they know are com-peting for their fish.

Later, we will use opinion data to examine how this process might have operated during a contemporary term-limit initiative campaign. Unlike many propositions that voters initially tend to be skeptical of (i.e., tax issues, spend-ing measures, bond levies), term limits enjoyed widespread support in early polls. When a competitive campaign occurs and voters are sensitive to the "Who's behind it?" question, however, opinion polarizes. When Democrats in the state of Washington and in California asked themselves this question, cam-paign information told them that the answer was "Republicans" (or that those in opposition were Democrats). This answer could allow many voters to make some inference about outcomes associated with term limits in their state. Con-sidering the dissension in political science about the consequences of term limits (for example, see Reed and Schansberg 1995 and comments; Mondak 1995 and comments), expert debate may have been more a source of confusion than clarity. For some voters, knowledge of "Who's for it?" might be enough to cast a vote that is consistent with their preferences or interests. Such cues might also allow some voters to make instrumental judgments about how a proposition can affect them.

Elite cues and endorsements by reference groups are but one source of information that voters might use as a shortcut for making decisions about ballot propositions. These shortcuts might allow them to decide what they are for and against, or perhaps even to decide how a specific proposal affects them personally.

Thus far we have identified three such shortcuts: voting *no* in the face of uncertainty, instrumental concerns ("What's in it for me?" or "What's this going to cost?"), and elite or party cues ("Who's for it?" or "Who's against it?"). When voters have such shortcuts and such minimal information, our theory suggests that many should form opinions about propositions that "make sense" in terms of their values or interests. As a means for developing a parsimonious theory, this approach leaves something to be desired. There are likely to be many other such shortcuts used for evaluating propositions that we can arrive at either a priori or through induction. We keep our analysis somewhat parsimonious by focusing largely on how decisions might be structured by partisan or ideological referents and by various instrumental concerns. These cues can be manifested in different ways among different propositions. For some, as we shall see, these "what's in it for me?" motivations might be applied easily on certain issues on the basis of personal costs or benefits associated with a proposition. On other issues, instrumental motivations might be bound up in group interests, or benefits or costs that might accrue to the local community.

Ideology and Decisions

So far, we have discussed the idea that voters act upon and identify self-interest and that they react to cues. In taking cues from leading politicians who represent established political movements and parties, voters are also likely to be able to identify whether the proposal will make them better or worse off. Moreover, and perhaps just as important, cues and campaign information are likely to allow some voters to relate propositions to their preexisting ideologies. Easily available information may thus allow some voters to understand a given proposition in terms of broader ideological and partisan concerns.

Not all propositions are alike, and not all propositions encourage self-interest and partisan or ideological concerns in equal measure. The context of each decision (i.e., the substance of the policy) might also determine what shortcuts voters use when casting their votes. For some (if not many) voters, reasoning about direct democracy is likely to involve more than the use of information shortcuts. As noted before, early voting studies (Converse 1964; Sniderman 1993) gave little credence to ideology as a major cognitive determinant of voting in the United States. If ideology constrains disparate views on an array of issues, however, we might expect that ideology helps some people order the political world in terms of the core values they hold prior to exposure to any individual issue or proposition. As a value orientation or as a way to organize views about politics, ideology may also allow people to judge issues with reference to past experiences and feelings (Kuklinski, Metlay, and Kay 1982, 619; Bennett 1980:17).

In a discussion of the correlates of vote choice found in earlier studies of proposition elections, Magleby noted that "[t]o a surprising extent, ideological self-classification appears to determine voting behavior" (1984, 176). If some number of voters are "sophisticated" in the sense that their opinions are constrained by ideology (or are consistent with general ideological orientations), we should not be surprised to find that ideological identifications are associated with vote choices on initiatives. Ideology can thus help voters reason about measures even though they might be minimally informed of specific details of the policy.

The consistent relationship we find between ideology and opinions on propositions is not surprising when we consider the choice context presented by direct democracy. Candidate races, particularly heavily studied presidential races and winner-take-all legislative races in two-party systems, present voters with choices between individuals who are often forced by electoral context toward the center of the political spectrum (Amy 1993; Downs 1957). Concerns about issues can be and are subsumed by candidate personality matters of competence, integrity, reliability, and so on (Miller, Wattenberg, and Malanchuk 1986). With a decision context that emphasizes candidate personality traits, it is perhaps not surprising that ideology—as a bundle of beliefs about polices and politics—displayed a limited role in some studies of choices in candidate races. When the decision context removes personality traits from center stage, however, and choices are about issues (ballot propositions) rather than candidates, then ideology might play a major role in structuring voting and voter opinions.

For example, if self-identified liberals have constrained opinions (in a manner conventionally associated with late-twentieth-century American liberals), we might find it easy for them to know what they are for or against when presented with many direct-democracy choices. Assume that some voters identify themselves as liberals because they are sympathetic to an active public sector—except perhaps in the arena of personal liberties.[1] Without knowing de-

---

1. That is, standard descriptions of contemporary liberalism associate this belief system with sympathy for government intervention in the economy and in the promotion of civil rights, while resisting government interference in personal and privacy issues.

tails of specific propositions, we might expect that self-identified liberal voters favor policies that maintain the public sector and oppose policies that constrain personal liberties. Because voters who have a grounding in abstract ideology possess the capacity to make deductive inferences about each ballot proposition on the basis of their ideological conceptions, the information shortcuts presented earlier might not be as necessary for making reasonable choices.

Furthermore, if ideology has an affective component rooted in likes and dislikes about groups, it can allow a great number of voters to evaluate policies in terms of who the voter likes (or dislikes; see Sniderman, Brody, and Tetlock 1991, chap. 8). Indeed, ideologies may give meaning to the cues available to voters. One example, which we consider later in greater detail, is that of a partisan voter receiving a cue from a well-known politician. That cue may tell the voter not only which side of the issue the voter's party favors, but also where the voter's position on the issue is likely to be located and something about where along the continuum the proposal lies. A single cue, then, can tell the voter much about the decision at hand. If we consider each point in figure 1 as something the voter needs to be aware of in order to make a decision, it may not be the case that voters need a different cue in order to decipher each and every detail. Some cues may allow a voter to clarify simultaneously a number of the aspects in figure 1.

Summary

If we agree that direct democracy places upon voters very different demands than those presented by candidate elections, it seems both unlikely and unreasonable to expect that voters will respond to proposition elections using exactly the same approach that they use in candidate elections. In addition, given that propositions may differ quite markedly in their content, it seems equally unreasonable to suppose that voting across many propositions can be explained by a single model with a single set of parameters that tap the impact of ideology, self-interest, or other possible motors of voter behavior.

Many observers of direct democracy have criticized voters' ability to make decisions on many new and complicated issues by pointing to empirical evidence, predominantly from national elections but also from a series of single-case proposition studies that show mass behavior to be ill-informed and lacking the capacity for reasoning. We take seriously the fundamental assumptions of this critique of voting—that there are too many different issues for voters to decide on and that relevant information is sparse—and we examine them in the following chapters. We illustrate that voters do appear able to draw inferences from available information and that they respond to cues when making decisions on ballot propositions. That does not mean that all voters, or even most of them, are well informed and in command of narrow factual details about the policies on which they are casting votes. Rather, we show that they vote in predictable ways, in ways that respond to information demands, and in ways that often are consistent with their ideology and (our conceptions of) their interests. At a basic level, then, direct-democracy voters appear sufficiently competent to make informed choices. If that is so, then criticism of the process of direct democracy—particularly regarding the policy outcomes of the system—might be better directed somewhere other than at the mass electorate.

CHAPTER 3

Responding to Demands: Information, Abstention, and Just Saying "No"

Theories of voting with limited information offer a picture of voters who have some basic default point of reference to anchor their evaluations and decisions. As noted in chapter 2, voters in presidential primaries can compare other candidates with front-runners. Voters in candidate contests can also defer to better-known candidates or candidates who share their party identification. They might also evaluate an incumbent candidate's performance retrospectively by taking cues from information about the state of the economy.

In direct democracy, these points of reference are largely absent. Propositions are listed on ballots without party labels. On occasion, voters might find party cues in ballot pamphlets or from campaigns. As we demonstrate later, voters can make choices on the basis of partisan cues if they are available, but many less-contested propositions create a situation in which the voter will find it difficult to identify party positions (Magleby 1984, 174). Given that nearly all propositions present new policies that change the status quo, retrospective evaluations are also problematic.

A Reference Point

We propose that direct-democracy voters nevertheless have a least one point of reference when they approach a slate of initiative and referenda choices. As Lupia (1992, 1994a) demonstrates, it is logical to assume that people know more about the status quo than they know about a given ballot proposition. The status quo is the current state of affairs that might be altered by passage of a ballot issue. For any voter who lacks perfect information, changes in the status quo will involve greater uncertainty and risk than maintenance of the status quo. As far as ballot choices are structured, a *no* vote on any proposition is essentially a vote that maintains the status quo.

If we assume, however, that few propositions are exactly alike, all choices do not present the same information demands. Indeed, nearly every ballot issue makes unique information demands on the voter. Given variety in campaign intensity, subject, language, ballot title, and other factors, some choices might be harder to make than others. Voters, if sensitive to the unique information demands associated with different types of choices, would vote *no* in a manner that varies systematically with information demands.

These assumptions might be seen as little more than conventional wisdom that suggests that when in doubt, voters vote *no*. We suggest that there is a bit more to it. As Magleby noted, confused voters often vote *no* because of their uncertainty (1984, 162). There are costs associated with reducing this uncertainty by becoming politically informed, however. Citizens have incentives (and opportunities) to minimize these costs. In addition, some choices present greater costs than others. For most voters, a decision on a $200 million school construction bond is likely to be qualitatively different than a decision on reorganizing regulations that affect chiropractors or denturists (these are real choices that voters have faced in the Pacific states). We assume that unless they happen to be a chiropractor or a denturist, most people would have an easier time with the school bond decision than with the regulations issues. The substance of the bond issue is less technical, there might be people discussing the issue, the costs are more straightforward, and the beneficiaries are more clearly defined—especially if there are no campaigns on any of these issues. In other words, there is greater uncertainty with the simpler decisions. Where information demands are greatest, uncertainty is highest.

As Downs suggests, a rational voter might reduce uncertainty by seeking "free" information from political parties, interest groups, paid ads, knowledgeable friends, published letters, speeches, and other sources (1957, 222). In such situations, voters might be more likely to defect from the status quo. But if gathering information about ballot propositions is costly and the voters' incentive to do so is limited, we might expect that they would respond by voting *no* where costs are greatest. Thus, it is not just that they vote *no* when in doubt, but that they do so on some other occasions—particularly when they are faced with the greatest information demands. Evaluating candidate races (where a simple vote that preserves the status quo is often less obvious), Downs contended that some voters might also abstain in such situations. Such behavior might be seen as rational when information costs are exceedingly high (Downs 1957, chap. 14).

This conception of reasoning raises several questions about how voters perceive information demands created by proposition contests and how they respond to those demands. In the analysis that follows, we demonstrate that California voters articulate serious concerns about participating in direct democracy. These concerns appear to center on the information demands required to manage the process: voters find proposition elections confusing, and they feel that they have little knowledge about the issues. Nevertheless, most seem to like the process, which suggests that many learn to cope with the information demands. After examining their concerns, we test several hypotheses about how election outcomes in Oregon and California reflect a systematic process in which voters respond to information demands by saying *no*. We then examine the sources of information that voters might use to cope with complex, lengthy ballots. In the end, we find that voters fall short of understanding the substance of the initiatives, but they find enough information to make reasonable choices.

Voter Perceptions of Information Demands in Direct Democracy

With its large population, numerous media outlets, and many academic institutions, the California electorate is one of the more heavily surveyed in the nation. The Field Institute, using its California Polls, has tracked opinion on candidate politics and public issues for decades. The institute frequently investigates proposition contests, and it has occasionally asked voters questions about the process of direct democracy itself. The results of these polls tell us a great deal about the information problems voters face, as well as how they might cope with them.

In November 1988, California voters were presented with one of the longest ballots in the state's history. Twenty-nine statewide propositions were listed, the most since 1922. Included were the five rival insurance initiatives that we discussed in earlier chapters (Lupia 1994a; Banducci 1992) and a highly contested smoking tax initiative. More than $100 million was spent on these six measures alone (in comparison, no presidential campaign has ever generated similar spending in a single state). Less than two months after facing this lengthy ballot and the barrage of advertisements associated with these initiatives, the Field Institute asked voters what they thought about the initiative process.

Respondents were asked an unprompted, open-ended question on their general concerns about proposition elections. Up to three responses were recorded per respondent. As figure 2 illustrates, over half of respondents could think of something that they did not like about the process. The most common criticism was that it was too confusing. Voters also cited worries about having too little knowledge of the issues, and they voiced concerns that there were too many issues on the ballot. Among those mentioning specific concerns, 26 percent of voters offered one of these worries as their most-pressing concern with direct democracy. Conversely, only 7 percent worried that the process was too expensive (Field Institute California Poll, January 1989).

In spite of these responses, California voters do not dislike direct democracy. In the same poll, roughly 70 percent of voters said that proposition elections were a good thing. In August 1990, prior to another election with a large crop of ballot measures, voters were asked if they thought that statewide ballot proposition elections were a good thing for California, a bad thing, or neither. Sixty-eight percent said the elections were a good thing. Conversely, only 8 per-

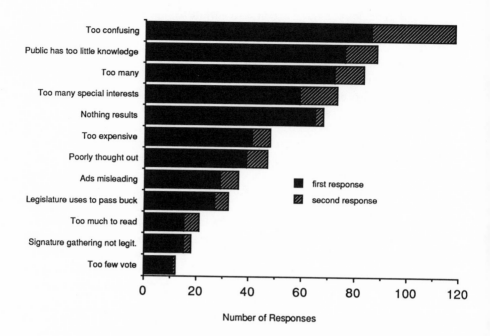

Fig. 2.   What is bad about state ballot proposition elections? (*N* = 1, 007; data from Field Research Corporation, California poll, January 1989.)

cent thought they were bad, and 24 percent thought they were neither good nor bad. In 1996 another California poll showed over 69 percent of respondents thought ballot propositions were a good thing, yet 71 percent thought most propositions were not "understandable to the average voter" (Field Institute California Poll, September 1996). And so we have an apparent paradox—most voters have something bad to say about direct democracy, yet most also *like* the process.

The findings seem less than paradoxical if we consider that voters' opinions about direct democracy are related to their ability to deal with the information demands that direct democracy creates. Voters with the most information about ballot issues have the highest regard for direct democracy. Table 1 reports a logistic regression analysis of the 1990 opinion data. Results illustrate that favorable evaluations of the process are affected by how familiar the voter is with the actual measures that are to appear in a forthcoming election. The survey included questions that asked voters if they had heard anything about individual propositions on the ballot, allowing us to create an index of how much information voters have about propositions. Even after controlling for education (the two are correlated at .18), the most informed voters are more likely to think the process is a good thing. The less-informed voters are significantly more critical.

These data demonstrate two things. First, despite information demands, large proportions of well-educated *and* less-educated voters think that California's demanding process of direct democracy is a good thing. Second, the more informed one is about ballot measures, the more likely that one is going to offer a positive evaluation of the process.

We suggest that voters at different educational levels approve of the seemingly confusing process because they can manage the information demands it creates. Different voters might manage these demands in different ways. As we see in this and in subsequent chapters, voters use different sources of information, and different cues apply to various types of ballot choices. One potential key to the "hate-it-but-like-it" paradox identified here is that people can respond to the information demands by abstaining on matters they know or care less about, or by voting *no* when they are uncertain. When information about an issue is available, voters can seek out the relevant proposition and make a choice. Choices for the well-educated and less-educated voters, moreover, can be made easier as they find cheap and useful sources of information that are relevant to the decisions they face.

TABLE 1.   Estimation of Voter Evaluations of Direct Democracy

Respondents were asked, "Do you think that proposition elections are a good thing?" $1 = $ Yes, $0 = $ otherwise.

Variable	
Strong GOP	.38[+]
	(.25)
Level of information about propositions	.26*
	(.11)
Age	$-.006$
	(.005)
Education	.06
	(.04)
Constant	.42
	(.30)
Number of cases	614
Percentage correctly predicted	66.1

Source: California Poll, August 1990.

Note: Logistic regression estimates. Level of information equals the number of ballot propositions listed on the November 1990 ballot that the respondent had heard of. Standard errors of estimates in parentheses.

*Significant at $p < .05$ (two tail)   [+]Significant at $p < .10$

With the status quo preserved by negative voting, these voters also have a reference point for making decisions. Using cues and information shortcuts, voters can deflect from this point and make informed choices with limited information.

Responding to Information Demands

Abstaining and Saying "No"

Does *no* voting or abstention serve as a way for voters to minimize information costs? If so, we would expect to see that each varies systematically with the demands created by the choice context that proposition voting creates. We can test this expectation by examining the relationship between *no* voting or abstention and the information demands associated with various ballot choices. Following Downs (1957), we also expect that the decision to actually participate on any given ballot proposition should be affected by the information demands associated with each specific proposition choice.

With direct democracy, information demands can increase as voters are faced with longer ballots, which require that they make more individual choices. Marginal increases in the length of the ballot increase costs and translate into additional decisions that must be made. Scholars of voting have noted that ballot structure can affect election outcomes (Darcy and McAllister 1990; Taebel 1975; Magleby 1989; Magleby 1984, 55). Longer ballots, then, can be expected to be associated with more *no* voting, and voters who wish to reduce costs can simply vote *no* or abstain.

Looking at ballots and election returns from Oregon and California, we see that such an increase in *no* voting when the ballot is longer appears to occur. Table 2 reports a bivariate regression analysis of Oregon general election

TABLE 2.   Estimation of Negative Voting by Ballot Length (aggregate data)

	Oregon 1910–90	California 1974–92
Number of propositions	.37**	.41**
	(.10)	(.12)
Constant	45.9**	38.1**
	(1.38)	(2.14)
N	400	268
R^2	.05	.05

Source: Mason 1994 (Oregon); California Secretary of State, Statement of the Vote, various years (California).

Note: OLS estimates. Standard errors in parentheses.

**Significant at $p < .01$ (two-tail)

propositions from 1910 to 1990. The results illustrate a weak but significant linear relationship between the percentage of the *no* vote and the total number of propositions on the ballot. For every additional proposition on the total ballot in an election, individual propositions drew 37 percent more *no* votes. A similar analysis of propositions appearing on California ballots from 1974 through 1992 produces a slope of .41. These bivariate data illustrate that when more proposition choices are placed on the ballot, voters cast more negative votes.

There is a more direct way to test the hypothesis that many uncertain voters end up voting *no* on ballot measures. In table 3, the percentage of undecided voters on individual propositions included in the final California Poll taken before each statewide election from 1982 through 1994 is regressed against the actual percentage of *no* votes on each proposition. We also include the percentage of those intending to vote *no* on each measure from the last poll to provide a baseline that controls for the initial level of opposition to the measure. When more voters are undecided about a proposition prior to an election, we find greater negative voting on that proposition.

Such findings are consistent with our theory, but they do not tell us much about how negative voting on a proposition is related to the context of choice. If voters simply tire from marking long ballots without any response to information demands associated with each individual choice, there would be a simple linear relationship between negative voting and ballot length. However, if voters search for information or if they make choices where demands are less burdensome, there is no reason to expect a simple linear relationship between ballot length and *no* voting or abstention. As noted before, it is easier to obtain

TABLE 3. Estimation of Negative Voting
on Individual Propositions, California, 1982–94:
Predicated by Percentage Undecided Prior
to Election (dependent variable = percentage
of *no* vote in election on proposition)

Variable	
% undecided before election	0.13*
	(.06)
% saying *no* before election	0.62**
	(.11)
Constant	25.74**
$N = 62$	
$R^2 = .34$	

Source: California Polls 1982–94 (opinion measures); California Secretary of State, Statement of the Vote, various years (election data).

Note: OLS estimates. Standard errors in parentheses.

*Significant at $p < .05$ (two-tail)

**Significant at $p < .01$ (two-tail)

needed information on some propositions. Some observers (Magleby 1984, Magleby 1989; Bone 1974) suggest that when controversy surrounds a proposition, voters receive more information. If that is the case, they may be encouraged to sort through a long ballot in order to cast a vote for or against the issue they have heard about. Controversy over an issue might be difficult to operationalize, yet it is reasonable to expect that voters are less likely to automatically abstain or to vote against those propositions with which they are most familiar.

A Model of Abstention and Negative Voting

California ballots provide an interesting opportunity for testing how (or if) voters respond systematically to the information demands associated with direct democracy. Statewide ballots in California include bond measures, citizen initiatives, and referenda drafted by the legislature. Table 4 provides a list of the measures appearing on the 1988 and 1984 general election ballots in California. Although the 1988 ballot was longer than average, the order that measures appear in is typical and is determined by law. Bond measures usually appear first, followed by constitutional measures referred by the legislature, with direct citizen initiatives at the end (Section 10218, Election Code of California). Of these, voters can be expected to be most familiar with initiatives.

Given the controversial topics that are included in many direct initiatives, these measures are probably associated with more readily available information. In addition to being associated with more campaign spending than are other propositions (Magleby 1984, 209–10), initiative measures reach the ballot only after petitioners receive signatures from registered voters that are the equivalent of 5 percent of the vote cast for governor in the previous election. This requirement creates a costly qualification process whereby a sizable number of voters are exposed to the measure before the campaign begins (Price 1988). Because bond measures are issues that affect the pocketbook, we might also expect less abstention with them. In contrast, legislative measures, which appear in the center of the ballot, are more likely to deal with governmental reorganization or minor revisions to existing laws. Because they lack the campaign and novelty that surrounds initiatives, voters have less exposure to these issues prior to an election.

Information demands are also affected by the nature of the individual propositions. Wordier propositions—all else being equal—increase the costs associated with making a choice. Because it takes more to read and time is scarce, a longer proposition title might be associated with greater abstention or with negative voting. Constitutional measures, which have longer titles than do other ballot propositions, present a problem in estimating these equations. Therefore, we estimate the effects of title length on each type of proposition

**TABLE 4.   A Sample of Referenda and Initiative Subjects
in California General Elections**

1988	1984

Legislative Bond Acts

Higher Ed Facilities	Parklands Bonds
School Facilities	Veterans Bonds
Prison Construction	
Drinking Water	
Water Conservation	
Clean Water	
Housing	
Library Construction	
Correctional Facilities	

Legislative Constitutional Amendments

Redevelopment Projects	State Capitol Maintenance
Tax Reallocation Revision	Low-rent Housing
Depositing Public Moneys	Freedom of Press
Governor's Review of Sentencing	Reapportionment
Property Tax Reappraisal Exemption	Disaster Assistance
Courts of Record	Alternative Energy Financing
Commision of Judicial Performance	
Property Tax: Revise Veterans Exemptions	
Permit Judges to Teach Part-time	

Citizen's Initiatives

Housing and Nutrition for Homeless	Income Tax Cut
AIDS Testing for Criminals	Rent
Reestablishing Cal-OSHA	Taxation: Surtax
Guaranteed Level for K–12 Funding	
Cigarette and Tobacco Tax for Health Care	
AIDS Reporting	
Insurance Rates: Trial Lawyers	
Insurance: Polanco	
Insurance: Nader	
Insurance: No-Fault	
Right-to-Know for Consumers	
Insurance: Tort Reform	

with interactive terms.[1] As Downs (1957) noted, voters might rely on free information from campaigns to compensate for demands that would otherwise cause them to abstain. Propositions having greater total spending on each side

---

1. Proposition type is determined by California state law. We identified measures as bond referenda, legislative-referred constitutional measures, or initiatives from the official ballot summary the state published for each proposition.

should thus have lower costs associated with decisions, and they would be associated with less abstention. Likewise, when spending is one-sided against a measure, we should expect increased negative voting.[2]

We have assembled data on all 190 California proposition choices appearing from 1974 through 1988 in order to model the relationship between information demands and abstention and negative voting. During this period, there were an average of thirteen propositions per election. In addition to ballot-specific and campaign-spending measures, we included measures of the composition of the participating electorate. Because presidential elections lead more people to vote, they also can alter the composition of the electorate. Higher turnout can be associated with the mobilization of less-informed and less-interested voters (A. Campbell et al. 1960), which means that more voters will be unable (or unwilling) to bear the costs of making decisions on all propositions. Our models include measures of turnout and a dummy variable representing primary elections.

Because many voters might seek out those measures that have lower information costs, we need to address the possibility of nonlinearity in the relationship between ballot position and abstention or *no* voting. Doing so is important in California because initiatives typically appear at the end of the state ballots. We test for nonlinearity by squaring the proposition's ballot position and including this squared term in the model. Used in combination with the regular measure of ballot positions, these two variables provide a test for a parabolic relationship between ballot position and voting. Abstention is measured as the percentage of voters who vote in candidate races at the top of the ballot but who "drop off" and fail to vote on a proposition. *No* voting is the percentage of votes cast against each proposition.

Table 5 reports the estimations of the following two equations.

$$
\begin{aligned}
\% \text{ Drop-off/Abstention} = {}& - \text{B*Campaign Spending} - \text{B*Initiative} \\
& - \text{B*Bond Measure} - \text{B*Primary} + \text{B*Pres.} \\
& + \text{B*Turnout} + \text{B*Const. Issue} + \text{B*Length*Init} \\
& + \text{B*Length*Bond} + \text{B*Length*Const} + \text{B*Ballot} \\
& \text{Position} - \text{B*Ballot Position}^2
\end{aligned}
$$

$$
\begin{aligned}
\% \text{ No Vote} = {}& + \text{B*Neg. Spending} - \text{B*Initiative ? B*Bond} \\
& \text{Measure} - \text{B*Primary} + \text{B*Pres.} + \text{B*Turnout} \\
& + \text{B*Const. Issue} + \text{B*Length*Init} \\
& + \text{B*Length*Bond} + \text{B*Length*Const} + \text{B*Ballot} \\
& \text{Position} - \text{B*Ballot Position}^2
\end{aligned}
$$

---

2. Our reasons for using spending against a measure are presented in chapter 8, where the effects of campaign spending are examined in further detail. Alternative specifications of spending (including spending in favor, or measures of spending differentials) were not significant predictors of the vote.

Although some of our hypotheses about responsiveness to information demands are not supported, the results demonstrate significant proposition-specific effects that correspond with demands. Abstention is significantly lower on initiatives, and lower still where there is greater spending, and it is significantly higher on constitutional items. Voters do appear to mark most often the last

TABLE 5.   Estimation of Drop-off from Top of Ballot (Abstention) and Percentage Voting "No" on Propositions, California, 1974–88

	Dependent Variable	
	Drop-off	"No" Vote (%)
Ballot position	0.32**	−2.12**
	(.17)	(.91)
Ballot position^2	0.01*	0.13**
	(.01)	(.05)
Initiative measure	−7.13**	1.74
	(1.71)	(8.4)
Bond measure	−0.71	−6.27*
	(.94)	(4.9)
Constitutional measure	2.63**	−4.13
	(.97)	(4.9)
Length* Init.	0.43**	0.74
	(.15)	(.79)
Length* Bond	0.15	0.66
	(.18)	(.92)
Length* Const.	−0.17**	0.47
	(.08)	(.45)
Presidential election	−0.56	−3.38
	(.54)	(2.8)
Primary election	0.17	3.72**
	(.39)	(2.0)
Time	−0.32**	0.40
	(.11)	(.12)
Turnout	0.12**	0.44**
	(.02)	(.12)
Spending (in 100,000s)	−0.019**	—
	(.008)	
Spending against	—	0.03*
		(.02)
Intercept	1.24	9.99
	(1.95)	(9.98)
N	190	190
R^2	.67	.29

Note: OLS estimates. Figures in parentheses are standard errors.
*Significant at $p < .05$ (one-tail)   +Significant at $p < .10$ (one-tail)

propositions on the ballot (that is, they drop off less) and the early propositions, while skipping more measures in the center of the ballot. The direction of the quadratic terms reflects the existence of a ∩-shaped relationship between percentage of drop-off (abstention) and ballot length. There is also evidence that some voters avoid lengthier initiative measures. Many voters do sort through lengthy California ballots, skip over the relatively esoteric legislative constitutional amendments in the center, and then locate and cast votes on initiative measures they probably have heard something about. When we consider the information demands associated with these ballots, this behavior makes some sense. Some voters respond to demands by seeking out those measures for which they have more information (initiatives) or those on which decisions are easier to make (bonds).

But what do voters do when they find the measures with lower information costs? Without survey data, we cannot yet say much (such data are presented in later chapters). Our estimation of *no* voting does illustrate that, other things being equal, many people vote against items toward the top and the bottom of the ballot (although there is no significantly unique effect for initiatives). The hypothesis that voters will mark *no* in response to specific information demands associated with wordier measures is not supported. People do vote against measures where the *no* side dominated campaign spending, and they are less likely to vote against bonds. The direction of the coefficients for the quadratic term for the percentage of the *no* vote illustrates a ∪-shaped relationship between the percentage of the *no* vote and ballot length.

When we examine the quadratic results from each estimation presented in table 5, we see that many voters appear to seek out the more visible contested measures at the end of the ballot, which they vote against. When considered with the Oregon results, our assumptions about a negativity bias in proposition voting associated with risk-averse behavior within a minimally informed electorate appear consistent. These findings stand in contrast to Magleby's descriptions of ill-informed direct-democracy voters playing "a form of Russian roulette, casting affirmative and negative votes at random" (1984, 198). Rather, voters abstain when information demands are greatest (the center of the California ballot), and negative voting dominates as a strategy in some situations, especially when information demands are greatest (i.e., longer ballots and when high turnout mobilizes less-informed voters). Trends in negative voting are examined further in chapter 4.

There is additional evidence that information demands affect this abstention and *no* voting. As turnout increases and more ill-informed voters are drawn into the electorate, abstention and negative voting both increase. The coefficients for longer ballot titles are each associated with more negative voting; however, none are significant. We suggest that the findings reflect a process in which voters with limited information participate more on the most visible choices. If we consider that these less-demanding choices are at the end of the ballot (in California), then many voters appear disposed to vote *no* on those issues that they seek out. These aggregate findings are consistent with our conception of risk-averse voters with limited information sorting through the demanding choices of direct democracy.

Finding Useful Information Sources

Abstaining and negative voting do show some systematic association with information demands (or information availability) presented by different types of proposition choices. Abstention and negative voting, however, clearly are not used by all voters at all times. All voters do not abstain and they do not always vote *no*. They might also gain information about propositions and make their choices on that basis. In chapter 4 we examine variations in *no* voting in greater detail. At this point we need to assess other ways in which voters cope with the information demands presented by proposition voting. With adequate information, voters not only have a greater ability to participate in proposition choices (rather than abstaining), but they also can begin to reason about individual choices (rather than simply voting *no*). If information that is relevant to the choice is available, voters can evaluate it and then decide how to vote. As we have demonstrated elsewhere (Bowler and Donovan 1994a, 419) voters with more sources of political information are more likely to have heard of a specific proposition and will therefore have an opinion on it.

This finding raises questions about the types of information that are available to direct-democracy voters and the types of voters who use the various sources of information. Lupia (1994a, 63) notes that voters can use multiple sources of information as potential shortcuts for evaluating propositions. Research conducted by Sniderman, Brody, and Tetlock (1991) on shortcuts that voters use when reasoning about politics indicates that people can use multiple sources of information for cues and that different voters might use different sources of information. Sniderman and colleagues also note that different voters are likely to use various kinds and different amounts of information when thinking about politics. Some voters, having greater information-processing abilities, can utilize different information sources and can reason differently. Lacking a better indicator of information-processing abilities, we (as do Sniderman and colleagues) focus on formal education as an indicator of this element.

To establish that most voters can reason about the direct democracy choices they face, we need to demonstrate that information sources are readily available to them. We should also demonstrate that both well-educated and less-educated voters are able to find information that allows them to make decisions. The research on reasoning with limited information suggests that less-educated

voters will utilize fewer sources of information than their well-educated coun-
terparts will but that they might nevertheless find something that allows them
to decide which outcome they desire.

The highly educated voters might, for example, utilize "hard" (objective,
noncampaign, print) information sources that are available prior to the last
weekend of a campaign. Hard sources might include newspaper editorials and
the public ballot pamphlet. The use of these sources requires activity on the part
of the voter, particularly in the form of time spent reading. Less-educated voters, on the other hand, might utilize fewer information sources, relying on
"easy" sources that are accessible at the close of a campaign. These sources are
received more passively and require little time to consume. Easy sources might
include television advertising and editorials, and conversations with friends that
turn to the subject of politics.

At the close of the state election campaign in late October 1990, the Field
Institute's California Poll asked respondents an open-ended question: "What information do you usually turn to to help you make up your mind on how to vote
on various statewide ballot propositions?" The poll recorded ten sources that
were mentioned most frequently. Respondents could mention multiple sources.
Those mentioned included the ballot pamphlet (54%), newspaper editorials
(47%), TV editorials (33%), friends (22%), TV ads (21%), direct-mail ads
(20%), newspaper ads (18%), radio editorials (10%), radio ads (6%), and the
League of Women Voters (2%). In table 6 we examine the utilization of "hard"
and "easy" information sources by voters with different levels of education in
1990. As expected, college graduates are significantly more likely than the less
educated to use information from the ballot pamphlet. Furthermore, the well
educated are more likely to use information that requires activity to consume,
such as newspaper editorials.

Contrary to our expectations, utilization of "easy" broadcast information
and direct information from campaign sources appears to occur independently
of education. Less-educated voters are only slightly more likely to acknowledge using television ads as one of their sources of information. Utilization of
radio ads, direct mail, and newspaper ads occurs at the same rates for each level
of education (results not reported here). The least educated are significantly
more likely to rely on friends and neighbors as a source of information about
ballot propositions. The least educated are also more likely to mention that they
use fewer sources of information (an average of 2.1 sources) than are the highly
educated (an average of 2.4 sources; t test for difference between group means
= 2.48, $p < .01$).[3]

---

3. In a 1996 survey, however, the less educated were significantly more likely to mention
television and less likely to mention the voter guide as their *single most important* source
(Field/California Poll, Sept. 7, 1996).

We suggest that these findings about the voter's pamphlet provide clues to how minimally informed voters reason about direct-democracy choices. In California and in many other states (including the high-initiative-use states of Arizona, Oregon, and Washington), public officials mail voters a pamphlet—or voter's guide—that includes the text of the legislation associated with each ballot measure, a synopsis of each measure, and brief statements in support of and in opposition to each measure (Magleby 1984, 38–39; 56–58). California's pamphlet also includes information about the potential fiscal impact of propositions.

What is striking about the results reported in table 6 is that the majority of voters (regardless of education level) reported that they usually turn to the ballot pamphlet as one of their sources of information about propositions. Moreover, it is the most frequently cited source for the less educated—half of the

TABLE 6. Differences in Utilization of Information Sources, California Voters (in percentages)

	Level of Education				
	Low	Medium	High	Total	N
	A. Use Ballot Pamphlet as Source				
Yes	50	51	62	54	(646)
No	50	49	38	45	(543)
$X^2 = 11.43$ $p < .004$					
	B. Use Newspaper Editorials as Source				
Yes	36	48	57	47	(565)
No	64	51	43	53	(624)
$X^2 = 31.30$ $p < .0001$					
	C. Use TV Ads as Source				
Yes	23	21	18	21	(246)
No	77	79	82	79	(943)
$X^2 = 2.57$ $p < .28$					
	D. Use Friends and Neighbors as Source				
Yes	25	22	17	22	(259)
No	75	78	83	78	(930)
$X^2 = 6.51$ $p < .04$					

Source: California Poll, October 30, 1990.

Note: For coding on education, low = high school, trade school, or less; medium = some college; and high = three of four years of college or more.

least-educated voters claimed to use the pamphlet. Compared to the use of sources such as newspapers, the rate of use of the state provided pamphlet by less educated voters is closer to that of the educated. Another survey found equal proportions of Californians (27 percent respectively) mentioning the voter guide and television (news and ads) as their *single most important* source of information about propositions (Field/California Poll, September 7, 1996). These levels of reported use stand in contrast to levels 15 to (40 percent) found from surveys in California conducted during previous decades (Magleby 1984, 136). Magleby's examination of 1972 California survey data found that only 7 percent of those having less than an eighth-grade education made use of the pamphlet (1984, 137).

Some scholars have claimed that these pamphlets provide valuable information and are used frequently by voters (Balmer 1972; Lee 1978; Mueller 1969; Cronin 1989, 81). Others (LaPalombara 1950) noted that those reading the pamphlets still could not understand the proposed legislation. As Magleby notes, there has been scant empirical evidence on either perspective (1984, 136). His analysis indicates that information contained in the pamphlets is written at a reading level that is too difficult for between one-half and two-thirds of the electorate (138). Thus, "given these readability scores, the vast majority of voters who receive the handbook could not effectively use it" (139; see also 198). This finding is presented as partial evidence that the process of direct legislation results in confusion and in "considerable misrepresentation" of voter interests (144). Given the apparent value of this information source to the voter, it is important that we examine what elements voters find useful in the pamphlet.

The Importance of Elite Endorsements

We suggest that minimally informed voters, even those with low information-processing or reading abilities, can nevertheless distill enough information from these pamphlets to reason about propositions. As we suggested in chapter 2, one possible shortcut that voters might use is the "Who's behind it?" cue. Without knowing anything about the text of a piece of legislation, a voter might nevertheless decide that she or he likes it (or opposes it) on the basis of credible endorsements. Furthermore, finding endorsements in the voting pamphlet need not require the advanced reading abilities that Magleby suggests are necessary for using the handbooks to make effective, informed decisions. The section of the pamphlet with pro and con arguments is one possible source of information that allows the use of the "Who's behind it?" shortcut. If voters seek out this information from the mass of material, they can come some way toward making informed choices about propositions.

In November 1990, a survey of California voters who read the pamphlets was conducted by a team of researchers at the University of California, Davis

(Dubois, Feeney, and Constantini 1991). Their results are consistent with what we would expect if voters use these pamphlets to seek out a limited amount of information for making their choices. Fewer than 20 percent of respondents claimed to read the actual text of a measure, yet more than 90 percent claimed to look at the arguments in favor of and against a measure—more than reported looking at the title and nonpartisan summary of the propositions. Moreover, most respondents found the arguments for and against to be the single most helpful part of the pamphlet. More than 80 percent claimed that the names of supporting groups and individuals (contained in the arguments) were important in helping them make up their minds. Fewer than than 20 percent found the title and summary helpful, and fewer than than 10 percent found the text of the measure helpful. Voters appear to use the pamphlets to find information on elite endorsements.

Elite endorsements by politicians and groups are thus a key part of the pamphlet. These cues are important because they might provide some political or party referent. Such cues can have an effect, however, only if voters understand the referent. To be influenced one way or the other by California Democratic party leaders such as John van de Kamp or Kathleen Brown, or by Common Cause's endorsement, requires that the voter knows something about the person who makes the endorsement. Elite endorsements might provide voters a means of anchoring decisions about ballot propositions to standing party attachments or to some preexisting stock of information, but the use of such information could itself be fairly demanding. Voters must have some existing knowledge of party cues, party elites, and public figures to be able to use an endorsement in forming an opinion. Endorsement cues might be more useful to the more attentive, more partisan, and more educated portions of the electorate.

To establish whether elite cues can act as a shortcut that voters use when deciding on ballot issues, we need to establish whether people are likely to have their opinions influenced by elite endorsements. We must also test whether the use of this cue is limited to those who are the most educated or is available to all voters. In a study of citizen knowledge relating to a nuclear energy initiative, Kuklinski, Metlay, and Kay (1982) predicted that the *less* knowledgeable would rely more heavily upon cues from "reference groups." They assumed that the less knowledgeable would require cues as information cost-cutting devices in place of the factual details that knowledgeable people use in making decisions, but such was not the case. In the end, they found that all voters used reference-group cues, but the more educated were more likely to accurately perceive the position taken by a group on an issue. We take as our point of departure the assumption that voters often lack factual knowledge on most propositions, but we hypothesize that voters with greater cognitive abilities might be able to associate more groups and elites with their own partisan orientation.

We also need to test whether the impact of these elite endorsements is associated with partisanship. We take these questions in turn, looking first at whether elite cues can shape opinion and then at which voters are more likely to shift opinions in light of elite cues. Finally, we examine how cue taking may be linked to partisanship.

A September 1988 Field Institute survey conducted in California helps illustrate the potential importance of endorsements. This survey split the sample into two random subsets and asked voters in each subset their opinion of the rival automobile insurance propositions (numbered 100, 101, 103, 104, and 106). The wording of the questions was different in each subset, thereby providing a natural experiment of the impact of elite cues. Respondents in Group A received a fairly detailed description of the proposition that noted, "Proposition 101 would reduce auto-insurance rates and limit compensation for noneconomic losses for four years." Those in Group B received a question that supplied the policy content given to Group A as well as a cue about the elites backing each measure ("Proposition 101 is sponsored by Assemblyman Richard Polanco and insurance executive Harry Miller . . . ").

Table 7 offers a description of the information given to respondents and the frequencies in each response category for each group. Because the samples were split randomly, we attribute differences in response patterns between groups to the effect of knowing who is backing each initiative. The effect of this knowledge is most clearly evident with Propositions 103 (the consumer group's

TABLE 7.   The Effects of Cues on Opinions

Group	Prop. No.	Yes (%)	No (%)	Undecided (%)
A	100	57	26	17
B	100	55	22	23
A	101	36	32	33
B	101	31	38	30
A	103	62	16	22
B	103	73	12	14
A	104	31	40	29
B	104	27	51	22
A	106	59	24	17
B	106	48	30	20

Source: California Poll, September 1988.
Note:
A = uncued group
B = cued group (knows who supports the initiative)
The main cues given are as follows:
100   California trial lawyers and state attorney general
101   An insurance executive
103   Consumer groups (Voter Revolt) and Ralph Nader
104   California insurance companies (general support)
106   California insurance companies (to limit lawyers' fees)

proposal) and 106 (the insurance companies' plan to limit lawyers' fees). Support for Proposition 103 was much greater among respondents who knew that the initiative was backed by consumer groups. Conversely, support for Proposition 106 was much lower in the groups receiving information that the initiative was backed by insurance companies.

Thus, once the cue is given that someone like Ralph Nader or his group backs a measure, support for the relevant proposition increases. Once it is seen that the insurance company backs an initiative, support drops. Arthur Lupia's exit poll of Los Angeles County voters (1994a) produced evidence of similar responsiveness to information about elite positions on these initiatives. These patterns make a great deal of sense if voters, as insurance consumers, believe that insurance industry actions are designed for the benefit of the industry rather than consumers.

The effects of knowing who's backing an initiative, furthermore, might transcend the impact of heavy "Yes"-side spending in some initiative campaigns. In chapter 8 we suggest that the failure of some initiatives backed by massive spending on the *yes* side is due to voters becoming aware of the major actors behind the proposal, then inferring (rightly or wrongly) that the proponents were acting on behalf of their own narrow interests, rather than on behalf of a broad category of voters, citizens, or consumers. For example, Philip Morris's $13 million expenditure on an initiative designed to repeal California's local smoking restrictions (Proposition 188 of 1994, written as an "antismoking" law) galvanized attention to the fact that the tobacco industry backed the measure. An opposition campaign with limited funds reversed widespread support (suggested by early polls) by using cost-free media and former U.S. surgeon general C. Everett Koop to inform voters that the "antismoking" initiative was financed by Philip Morris (Williams 1994, 24). Revealing "Who's behind it" was the key element to the successful opposition campaign. In the end, only 30 percent of voters cast their votes in favor of Proposition 188.

Some industry groups appear well aware of the idea that credible endorsements in the ballot pamphlet can weigh as heavily as—if not more heavily than—campaign spending itself. In 1996, three well-financed tort-reform initiatives backed by the California technology industries (Propositions 200, 201, and 202) were qualified and presented to voters as proconsumer. To solidify their claim to the proconsumer argument, initiative proponents included in their ballot pamphlet statement one of Nader's recent organizations as a supporter of Proposition 201. The organization—Voter Revolt of Santa Monica— was Harvey Rosenfield's grassroots group that drafted and qualified the successful 1988 Proposition 103 insurance rate reduction initiative.

Media reports (following claims by the anti-200s campaign) suggested that by 1996, Voter Revolt had become little more than a front for the industry group sponsoring Propositions 200, 201, and 202. One report stated that the group had been renounced by Rosenfield and by Nader and that its former volunteer staff had been replaced by paid workers (*San Jose Mercury,* 22 March 1996, 3B). Nevertheless, the same Voter Revolt logo used by the Rosenfield-Nader consumer group in 1988 was displayed prominently on omnibus pro-Proposition 200, 201, and 202 mailings. Over the din of the arguments and countercharges leveled by attorneys' groups at industry groups sponsoring the 1996 measures, Rosenfield and Nader's opposition to the initiatives became visible. Rosenfield's name was included in the ballot pamphlet as an opponent of the initiatives, and Nader's was used in opposition commercials. The industry coalition backing the initiatives was apparently unable to convince voters that their proconsumer endorsements were credible. All three initiatives failed, even after one had appeared to be quite popular in early opinion polls.

Clearly, there are limits to the impact of these endorsements. For one thing, voters have to know enough to be able to recognize the cue before taking it, which suggests that there will be some distinctions in cue-taking behavior between groups of voters. We can address this issue, and the attendant issue of the links (if any) between cue taking and partisanship through survey data that ask more extensive questions of voters on the impact of cues.

Respondents to the Field Institute's August 1990 California Poll were asked if the initiative positions of twenty-six politicians, political groups, and elites would have a positive or a negative influence on their vote. The twenty-six endorsees had actually adopted public positions on measures appearing on that election ballot. Only about one voter in eight said they would not be influenced by any of the endorsees mentioned. It is relevant to the issue at hand to ask which voters should be most influenced by these elite endorsements. We expect that voters with higher education levels are somewhat more likely to use the pamphlet (table 6), and we also assume that these voters have greater cognitive capacity. If that is so, such voters would be more likely to respond that they are influenced by the issue positions taken by key elites. Furthermore, we expect that partisanship is associated with attentiveness to elites within each party, because the respondent's ability to use partisan endorsements could be greater among strong party identifiers. If such is the case, independents should be less likely to be swayed by endorsements (because many of the endorsees are party figures).

Table 8 reports an ordinary least squares (OLS) regression estimate of the number of times respondents claim that an elite endorsement would have no influence on their ballot proposition decisions. Income, race, gender, and age are included as control variables in the estimate. These results demonstrate that educated voters are less likely to say that endorsements have no impact. Educated people are thus more likely to utilize endorsement information when making decisions. Our expectations about partisanship are also supported by the data in table 8. Independents are more likely to claim that endorsements will not influence their decisions. The opposite result is produced if a measure of partisanship is used in the equation: partisans are less likely to claim that an endorsement will not affect their decision.

The relationship between the influence of endorsements, partisanship, and education can be represented in another way. Splitting the sample by educational attainment also buttresses the point that these effects differ among voters with higher and lower levels of education. Splitting the sample also demonstrates that education is associated with the ability to translate a greater number of elite endorsements into a partisan referent. Table 9 reports a series of correlations between an ordinal measure of the self-reported strength of partisanship and the direction of the self-reported impact of elite endorsements. Correlations with higher absolute values reflect a stronger association between strength of partisanship and influence.

Results in table 9 illustrate that only eight of twenty-six endorsements are associated with respondents' partisanship among the less-educated half of the

TABLE 8. Estimation of Number of Times Respondent Claimed that Elite Endorsement Would Not Influence Vote on Ballot Issue

Variable	
Independent	.638*
	(.263)
Income	.287*
	(.119)
Nonwhite	−.083
	(.415)
Gender	−.015
	(.250)
Age	.007
	(.006)
Education	−.209**
	(.056)
Constant	5.479**
	(.556)
$N = 941$	
$R^2 = .023$	
$F = 3.68$	
$p < .0013$	

Source: California Poll, August 1990.

Note: OLS estimates. Standard errors in parentheses. Independent is a dummy variable reflecting respondents who do not identify themselves as Democrats or Republicans. Nonwhite is also a dummy variable representing all respondents who are not white.

*Significant at $p < .05$ (two-tail)

**Significant at $p < .01$ (two-tail)

sample. Strong partisanship is more commonly associated with being influenced by elite positions among the better educated. Among voters with more education, sixteen of these endorsements are associated with partisanship. The relationship between a voter's partisanship and the influence of endorsements by environmental groups, Common Cause, Diane Feinstein (then a candidate for governor), and most elected officials (David Roberti, Tom Hayden, John Van de Kamp, George Dukmejian) is strongest among the well-educated voters. This finding suggests that when these party figures (or groups) take a position on a ballot measure, these voters might evaluate the issue in partisan terms.

TABLE 9.   Correlation between Strength of Voter's Partisanship and Direction of Impact of Elite Endorsement (by level of education)

	Lower	Higher
Van de Kamp	.0948	.2031**
State legislature	.0681	.1802**
Farm lobby	−.0495	−.0597
Chamber of Commerce	−.0209	−.0651
Environmental groups	.2147*	.3601**
Dianne Feinstein	.2683**	.3105**
Common Cause	.1174	.2794**
Pete Schabarum	.0955	−.0052
Drug prevention group	−.0072	.0686
George Dukmejian	−.3314**	−.4216**
Joel Fox	−.0227	−.3490**
David Roberti	.0661	.2325**
Tom Hayden	.0492	.2934**
Chemical companies	.0224	−.0888
Consumer groups	.1402	.1338*
Willie Brown	.3178**	.3244**
Alcohol industry	.0070	−.0340
Logging industry	−.0591	−.0535
Pete Wilson	−.3135**	−.3526**
Wildlife preservation	.1638*	.1693**
CA Taxpayers Association	.0264	−.0685
State labor group	.2842**	.2061**
League of Women Voters	.2414**	.2074**
Ralph Nader	.0663	.1630**

Source: California Poll, August 1990.

Note: Party identification is a 5-point scale: $+2$ = strong Democrat, -2 = strong Republican. The impact of each of these groups or individuals was coded on a 3-point scales: 1 = positive influence, 0 = no impact, -1 = negative influence.

*Significant at $p < .05$ (two-tail)   **Significant at $p < .01$ (two-tail)

We should note that the correlation between strength of partisanship and influence of endorsement is usually, but not always, stronger among the well educated. The endorsements of state labor groups and the League of Women Voters appear to have greater resonance among less-educated partisans, and there is no difference between education levels in the relationship between partisanship and the influence of former speaker of the California Assembly Willie Brown and Governor Pete Wilson. Thus, for less-educated voters, it is possible that there is a smaller set of public figures whose positions on ballot measures can also be used to evaluate ballot issues in partisan terms. Although these data suggest that the relationship between the influence of elite positions and partisanship is stronger among the better educated, and that the better educated can make use of more endorsements, the impact of elites probably varies with the type of issue on the ballot.

Conceivably, it is through the ballot pamphlet that many voters use these endorsements as shortcuts when making choices about propositions. For many well-educated voters, knowing something about who is behind a proposition is something like knowing how one's party (or a relevant interest group) might stand on an issue. If voters know who Ralph Nader is and which side of an issue he supports, this knowledge might provide sufficient information to make their decisions. For some voters, this knowledge could hold even if they are unsure about (or unaware of) the nature of the issue at stake. Although these data are not perfectly suited for assessing that, they do suggest that strong party identification might represent the ability to utilize elite cues. For this reason, we include measures of strong party identification in our models of opinions and voting on propositions.

These results also demonstrate that there are some public figures or groups that even the less-educated voter might use to link a proposition to his or her own party identification. A less-educated voter apparently might not know who John Van de Kamp (Democratic candidate for state office) is or who Ralph Nader is, much less what party either might be associated with, but the significant correlations for less-educated voters in table 9 indicate that they do know more prominent figures such as Willie Brown and Pete Wilson. Knowing them, knowing their own party, and knowing that someone important in their party is against (or is in favor of) a measure might be sufficient decision information for some. In California, that is the information that many voters appear to seek in the voter's pamphlets. Our analysis here illustrates how they might use this information.

Summary

In this chapter we establish that voters find direct democracy challenging but respond to the demands created by these elections. Voters' decisions to participate or abstain are affected by the information demands associated with proposition ballots. When ballots are lengthy, voters also vote *no* more frequently. Many voters also appear to seek out higher-profile measures, and they vote against them. In addition, they also seek out multiple sources of information that might aid them as they make their decisions. Although we do not establish that voters understand the issues they decide on, we illustrate how many voters might nevertheless find one source of information that allows them to decide if they are for or against a particular issue. When evaluating propositions, voters seem keenly interested in knowing "Who's behind it?" Our analysis suggests that such information might allow many voters to place the proposition within a partisan frame.

We also illustrate that endorsements (the "Who's behind it?" cue) might be of greater use to the well educated because they are able to use more elite cues that allow them to see propositions in partisan terms. Nevertheless, those with less education might also be able to associate some endorsements with partisanship. In chapter 4 we examine additional reasoning shortcuts that might be used by voters who have less information or lower cognitive abilities. Because they lack the cognitive capacity to see propositions in terms of party or ideology, less-educated voters might compensate by evaluating propositions in terms of general concerns over the state's economy.

Economic Conditions and Voting on Ballot Propositions

As noted in earlier chapters, theories of voting under limited information suggest that different voters utilize different cues and shortcuts when reasoning about politics. In particular, well-educated voters simply use more information. We also find that the highly educated are more likely to say that elite endorsements will impact their choices and that the strong partisans among them are more likely to be influenced by elite positions on ballot measures. Voters with higher levels of education thus appear to reason differently than do other voters.

Sniderman, Brody, and Tetlock (1991) demonstrate that voters with greater cognitive abilities do not simply use more information when deciding what they are for or against politically. They also use different information shortcuts. They think in ways that might be seen as more sophisticated, if not in ways that are more cognitively complex. Ideology, as we mentioned in chapter 2, allows some voters to think about politics—and ballot propositions—in terms of complex abstractions such as liberalism and conservatism. From the behavioral perspective, political ideology has been defined as "a set of inter-related attitudes that fit together into some coherent and consistent view or orientation toward the political world" (Flanigan and Zingale 1994, 131). It is a "constrained" belief system (Converse 1964) or a store of conceptual political information that allows some voters to reason about the individual issues of the day. Just as voters with greater cognitive abilities might be better suited for linking elite endorsements to party, they should also be more capable of evaluating propositions in terms of their self-identified ideology.

But what of voters with less-than-average cognitive abilities? Voters with different cognitive abilities can reason differently when evaluating the same proposition. We know (as we saw in the previous chapter) that the less educated have fewer information sources and that the opinions that less-educated voters have on ballot issues are influenced less by groups and elites, at least in their propensity to associate these cues with their own party attachments. Likewise, Kuklinski, Metlay, and Kay (1982) found that less-educated voters might have a harder time making accurate assessments of the positions that groups take on a ballot proposition. Behavioral research has also held that ideological responses to issues—reasoning on the basis of some general orientation about the political world—is difficult for people with less-developed cognitive abilities (Converse 1964). Others (Sniderman, Brody, and Tetlock 1991; Sears, Hensler, and Speer 1979) suggest that ideology has an affective or symbolic component that allows the less educated to reason about politics on the basis of their ideological dispositions. If we assume that ideology does have a cognitive aspect, we should expect that less-educated voters approach proposition elections far differently than do other voters. They may often have less information and less opportunity to use standing belief systems when making choices.

We suggest that when in doubt and faced with great information demands, many voters use *no* voting as a default when evaluating propositions. If we assume that *no* voting is in fact associated with doubt and uncertainty, then we must consider how negative voting is used more frequently by those voters with fewer cognitive resources. This does not mean that the less educated or less informed cannot reason about direct democracy measures, but rather that they might reason differently. We suggest that because they have fewer information resources and therefore less capacity to use party or ideology to evaluate propositions, less-educated voters turn to another shortcut: evaluations of the condition of the state's economy.

Substantial scholarly attention has been directed at the relationship between economic conditions and voting in national elections (e.g., Kramer 1971; Lewis-Beck 1988). Indeed, economic conditions are thought to be one of the major cues that voters use to form decisions in candidate races. In demonstrating that American voters are not "fools," V. O. Key (1966) noted that retrospective evaluations of the economy were one subtle manifestation of issue voting in the mass electorate. Despite the wealth of studies addressing the interplay between economic conditions and voting, limited attention has been directed toward the question of how these conditions might affect support for ballot propositions.

This lack of attention is not surprising, considering that economic evaluations applied by voters are typically seen as retrospective. In direct-democracy elections, voters would obviously need to use something other than retrospective judgments such as "Am I better off now than when candidate X took office?" when evaluating ballot propositions. We demonstrate that some voters appear to utilize perceptions of the state's economy when making choices about propositions. Unlike candidate contests, they appear to be guided by the heuristic, "Is this a good time for the state to adopt a new policy?"

Direct Democracy, Risk Aversion, and Economic Voting

In contrast to candidate contests, economic evaluations are not assumed to be used only for instrumental purposes: they might also be associated with a mood in the electorate that mitigates policy expansiveness. Others have noted that a mood in the electorate results in good and bad years for ballot propositions (J. Mueller 1969). We contend that the general willingness of the electorate to adopt new policies varies with economic conditions. This contention assumes that the evaluation of propositions need not result exclusively from an issue-by-issue analysis of each proposition on a ballot. Such evaluations can place great information demands on voters. Rather, some voters might respond to information about general state conditions when making decisions about propositions of which they have limited knowledge. They might ask themselves a question such as, "Is this a good time to adopt something new?" As economic conditions deteriorate, levels of electoral support for propositions should change as additional voters answer this question in the negative. Thus, we propose that support for ballot propositions should be lower in years when state economic conditions are poor.

This aggregate expectation is based on specific assumptions about individual-level behavior. We assume that many direct-democracy voters experience a lack of knowledge of ballot issues, which causes them to adopt risk-averse behavior. This behavior is expected to be associated with poor state economic conditions and is manifested in negative voting on propositions. In some instances, a majority of voters are unaware of and have no opinions on ballot issues (Bowler and Donovan 1994a). Empirical tests of rational decision theories have produced results indicating that lack of knowledge affects voters' choices through risk aversion. Other things being equal, people tend to avoid deciding in favor of choices (candidates) they are not familiar with (Brady and Ansolabehere 1989). In addition, econometric studies of elections that estimate vote choice with utility functions find that voters are primarily risk averse (e.g., Ansolabehere and Iyengar 1993, 329), and studies of candidate contests indicate that negative voting is a function of risk aversion (Lau 1985).

Our theory of direct-democracy voting views choices as a decision between an uncertain outcome (the new policy) and a more certain outcome (the status quo). If some portion of the electorate associates the risk of altering the status quo with concerns about the state economy, then we should see negative voting ebb and flow with the health of the economy. With little information available on many of the propositions, evaluations of state economic conditions can act as a source of information that increases (or decreases) risk aversion, at least for those who are unable to use ideology or party to evaluate propositions. Many uncertain voters might simply decide "We can't afford it" when evaluating ballot issues in poor economic periods. Because risk aversion has been shown to be associated with negative voting (Lau 1985), we expect that poor economic conditions in a state will cause more voters, in aggregate, to vote against ballot propositions.

We noted in chapter 3 that various issues present to voters different sorts of information demands. We might then expect that the use of economic evaluations varies across different types of ballot measures. We initially expected that less-publicized issues would be one arena where concerns about the state's economy play a factor in evaluations of propositions, because other information sources and cues are largely absent. Many propositions, particularly legislative constitutional amendments and legislative bond referenda (see table 4 for samples), involve no campaign and little press coverage (Magleby 1984). In this sense, economic concerns could be associated with a general mood of risk aversion to new policies that increases when times are bad.

Conversely, some initiatives and propositions are concerned with tax and revenue issues. Economic evaluations might be used by voters to decide on these propositions because they have more readily identifiable economic (or pocketbook) content. Some voters, particularly less-educated ones who are less able to evaluate propositions in terms of a comprehensive political ideology, might use these cues across all sorts of propositions. Thus, if some proportion of less-educated voters participates in many referenda decisions, and they lack other cues, we could expect to see a relationship between economic conditions and support for propositions on economic as well as noneconomic issues.

Some caveats are in order at this point. Our assumptions about uncertain, risk-averse voters might be most appropriate in electoral contexts in which ballots routinely require voters to make decisions on a fairly large number of propositions (e.g., California, Arizona, Oregon, Colorado). In such demanding contexts, it might be likely that more voters lack a complete understanding of the policy consequences of all ballot issues and thus rely upon easily available economic evaluations. This logic assumes that people prefer simple decision rules when faced with substantial information demands and that many individuals seek "to conserve cognitive resources in seeking and processing information" (Jervis 1993, 339). When only one proposition appears on a ballot, people might not face information costs that are as demanding and thus might not need to rely as much on this cue.

It should also be noted that, contrary to the econometric findings discussed earlier, experimental research suggests that people might actually be more risk acceptant in bad times when policy outcomes are known (Quattrone and Tversky 1988). Furthermore, ballot issues authorizing bond spending could indeed promote economic development. Rational voters with complex reasoning processes could thus be expected to approve bonds when economic times are poor if they are risk acceptant or if they subscribe to classic Keynesian stimulus practices. We are working from the perspective that minimally attentive and minimally informed voters seek easily available references for decisions, references that conserve cognitive resources in the face of steep information demands. We think negative voting in response to a "Can we afford this now?"

evaluation is more plausible than risk acceptance in a context of limited information and relatively crowded ballots.

Economics and Voting in State Elections

Little is known about how economic evaluations affect decision making in state-level direct democracy. Although economic voting in state elections has become the subject of several studies (Peltzman 1987; Chubb 1988; Howell and Vanderleeuw 1990), virtually no attention has been given to the question of how economic conditions affect support for state ballot propositions. That is unfortunate, given the prominence of ballot propositions in many states.

Economic models of voting are based on assumptions made about the evaluations of economic conditions that individuals form and their use of those evaluations when deciding between candidates or parties. In their simplest form, these studies assume that voters withdraw support from incumbents (or their parties) when conditions worsen. Vote decisions on statewide ballot proposals present a situation that is far removed from standard economic voting studies, because party labels and incumbency are lacking. We suggest that economic conditions can nevertheless affect decisions about propositions, because economic conditions might be associated with voter willingness to adopt new policies. This argument is tested subsequently.

There is some evidence demonstrating that state economic conditions fail to affect election outcomes in states when national conditions are accounted for (Holbrook 1991). Stein (1990, 30) has shown that voter evaluations in state contests are "constrained" by the content of functional economic responsibilities assigned to each level of government. State officials are less likely to be assigned responsibility for the economy than are national officials, and they are less susceptible to electoral punishment as the economy sours (Stein 1990). Chubb's (1988) conclusion that state politicians do not suffer at the polls for state economic conditions is consistent with this finding, although some of Chubb's results suggest that state economic conditions do affect state legislative seat changes. Howell and Vanderleeuw (1990) have demonstrated that state economic conditions do affect gubernatorial approval ratings. In short, evidence of economic voting in state elections in response to state economic conditions is somewhat mixed.

Direct democracy provides a unique opportunity to test for a relationship between state economic conditions and state election outcomes. With direct democracy, voters have less need to assign responsibility for economic management to state officials. Direct democracy charges voters with making policy decisions themselves. In this context, voters might utilize evaluations of state economic conditions when they make decisions to adopt new public policies.

Economic Evaluations of Propositions

Individual-Level Analysis

Our foregoing discussion suggests that voters use economic evaluations readily on economic issues, that their use is more visible among the less educated, and that such evaluations might be used on those issues where other information sources are most lacking. Ideal tests of these propositions require survey data that asked detailed questions about voters' economic concerns and their vote intentions on numerous issues. Sadly, statewide opinion polls taken during proposition elections rarely focus on less-visible issues, which tend to be more numerous. Nor do they typically ask about statewide bond referenda. It is also difficult to find polls that include questions on initiatives and on economic evaluations.

Fortunately, one of the Field Institute's 1990 California Polls used questions measuring respondents' economic concerns, including their evaluations of state conditions. The survey also measured support for selected issues placed on the November ballot. Although the survey intentionally focused on the more visible initiatives on that year's ballot (e.g., term limits and the "Big Green" omnibus environmental proposition), the poll provides a rare opportunity to examine how individual voters use economic evaluations as a cue when forming opinions about ballot propositions. A 1992 Colorado poll also asked voters about propositions on their ballot and included an open-ended question that allowed voters to voice their concerns about the "most important issue" facing Colorado at the time. This question allows us to identify those voters who also have concerns about that state's economy.

We examined opinions on all the California propositions in which respondents were asked their vote intention and their economic concerns. These include Proposition 128 (Big Green), Proposition 140 (term limits), and Proposition 135 (an industry-sponsored regulatory measure). One of four propositions from the Colorado poll is also included.[1] Colorado's Amendment 1 required that future legislative tax increases be put to a public vote. To assess how voters with different cognitive abilities might reason about these propositions, we estimate opinions of well-educated and less-educated voters separately. Each equation includes measures of state economic concerns, ideology, and partisanship, and controls for age and income. Table 10 reports logistic regres-

---

1. The four Colorado propositions were Amendment 1, voter approval for tax increases; Amendment 2, limits on gay rights; Amendment 6, sales tax for public education; and Amendment 7, school vouchers. Three of the four Colorado propositions showed a pattern where economic evaluations were correlated with the vote by the less educated in the expected direction, but the pattern did not hold with the more-educated voters. The pattern was significant with one proposition (Amendment 1), and it is included here for comparative purposes.

TABLE 10. Estimation of Use of Economic Evaluations as Cues: Opinion Data

	CA Term Limits		CA envr. regs.		CA "Big Green"		CO taxes	
	Hi Ed	Lo Ed	Hi Ed	Lo Ed	Hi Ed	Lo Ed	Hi Ed	Lo Ed
Liberal	−.76*	.64	−.16	−.35	1.58*	.39	−.73+	-.18
	(.38)	(.90)	(.40)	(.92)	(.53)	(.92)	(.45)	(.39)
Income	-.02	.16	−.19	.05	−.29*	−.34	−.14	−.62
	(.16)	(.23)	(.15)	(.24)	(.17)	(.22)	(.12)	(.43)
Age	.00	.02+	-.00	−.01	.03*	−.00	−.10	.00
	(.01)	(.01)	(.01)	(.01)	(.01)	(.01)	(.13)	(.11)
Strong GOP	.32	.19	−.76*	−.46	−.94*	−.26	−.11	−.14
	(.42)	(.54)	(.38)	(.53)	(.40)	(.50)	(.45)	(.10)
State econ.	−.14	−.10	−.22	−.53*	.38	−.43+	.70	−.73+
evaluation	(.23)	(.26)	(.23)	(.26)	(.26)	(.24)	(.49)	(.43)
Constant	1.19	−0.55	2.10	2.96	1.53	2.55	0.80	1.37
	(.95)	(1.13)	(.95)	(1.27)	(1.00)	(1.15)	(.69)	(.56)
Number of cases	172	117	172	117	172	117	115	168
% correct	68	67	62	71	69	62	61	64
−2 log likelihood	215.3	145.5	223.7	138.7	198.7	152.2	158.9	218.9

Source: California Polls. August 1990; Colorado Poll, Fall 1992 (Department of Sociology, University of Colorado).

Note: Logistic regression estimates. Standard errors in parentheses. Dependent variable coded 1 = support proposition, 0 = otherwise. Low education is high school, trade school, or less. High education is three or four years of college or more. Strong GOP is a dummy variable representing strong Repulican identifiers. Liberal is a dummy variable representing self-identified liberals.

*Significant at $p < .05$ (two-tail)   +Significant at $p < .10$ (two-tail)

sion estimations of opinion on the four propositions.[2] The dependent variable is support for the proposition (1 = support, 0 = oppose or have no opinion). California respondents were asked, "How are things going in California?" to assess their concerns about the state's economy. Responses ranged from "well" and "fairly well" through "pretty bad."

Given the fact that these are not the ideal data for our test and that the number of cases for analysis drops when we divide our samples by level of education, the survey results should be treated with caution. These models are overly simple, in that opinions on many of these issues obviously can involve additional factors (we examine some of these propositions in greater detail in subsequent chapters). The results do seem to illustrate that on some issues, well-educated voters reason about direct democracy differently than do less-educated voters. They also suggest that both sets of voters are nevertheless capable of reasoning about these issues.

---

2. The California poll included questions about several additional ballot issues, but a split-sample method of polling limited the number of issues in which relevant economic questions were asked.

On each ballot issue, the vote intentions of well-educated voters are associated in a sensible manner with their self-reported ideology or partisanship. Well-educated voters make a connection between their ideology and their vote intentions. Liberals are opposed to term limits (we examine this issue in chapter 7) and rules that make tax increases harder, and they are supportive of Big Green. Strong Republicans oppose both proposals for environmental regulation. All of this makes sense if ideology and party identification allow these voters to evaluate propositions in terms of their larger orientation to politics. With these voters, economic concerns or reflections on something as ethereal as "how things in the state are going" are not important.

Among the less educated, things are different. Here, neither party nor ideology matters much. Less-educated voters who identify with a party or who describe themselves in terms of an ideological orientation appear unable to arrive at vote intentions that match conventional definitions of the political views associated with liberalism. It does appear that these voters might form opinions on three of the measures on the basis of concerns about the general economic condition of the state. Less-educated California voters who say that things in the state are "bad" or "very bad" are more likely to oppose these initiatives. Less-educated Colorado voters who cite the state's economy as "the most important issue" in the state are opposed to Amendment 1. Because they lack the capacity to translate the store of political information associated with partisanship or with their ideological orientation into opinions on propositions, these voters use different concerns when evaluating propositions. Although these concerns might be less "sophisticated" when compared to ideological thinking, they might nevertheless be real if they are associated with objective economic conditions.

Minimally informed and minimally cognizant voters thus appear to have a way to reason when they decide why they are for or against some propositions. When voters are worried about the state in general or its economy in particular, they are less likely to accept a change in the status quo. Recall that these are issues we were forced to examine due to the availability of data. In a sense, they represent a "least likely scenario" for testing the hypothesis that minimally informed voters evaluate propositions in terms of economic conditions. Because these are propositions with higher-than-average visibility, voters are likely to have some additional information relating to them. To assess how voters respond to a wider variety of propositions, we turn to aggregate data. We suggest that more voters have economic concerns when times are bad. Consider that minimally informed voters might make up roughly one-third of the participating electorate in any state election. If the concerns of these voters about state conditions are the product of real economic conditions, we should expect to see less aggregate support for propositions when the state's economy is doing poorly. We now turn to this issue.

Aggregate-Level Analysis of Economic Voting on Propositions

We account for some variation in policy content by examining proposition voting in California and comparing the relationship between economic conditions and voting on specific types of propositions. The Results of an analysis of voting on propositions with economic content, noneconomic propositions, and bond propositions are compared to analyses of voting on all issues appearing on the California ballot from 1974 through 1992. A key to our argument is that on long ballots, voters face many issues they know little about, so some decide on the basis of broad economic worries.[3] In a given year, a few propositions may receive notoriety (e.g., tax revolts, term limits), yet many others do not.

If voting on ballot propositions is a function of an evaluation of state conditions, then we should expect to find aggregate patterns of association between indicators of state economic performance and ballot-issue voting. We conducted tests using election results from all statewide issues appearing on the California ballot from June 1974 through June 1992. This time period in California provides a useful arena for analyzing the relative impact of state and national economic conditions. During much of this period, the California economy was relatively insulated from national economic trends, which frees measures of economic indicators from collinearity.[4]

A pooled cross-sectional design is used to test for an association between economic conditions and negative voting on propositions. In chapter 3 we indicated that voting on California propositions is dependent on proposition-specific effects, such as each proposition's ballot position and the issue it concerns. A pooled design estimating the *no* vote on individual propositions allows us to control for proposition-specific effects. To account for issue-type effects, we conducted our analysis on homogeneous issue groups, where we estimated models of voting for each group. The first group included all propositions ($n = 268$), and a second included all overtly economic propositions (fiscal measures and bond issues, $n = 107$). We further refined the homogeneity of issue content by estimating models for a third subgroup of propositions that lacked explicit economic content ($n = 161$) and for a fourth subgroup that included only bond measures ($n = 75$).[5] We modeled negative voting (proportion of *no* vote received for each proposition) as a function of change in per capita state per-

---

3. For example, in 1990 voters in Los Angeles received ballots asking them to make more than one hundred choices on candidate offices (statewide, congressional, judicial, etc.) and propositions ("Government in California" 1993, 21).

4. Our measures of California state and national unemployment are correlated at $r = .47$ for this period. California state and national income growth measures are correlated at $r = .62$.

5. There were 268 propositions on the California ballot in this period. The California secretary of state clearly identified all propositions that involved issuing public bonds ($n = 75$). The

sonal income (over the period from the calendar year prior to the election to the election year) and annual state unemployment levels (during the year of the election). Corresponding measures of national economic conditions were included to test voting as a function of state or national conditions. Indicators of each proposition's position on the ballot are also included in the models.

Previous analysis of proposition voting suggests other variables that might be needed as controls in the models. Negative voting and drop-off can be related to turnout levels (Bone and Benedict 1975). Furthermore, the composition of the electorate participating in primary elections can be different than that in the general election electorate with respect to levels of political interest (A. Campbell 1960). Each of these factors was shown in chapter 3 to affect aggregate outcomes in proposition elections. The models were thus estimated with levels of turnout, and a dummy for primary elections was included as an additional control variable.

Estimation and Results

Aggregated Data from California

Pooled ordinary least squares (OLS) regression is used to estimate models of negative voting on propositions. The likelihood of serial correlation is minimized here because our economic data are measured at two-year intervals, and a limited number of periods are pooled. Furthermore, we include a trend variable accounting for time periods (first period = 1, second period = 2, etc.) to control for some of the possible sources of heteroskedasticity and to indicate whether negative voting increased over the period under study. The models were also estimated with a dummy variable least squares (DVLS) method (not reported here) that included dummy variables representing each year, except for one reference category. F tests (Pindyck and Rubinfeld 1981:204–206) were used to determine whether the DVLS method resulted in significant reductions in error, compared to the OLS models. In all cases, the significance of the F values was greater than .10. Thus, the more parsimonious OLS results are reported here.[6]

---

analysis of 107 economic (fiscal and bond) measures included these 75 issues, plus 32 additional propositions in which ballot descriptions indicated a specific appropriation of state funds for the policy, a change in state law that provided for revenue increases, and tax changes. For the 161 noneconomic issues, bond measures were excluded, as were the 32 additional fiscal issues. A list of the propositions included in each subgroup is available from the authors upon request.

6. The results of the DVLS estimations are available upon request. The substantive interpretation of the results remains unchanged with the DVLS method. See Pindyck and Rubinfeld 1981, 205 for a criticism of DVLS in pooled analysis.

Three separate models are estimated for the four groups of propositions. Multiple estimations are reported because we are interested in testing whether state economic conditions structure voting after national conditions are accounted for. Thus, Model 1 from tables 11 and 12 includes state income and national income measures, and the model is estimated for each group of propositions. Model 2 is estimated for each group and includes indicators of state and national unemployment. Model 3 includes all the economic indicators for the purpose of comparing their relative impact.

Table 11 displays the results of these estimations for all California ballot propositions and for a subgroup of economic propositions. Models estimating negative voting on all propositions (the left side of table 11) indicate that state income growth and state unemployment levels each structure the vote. Negative voting increases when per capita state income growth is low, and it increases

TABLE 11. Estimated Effects of Economic Conditions on Negative Voting, California Ballot Measures, 1974–92: All Propositions and Propositions with Economic Content

Variable	All Propositions			Economic Propositions[a]		
	Model 1	Model 2	Model 3	Model 1	Model 2	Model 3
Calif. p/c income chg.	−.021**	—	−.012*	−.031**	—	−.030**
	(.007)		(.007)	(.008)		(.010)
California unemployment	—	.017*	.025*	—	−.002	−.006
		(.010)	(.012)		(.016)	(.017)
U.S. unemployment	—	.001	.001	—	.003	.006
		(.005)	(.005)		(.010)	(.101)
U.S. p/c income chg.	.007	—	−.018	−.011	—	−.013
	(.010)		(.016)	(.015)		(.019)
Primary dummy	−.003	−.006	−.008	−.038	−.036	−.068*
	(.023)	(.023)	(.023)	(.037)	(.039)	(.038)
Position on ballot	.004**	.006**	.005**	.002	.004*	.002
	(.001)	(.001)	(.0014)	(.0016)	(.002)	(.002)
Turnout	.002*	.001	.002*	.001	−.001	.001
	(.001)	(.001)	(.0011)	(.001)	(.001)	(.001)
Trend	−.004	.007	.001	−.014*	.000	−.017*
	(.004)	(.005)	(.006)	(.006)	(.000)	(.008)
Constant	.323**	.344**	.225*	.491**	.331*	.523**
	(.072)	(.111)	(.128)	(.116)	(.171)	(.180)
N	268	268	268	107	107	107
R^2	.13	.13	.16	.25	.15	.26
adj. R^2	.11	.11	.13	.21	.10	.20

Source: Voting records, California secretary of state; economic data, U.S. Statistical Abstracts and Economic Reports of the President.

Note: OLS coefficients for pooled data. Standard errors are in parentheses. Dependent variable = percentage of *no* vote.

[a]Includes bond measures and fiscal propositions

*Significant at $p < .05$ (one-tail)   **Significant at $p < .01$ (one-tail) when state unemployment is high. Moreover, the coefficient for state income remains significant when national income is included in the analysis (Model 1). The same pattern holds for state unemployment levels (Model 2). The full model (Model 3) indicates that state unemployment and state income growth structure voting when we examine all propositions. The control variable representing ballot position indicates that issues farther down the ballot receive more negative votes (recall that in California these tend to be the initiatives).

A comparison of results from tables 11 and 12 indicates that the relationship between economic conditions and proposition voting might vary with issue content. Table 11 (right side) illustrates that per capita state income change is associated with voting on economic propositions, but unemployment is not. Furthermore, models of voting on economic propositions employing the state income indicator fit better than those estimating support across all propositions.

TABLE 12.   Estimated Effects of Economic Conditions on Negative Voting, California Ballot Measures, 1974–92: Bond Measures and Propositions Lacking Economic Content

Variable	Bond Measures Only			Noneconomic Propositions		
	Model 1	Model 2	Model 3	Model 1	Model 2	Model 3
Calif. p/c income chg.	−.026**	—	−.021*	−.018*	—	−.007
	(.010)		(.011)	(.010)		(.011)
California unemployment	—	.001	.003	—	.028*	.024**
		(.014)	(.015)		(.014)	(.009)
U.S. unemployment	—	.010	.008	—	.004	.001
		(.014)	(.009)		(.007)	(.001)
U.S. p/c income chg.	.011	—	.002	.014	—	−.023
	(.016)		(.020)	(.014)		(.016)
Primary	−.026	.002	−.023	.007	−.002	−.001
	(.035)	(.034)	(.036)	(.030)	(.031)	(.001)
Position on ballot	.004*	.008**	.005*	.007**	.008**	.009**
	(.002)	(.002)	(.005)	(.002)	(.003)	(.002)
Turnout	.001	.001	.001	.001	.000	.001
	(.001)	(.001)	(.001)	(.001)	(.001)	(.001)
Trend	−.014*	−.009	−.016*	−.003	.009	.006
	(.006)	(.007)	(.008)	(.006)	(.007)	(.009)
Constant	.442**	.307*	.440**	.351**	.216	.143
	(.111)	(.161)	(.178)	(.101)	(.151)	(.204)
N	75	75	75	161	161	161
R^2	.33	.31	.34	.12	.15	.17
adj. R^2	.27	.25	.26	.09	.11	.13

Source: Voting records, California Secretary of State; economic data, U.S. Statistical Abstracts and Economic Reports of the President.

Note: OLS coefficients for pooled data. Standard errors are in parentheses. Dependent variable = percentage of *no* vote. Primary is a dummy variable reflecting measures appearing in primary elections.

*Significant at $p < .05$ (one-tail)   **Significant at $p < .01$ (one-tail)

Table 12 reports the estimates of voting on bond issues, a subset of the economic propositions (left side). The fit of these models is even greater, suggesting that economic voting might be more pronounced on bond measures.

This finding is not surprising if we consider the potential uncertainty associated with these issues: they are some of the least visible and most routine items on the California ballot, yet they typically involve no campaign activity. If uncertainty is associated with risk aversion and negative voting, we would expect risk-averse negative voting to be more pronounced on less-visible issues. These measures also have tangible economic stakes, and thus they provide a more apparent connection between voters' economic concerns and the proposition decision. Negative voting on bond issues associated with lower per capita state income growth also suggests that the individual-level foundations of these patterns might be more likely to involve risk-averse behavior than risk-seeking behavior. In the aggregate, fewer people appear to accept the risk (or the uncertainty) of bond spending when the economy is weak. Ballot position also conditions voting on bond measures, with those propositions farther down the list of ballot measures receiving more negative votes.

Estimates of votes on noneconomic issues are reported in table 12 (right side). Results here show a slightly different pattern than those found with economic and bond propositions. The coefficient for state per capita income change is significant in Model 1. When all economic indicators are included (Model 3), however, negative voting on noneconomic issues appears to be associated with state unemployment. The state income coefficient fails to remain significant in Model 3, although the sign remains in the expected direction. As with the other types of propositions, state conditions continue to structure the vote when national conditions are accounted for.[7]

Aggregated Data from Michigan

Similar aggregate-level models of voting on statewide propositions were estimated with data from Michigan. Data available from Michigan ran from 1948 to 1990, when a total of ninety-seven issues appeared on the state ballot. Of these issues, most (seventy-five) were noneconomic. Because Michigan voters are not required to approve all legislative bond issues by referenda, nearly all issues classified as economic were tax related. Thus, direct comparisons between Michigan and California are difficult, and we estimated the vote over all

---

7. Different methods of estimation produce rather consistent results. Pooled models were estimated using each economic measure individually. State measures that are significant in tables 11 and 12 are also significant when used without the national measures. National indicators, when used without state measures, were seldom significant. The only exception is when national unemployment is used in an estimation of support for noneconomic measures. The effect disappears when state unemployment is introduced.

propositions and noneconomic propositions only. Because state-level economic data were not readily available for the entire time series, we report models using measures of national economic conditions.[8] Again, three models are estimated for each set of propositions. Model 1 includes income measures, Model 2 includes unemployment measures, and Model 3 includes both.

Table 13 reports results from the Michigan estimations. Once again, when we examine voting across all issues, unemployment levels appear to act to condition support for ballot measures. When unemployment is up, negative voting is also up. Unlike the case in California, income does not appear to affect support, although the sign is in the anticipated direction. When we examine noneconomic propositions in Michigan, we find that the effect of unemployment is in the expected direction but is much less significant.

Given differences in the economic data available for analysis, it is difficult to explain why income and unemployment measures are associated with support in California, but unemployment alone is associated with support in Michigan. It is clear, however, that these aggregate data suggest that economic

TABLE 13.   Estimated Effects of Economic Conditions on Negative Voting: Michigan Ballot Measures, 1948–90

Variable	Economic Propositions			Noneconomic Propositions		
	Model 1	Model 2	Model 3	Model 1	Model 2	Model 3
Unemployment	.012[+]	—	.021*	.010	—	.016[a]
	(.007)		(.010)	(.076)		(.011)
Income	—	−.001	.006	—	−.001	.005
		(.423)	(.005)		(.035)	(.006)
Trend	.005	.003*	−.001	.001	.003[++]	.001
	(.010)	(.001)	(.012)	(.001)	(.001)	(.002)
Primary	−.019	−.024	−.029	−.046	−.047	−.056
	(.057)	(.055)	(.053)	(.058)	(.038)	(.160)
Position on ballot	.006	.003	.007	.004	.002	.004
	(.008)	(.004)	(.007)	(.005)	(.003)	(.004)
Turnout	.002	.002	.002	.001	.001	.001
	(.0015)	(.0015)	(.0015)	(.001)	(.002)	(.002)
Constant	.243*	.301*	.172	.314**	.361**	.265[++]
	(.109)	(.108)	(.124)	(.119)	(.119)	(.146)
R^2	.148	.122	.161	.164	.147	.173
$N = 97$						

Note: OLS coefficients for pooled data. Standard errors are in parentheses. Dependent variable = percentage of *no* vote. Primary is a dummy variable reflecting measures appearing in primary elections.

[a]t-ratio = 1.43

*Significant at $p < .05$ (two-tail)   **Significant at $p < .01$ (two-tail)   [++]Significant at $p < .05$ (one-tail)

8. Models estimated for the period from which state and national economic data were available produced results similar to those displayed in tables 11 and 12.

TABLE 14. OLS and GLS Estimates of Effects of Economic Conditions on Aggregate "No" Votes, California and Michigan

| | California, 1974–92 | | Michigan, 1948–90 | |
	OLS	GLS	OLS	GLS
Unemployment	2.01*	1.53*	1.96*	1.56+
	(1.06)	(1.03)	(.82)	(.92)
Total on ballot	.46*	.38*	−.59	−.16
	(.24)	(.19)	(1.05)	(1.14)
Constant	22.99**	17.78**	35.26**	33.43**
	(9.53)	(5.90)	(6.94)	(6.82)
N	21	20	24	23
R^2	.24	.23	.21	.13
Durbin-Watson d	1.14	1.76[a]	1.73[a]	1.36[a]

Note: OLS and GLS estimates. GLS coefficients estimated by two-step Cochrane-Orcutt procedure (Ostrum 1990). Standard errors in parentheses. Dependent variable = mean *no* vote for all propositions in each election having statewide propositions on the ballot. Michigan did not have statewide propositions on the ballot in every year during this period.

[a]For given N and K, Dubin-Watson indicates we should retain the null hypothesis of no serial correlation.

*Significant at $p < .05$ (one-tail) **Significant at $p < .01$ (one-tail) +Significant at $p < .10$ (one-tail)

conditions are associated with voting on ballot propositions. Table 14 demonstrates that the patterns found are not simply a function of the pooled cross-section estimation techniques. Controlling for the number of issues on each ballot, OLS and GLS estimates of the average annual *no* vote in each state indicate that economic factors are associated with aggregate vote totals.

Summary

Our results provide support for the idea that economic conditions structure the fortunes of ballot propositions, at least in California and Michigan. In all but one aggregate estimation from California using income, lower rates of per capita state income growth are associated with greater negative voting on ballot issues. Moreover, state conditions in California remain significant predictors of proposition votes when national conditions are accounted for.

The individual-level results illustrate that these patterns are related to voters' concerns about state conditions. Many less-educated voters appear to evaluate propositions negatively if they are worried about conditions in their state. New bond sales and new taxes, for example, involve perceptible economic stakes for many voters, particularly when they are adopted in correspondence with new public programs. Voters might not know details about the specific proposition, but at times they seem to make decisions about economic measures on the basis of general economic concerns. As state income growth stagnates, more voters are likely to become aware of problems with the state's economy (i.e., from media coverage, personal experience, or local government fiscal problems), and they are less disposed to accept the risk that comes with changing policy. Examination of individual-level data reveals that the use of these economic evaluations appears to be limited to less-educated voters—the part of the electorate that has fewer information resources available and less ability to use partisan or ideological references when evaluating propositions.

Our conclusions assume that many voters will not look upon the issuance of debt (or increased public spending) as would classic Keynesians, nor do they look at new policies as rational utility maximizers or optimizers. Rather, we assume that many uncertain voters—namely, those facing the greatest information costs—adopt an information cost-cutting behavior. Direct democracy places substantial information demands on these voters. Uncertain voters might look at new policies or programs as a greater risk when times are bad, a risk they are unwilling to take given the prevailing uncertainties involved with proposition voting. If they are responding to objective economic conditions when forming assessments about state conditions and then they use those evaluations to decide when it is a good time to alter the status quo (as the aggregate data suggest), we might say that they are reasoning about ballot propositions on the basis of minimal information. Voters with higher levels of education might reason differently.

At this point we cannot evaluate why aggregate unemployment levels appear to be associated with support for noneconomic issues in California and economic issues in Michigan, but not with support for bond and economic propositions in California. Differences might be because of the use of a different time series for each state or because of different economic measures (each a function of data availability). Results might also differ between states because far more California propositions are bond measures referred by the legislature. Differences in aggregate results across states might be explained with further survey data that assess voters' use of personal or sociotropic evaluations of the state economy when evaluating different types of propositions. Nevertheless, at a basic level, it appears that economics matters in these direct-democracy elections.

Our findings also offer some further evidence of *state* conditions affecting *state* election outcomes. The discrepancy between our findings and those of previous studies of economic voting in state elections is likely to be a function of the decision contexts investigated. In state candidate contests, voters first assess the candidate's responsibility for state economic conditions, and then they decide if the candidate should be blamed or rewarded for those conditions. With ballot propositions, the voter does not need to determine who is to blame or who is responsible for economic performance. State economic conditions can simply act as an information source that some voters utilize when making decisions on policies. Additional research is needed to assess the decision process involved with the utilization of this information.

In this chapter we demonstrate that economic concerns might be but one piece of information that some voters refer to when evaluating ballot propositions. Thus far, we have not established that economic voting necessarily reflects instrumental, self-interested voting, nor have we established which voters might utilize instrumental concerns when making decisions on propositions. Given the analysis so far, we cannot interpret these data as evidence that rational voters conduct a cost-benefit analysis of the fiscal impacts of each ballot measure. Rather, some voters appear to use economic concerns as a cue, particularly when propositions have clear economic stakes. Economic voting might be of more use to the less educated, because those voters have less ability to translate their party and ideology into evaluations of propositions.

In later chapters we look at how voters might use instrumental evaluations (or narrow self-interest) to form opinions about propositions. We find that narrowly defined indicators of self-interest are associated with support for tax and expenditure referenda. We also demonstrate that voters with limited cognitive abilities (the less educated) might be more frequently disposed toward evaluating some propositions in terms of self-interest, while well-educated voters rely more commonly on ideology and party. In chapter 5 we examine these differences between cognitively narrow reasoning based on self-interest and cognitively complex reasoning based on ideology and party.

CHAPTER 5

Private Interests
and Instrumental Voting

To this point we have said little about the prospects for self-interested or instrumental voting on ballot propositions. As noted earlier, there is a body of literature suggesting that voters should not be expected to engage in much systematic reasoning when making decisions about propositions. Early and contemporary commentators note that many voters lack the requisite information and ability for it. Our use of limited-information theories illustrates how this pessimistic evaluation of voters might be inaccurate, or at least overstated. Many voters seek out and find useful information, cues, and references.

We have not yet established that voters can also make decisions on the basis of personal (private) interests. We suggest that some voters do so when evaluating certain propositions. If we consider the information required to translate ballot proposals into an understanding of the personalized benefits (or costs) that an individual might derive from altering the status quo, we might see voting based on self-interest as more complex than (or at least as demanding as) voting based on the information shortcuts discussed in earlier chapters.

To vote on the basis of private interests instrumentally so that a desired outcome might be produced, voters must know something about their own policy preferences, the proposition, and how (or if) the proposition will make them better or worse off. Some cues and shortcuts could help voters make self-interested evaluations of propositions, but it is another matter for voters to employ self-interested motivations when evaluating propositions. Evidence of that would bring us closer to establishing that voters do indeed reason systematically when they make their decisions in direct democracy.

In this chapter we examine the motivations of voters in elections that are focused primarily on tax and spending (school voucher) initiatives. We advance the argument that voters are not simply motivated by the factors frequently cited to explain support for these issues (i.e., symbolic or "public-regarding" concerns), but that they can also utilize private, instrumental interests when evaluating propositions. This argument is not entirely new, but we illustrate how the use of narrow private-interest motivations might be distinguished by available information and the voter's level of cognitive ability.

The Case against Instrumental Voting

The "Public-Regarding" and "Symbolic Politics" Traditions

Given the portrait of direct-democracy voters we receive from the behavioral political science studies of the 1960s and 1970s (see chapter 2), instrumental motivations have not typically been seen as part of an accurate explanation of how voters decide what they are for or against when they evaluate ballot measures. One body of literature grants limited weight to the idea that direct-democracy choices reflect instrumental behavior or the private interests of individual voters.

As Wolfinger and Greenstein noted, "it is common to assume that asking voters to pass judgment on substantive policy questions strains their information and interest, leading them to decisions that may be inconsistent with their desires" (Wolfinger and Greenstein 1968, 767). From this perspective, people lack information about the details of policy and have a limited capacity for deciding how a complex policy might affect them personally. Many voters are thus unable to translate their policy preferences into accurate votes on real propositions (Magleby 1984, 142; conversely, see Cronin 1989, chap. 4).

It is also said that many people intentionally vote against their interests. Wilson and Banfield claim that "a considerable portion of voters, especially in the upper income groups, vote against their self-interest" in direct democracy (1963, 885). These authors claimed that a "public-regarding" ethos motivated these voters, but that some lower-status ethic groups might be motivated by a "private-regarding" ethos (see chapter 2). Since the publication of the Wilson and Banfield article, a substantial amount of literature (typically employing aggregated data) has illustrated that upper-status constituencies favor proposals that require them to finance broad public benefits (e.g., Minar 1966; Hicks 1972; Piele and Hall 1973; Jennings and Milstein 1973; Alexander and Bass 1974; Schroeder and Sjoquist 1978; see Hahn and Kamieniecki 1987, 115, esp. n. 21, for a summary of various studies). Wilson and Banfield's aggregate analysis produced positive correlations between spatial indicators of higher social status and support for tax and expenditure measures. A more recent aggregate study produced similar results, showing that these patterns reflect that "high-status voters can afford the luxury of a diverse range of public expenditures" (Hahn and Kamieniecki 1987, 121).

Given that voters might have an easier time identifying costs and benefits contained in a tax or spending proposition than one contained in a regulatory proposition, we might expect that tax and spending measures are occasions when self-interested behavior would be identified frequently. Yet studies of these propositions rarely produce systematic self-interest effects (for a review, see Sears and Funk 1990, 170). Older voters, for example, have been found to be no more likely to oppose school tax referenda than are voters with school-age children (Rosenbaum and Button 1989; Rubinfeld 1977; Hall and Piele 1976). Such findings are seen to reflect a broad social consensus in favor of education that cuts across generational interests. Correspondingly, Lowery and Sigelman (1981, 964) noted that "previous studies have produced little evidence supporting the self-interest explanation" for tax referenda voting (see also Hall and Piele 1976). They found that measures of self-interest such as home ownership failed to explain individual-level support for property tax rollbacks (however, see Citrin 1979, 127). That being the case, they concluded that "the symbolic politics interpretation of the tax revolt goes a long way toward explaining the inadequacies of the [self-interest] explanation" (Lowery and Sigelman 1981, 972).

Alternatively, there is a smaller body of literature that emphasizes instrumental voting in direct democracy. Recent formal, experimental, and empirical studies suggest that direct-democracy voters can translate individual preferences into votes on policy when given minimal information cues (Lupia 1992, 1994a, 1994b). Tedin (1994), although not focusing explicitly on referenda, found evidence of a relationship between indicators of self-interest and opinions on legislation pertaining to financial equalization of schools. Sears and Citrin (1982) examined opinions on California's tax revolt (Proposition 13) and concluded that both symbolic and self-interested motivations structured support for tax rebellion.

Two perspectives emerge from this literature. The first of these suggests that a range of factors unrelated to self-interest (or unrelated to narrow private interests) might structure voting on referenda. A second perspective—perhaps a less common perspective among the findings in the empirical literature—suggests that choices on tax referenda might reflect the narrow, private interests of individual voters. One set of factors need not operate to the exclusion of the other (indeed, standard measures of each are not always mutually exclusive); however, much of the literature on referenda voting might lead us to expect that narrow, private interests are not a significant factor. If such is the case, then idiosyncratic, symbolic, or public-regarding motivations could influence the vote to the exclusion of factors associated with private interests. This dichotomy and this conclusion are not unique to the study of referenda voting. Indeed, many empirical studies that attempt to link individual behavior to the impact that policies have on individuals fail to detect self-interest effects (for reviews, see Lau, Brown, and Sears 1978; Sears et al. 1980; Citrin and Green 1990; Sears and Funk 1990, 1991).[1]

---

1. Green and Cowden's study of opinion on school busing (1992) found that although attitudes might not be affected by indicators of interest, it is possible that self-reported behavior is more likely to be affected.

Self-Interested and Non-Self-Interested Motivations

Non-Self-Interested Motivations on Propositions

Defining what is meant by self-interested and non-self-interested motivations tends to be a fairly difficult enterprise. Non-self-interested motivations are often grouped in the broad category of symbolic or affective motivations. Sears defines political symbols as referring to "emotion based on some enduring predisposition rather than on tangible costs and benefits of the matter to which the symbol refers" (1993, 114). On the other hand, Jacoby (1994) uses ideology and party identification as indicators of symbolic predispositions. As noted in earlier chapters, however, ideology can also be seen as a cognitive device that allows people to organize thoughts about the political world.

Either way, ideologies are likely to be important devices that allow voters to see a "broader picture" or to act on the basis of enduring predispositions, values, or orientations about politics. In this way, evaluating a proposition in terms of ideology represents something other than the use of narrow, self-interested motivations. Rather, ideology might enable voters to place a ballot issue in a broader social or attitudinal framework. In addition to ideology, a list of "symbolic" motivations might include a broad category of attitudinal motivations (e.g., racism, cynicism about government, generic hostility to taxation). Indeed, referenda voting was viewed by some of the earlier behavioral sociologists as a manifestation of alienation and anomie (Gamson 1961; Gold 1962; Horton and Thompson 1962; McDill and Ridley 1962; Tempelton 1966; Agger and Goldstein 1971; see also Stone 1965). In testing for self-interested motivations, we must include broad indicators of ideology and attitudinal concerns about taxation as controls. Given findings from previous research and from chapter 4, these concerns are expected to have substantial effects on support for these measures.

Private, Self-Interested Motivations

For self-interest, we focus more narrowly on factors that can be seen to represent the private, instrumental motivations people could have for supporting an initiative. Data limitations prevent us from letting voters define their own interests. We thus impute a set of narrow interests to individuals. For example, we assume that having children presently in school (or being of a corresponding age) is likely to affect support for school taxes. Furthermore, private interest in supporting voucher programs might be associated with the prospects of personally receiving a cash windfall from the policy. Instrumental voting motivations could also be reflected by the type of school the voter's children are in (public or private). Home ownership also serves as an imputed indicator of private self-interest when we examine support for propositions affecting property tax increases. In this chapter, we present hypotheses of how these narrow interests might affect support for various policies.

We suggest that the plausibility of private, self-interested motivations as an explanation of vote choice relates to the type of issue on the ballot and the timing of the election. It should be easier for voters to act on their private interests if they have information about the policy. Given the nature of campaigns, we assume that voters have more information at the close of a campaign. Thus, we examine data from surveys conducted near the close of actual proposition campaigns.[2] It might also be easier for a voter to perceive self-interest when the costs and benefits produced by the policy are directly tangible (e.g., fiscal issues). Our primary analysis examines whether self-interested behavior is evident near the close of campaigns for tax and spending issues. Tax and spending issues, however, might be "most likely case" scenarios when testing for self-interest effects. Self-interested motivations might be less likely to operate on other propositions with costs or benefits more widely distributed or not clearly defined—such as public morality issues. For the sake of expanding the potential generalizability of the results that follow, we begin with an examination of possible self-interest effects operating on a public morality issue. We leave to future research the issue of how far this behavior might extend to other contexts.

A Case for Self-Interest: Aggregate Examples

Prohibition Measures

We have noted the importance of symbolic factors and the argument that self-interest may affect choice on some propositions but not on others. We now examine some preliminary evidence that is consistent with the hypothesis that self-interest explains voting behavior on many propositions. We then present some simple evidence using aggregate data from Prohibition measures around the time of World War I. Prohibition, of course, raised fundamental religious and moral issues that were not easily resolved in legislatures (Morgan and Meier 1980; Franklin 1971). Prohibition measures appeared repeatedly on state ballots in the early years of American direct democracy, and they appeared with such frequency on California ballots that in 1914 an unsuccessful attempt was made to prevent any Prohibition measures from appearing for eight years. In addition to religious and moral concerns, those associated with the production

---

2. Previous research occasionally examined the opinions of voters who were detached from the context of a real campaign, or it examined opinions about hypothetical choices (e.g., Lowery and Sigelman 1981; Tedin 1994).

of alcohol were likely to have a keen interest in the issue, an interest that we would be hard-pressed to attribute to morality.

Table 15 presents a simple regression analysis using county-level data relevant to three Prohibition propositions from 1916, 1918, and 1920. We model county-level support for the three Prohibition propositions as a function of county-level religious affiliation and the level of "dry" wine production in millions of barrels. The classification "dry" wine excludes production of "sweet" wines such as sherry, which were typically unaffected by Prohibition measures. The analysis does not consider the production of beer or other liquors because figures for them are unavailable for this period.

Dry wine production serves as our indicator of the narrow economic interests associated with wine production in each county's electorate. Given this interest, we would expect wine production to be inversely associated with support for the propositions. Religious affiliation, and especially affiliation with some Baptist churches, was clearly a factor in helping shape attitudes toward Prohibition (Morgan and Meier 1980; Franklin 1971). A higher percentage of Baptists in a county should cause greater support.

It is more complicated to explain opposition to these measures as they relate to Catholic affiliation, however. Some Catholics could be expected to oppose Prohibition on personal rather than on religious grounds, yet the use of wine in Catholic church services did mean that total Prohibition created the possibility of offending many Catholics. The propositions of 1916 and 1920 actually made explicit and express exceptions for alcohol use for "sacramental" and "religious" purposes, respectively, thus allowing Catholics the use of wine for

TABLE 15.   Aggregate Indicators of Voter Self-Interest on Prohibition Propositions

	1916 (No. 1)	1918 (No. 22)	1920 (No. 2)
Constant	0.39	0.55	0.48
Dry wine production	−.031**	−0.037**	−0.021+
	(.01)	(.016)	(.013)
% Baptist	1.33**	.65+	.90**
	(.37)	(.43)	(.35)
% Catholic	0.05	−.15**	−.05
	(.07)	(.08)	(.06)
N	58	58	58
R^2	.28	.26	.23

Source: Wine production is denoted by millions of barrels of "dry" wine produced (excluding "sweet" wines such as sherry) in 1919, as given by the 1921 State Board of Viticulture Report. Percentages of Baptists and Catholics are from the 1926 Census of Religious Bodies.

Note: OLS estimates. Figures in parentheses are standard errors. Dependent variable = percent of county vote in favor.

+Significant at .10 level (two-tail)   **Significant at .05 level (two-tail)

"religious" purposes. The "Bone Dry" measure (Proposition 22) of 1918, how-ever, made no exceptions at all. We should expect that while areas with a strong Baptist presence would favor Prohibition, those with a high proportion of Catholics are likely to be opposed. If voters respond to differences in the con-tent of various ballot measures, the effect for Catholics should be particularly pronounced with the 1918 measure.

The results presented in table 15 are consistent with the idea that many voters evaluate "morality" issues in terms of economic interests, and they are also consistent with the idea that voters differentiate among relatively similar ballot measures. Wine production (our surrogate for interest) and religious af-filiation were related to support for each Prohibition initiative. In each estima-tion, we see strong and consistent opposition associated with wine production. The noticeable increase among Catholics in opposition to Prohibition in 1918 suggests that Catholic voters were somehow able to distinguish between mea-sures that most adversely affected them and those that did not.

California's Proposition 13 of 1978

Rather than dwell on the relatively distant past, we turn now to the more recent, and far more (in)famous Proposition 13. Recall that Proposition 13 would re-duce revenues available to governments in California (Neiman and Riposa 1986).

In 1978, after several failed attempts to pass property tax relief measures, Howard Jarvis and Paul Gann qualified a measure for the California ballot that would roll back property assessments dramatically. Proposition 13 was widely seen as part of an ongoing nonelite, populist antitax insurgency that reached the ballot at a time of rapid property tax increases. The measure was opposed by many members of the state's political elite, including elected officials from both major parties. Property taxes had inflated wildly as counties reassessed prop-erty every two to three years. By 1978, California property taxes were 52 per-cent above the national norm, with assessments increasing nearly 30 percent per year in some counties (Sears and Citrin 1982, 21–22). Prior to the initia-tive's qualification, the state legislature had been unable to pass major legisla-tion addressing the rapidly increasing property tax burdens.

Commercial and residential property holders were the major beneficiaries of the initiative's provisions. An active campaign was waged against Proposi-tion 13 by public employee unions (including the California Teachers Associ-ation), in conjunction with much of the state's political elite. Opponents em-phasized that much of the tax savings would accrue to nonresidential property holders, that renters would be shut out from any savings, and that services such as education would be heavily damaged by spending cuts if property tax rev-enues were lost.

We present a relatively simple aggregate test of self-interest here by assuming that employment in government is a reasonable indicator of those with a personal interest at stake when government revenue bases are threatened. While ideology and partisanship are likely to shape attitudes toward taxation, the source of a voter's livelihood and the voter's share of the actual tax burden might also affect support. An individual-level study of this proposition is presented at the end of this chapter; however, our survey data do not allow us to measure public-sector employment status. These aggregate data allow us to examine, indirectly, how public-sector employment might have affected support.

Support for Proposition 13 is assumed to be higher in counties with heavy Republican registration (a surrogate measure of ideology). It is also assumed to be lower in counties with more people employed in the public sector, because Proposition 13 had the potential to affect the economic prospects for public-sector workers and their dependents. If people who faced the highest taxes voted for Proposition 13 as a means of receiving tax relief, we would also expect support to vary according to county tax level and by median home prices. As can be seen in table 16, these measures of narrow economic self-interest have a significant affect on the vote.

TABLE 16.   Aggregate Indicators of Voter Self-Interest
and California's Proposition 13

	(1)	(2)	(3)
Constant	59.2	29.28	-47.74
% Government employment	-0.10^{**}	-0.10^{**}	$-.12^{**}$
	(.04)	(.04)	(.03)
% Republican	0.31^{**}	$.022^{+++}$	0.23^{+}
	(.14)	(.14)	(.12)
Property tax	-0.35	7.17^{*}	5.1^{+}
	(.51)	(4.1)	(3.6)
Property tax^2	—	-0.42^{+}	-0.32^{+++}
		(.23)	(.20)
House prices	—	-0.07	46.85^{**}
		(1.19)	(11.3)
House prices^2	—	—	-6.11^{**}
			(1.4)
N	58	58	58
R^2	.22	.27	.45

Source: California Field Poll data.

Note: OLS estimates. Figures in parentheses are standard errors. Dependent variable = percentage of county vote in favor.

$^{+}$Significant at .10 level (two tail)

**Significant at .05 level (two-tail)

$^{+++}$Not significant, but $p <$ at .20 level (two-tail)

One technical point carries with it substantive implications. A linear estimation of the effects of tax rates and home prices on support for Proposition 13 is not significant. There is, however, a substantive reason for expecting that linear measures are not especially useful in capturing public concerns about taxation. If responses to tax burdens are triggered only at some threshold beyond which additional taxes are not felt to be more burdensome, then we should use nonlinear measures (Vote $= a + b_{\text{tax}} + b_{\text{tax}}2 + bX_n \ldots$) to capture the middle range of taxes and home values that correspond to the greatest level of voter discontent with taxes. In other words, it is the middle range of taxation that tends to elicit the most hostility from minimally attentive voters. Very low taxes do not attract much notice; it is when they reach a certain, burdensome level that voter anger can be so high that even additional marginal increases are met with the same (high) level of anger.

Work by Bowler and Donovan (1995) contains a fuller discussion of the theoretical aspects of this argument, one part of which argues for the use of squared terms (similar to those used in table 5) to capture the ∩-shaped relationship between tax levels and citizen concerns about taxes. Once we do so, as shown in columns 2 and 3 of table 16, we see a large effect for tax levels. The substantive implication of these results suggests that voters acted instrumentally in response to objective tax rates and that most hostility to Proposition 13 was in the middle range of taxation and home values.

These simple examples provide evidence consistent with the hypothesis that voters evaluate some ballot measures in terms of their narrow self-interest. These aggregate results are suggestive, but they are not necessarily thoroughly convincing. Data limitations restrict the kinds of models we can estimate. These results rely on aggregate-level data and, as such, they are subject to criticism that they may not actually reflect individual-level behavior (the ecological fallacy). More persuasive evidence would come from individual-level data on less-publicized measures. We examine these in the next section.

Hypotheses and Cases for Individual-Level Analysis

Our selection of propositions for individual-level analysis was limited again by available survey data. In selecting cases, we were guided by a desire to examine initiatives that appear and reappear in various forms on many state ballots. In addition to California's famous property tax reduction initiative (Proposition 13 of 1978), ballots in California in 1993 and in Colorado in 1992 provided opportunities to test hypotheses about opinions on initiatives affecting property taxes, sales tax measures, voucher spending issues, and proposals for changing rules to increase state taxes.

We have data from two states on sales tax increase questions (Colorado's Amendment 6 of 1992 and California's Proposition 172 of 1993) and school "choice" plans (Colorado's Amendment 7 of 1992 and California's Proposition 174 of 1993). In addition, the 1993 California ballot and the 1992 Colorado ballot included measures that asked voters to alter requirements for increasing future taxes (Colorado's Amendment 1 and California's Proposition 170). Due to the richness of the Field Institute's California Poll survey, the primary analysis will be of the California cases. Wherever possible, Colorado data are used to cross-validate findings from California.[3]

We have, up to this point, attempted to split survey samples by level of education to demonstrate how voters at each level of cognitive ability might reason differently. Some of the samples used here were too small to conduct meaningful tests if the samples were split. In our final test of self-interested reasoning (another look at support for Proposition 13), we once again have a sample large enough to split by level of education, and we find important differences in the use of self-interested reasoning across education levels. Before we return to this test, however, we examine voting on tax and spending measures from the 1990s. Survey data collected during this time allow us to divide our sample into groups distinguished by the amount of specific, factual information they have been given about each initiative. This division provides another way of testing for instrumental reasoning as it reveals that voters can come to support (or oppose) a measure once they become aware of how it will benefit (or cost) them personally. We see evidence suggesting that once voters learn that a measure might make them better off personally, they then support the measure. We examine this finding across three issues.

School Choice or Vouchers

For the school voucher initiatives, we expect that voters with children in private schools would favor vouchers. Adoption of the policy would provide them with a direct cash windfall for which no action is needed. Under the Proposition 174 plan, vouchers would have been extended to all parents in California. All parents with children in school would be provided a voucher worth about $2,600 (Locke 1993), including those with children in private schools. For the latter parents, the voucher would reduce their existing tuition payments. Thus, such parents would have strong private (personal) motivations for supporting Proposition 174. Alternatively, if parents with children in private school were "public regarding" or were interested in preserving the existing public school system, we might see no differences between these parents and other voters.

---

3. The California data were obtained from University of California data. Colorado data were obtained from the University of Colorado Social Science Data Lab, administered by the Departments of Political Science and Sociology. John McIver was the principal investigator on the Colorado Poll.

Unlike voters with no children, parents with students in public schools also faced the *possibility* of receiving the economic benefit of the voucher if they eventually enrolled their children in a voucher school. If they too were motivated by private (personal) interests associated with the prospect of receiving the voucher, they would also be more supportive than would be voters with no children. These parents could have at least a moderate interest in supporting Proposition 174, albeit not as strong an interest as private-school parents.[4] If personal motivations structure voting, those with no children should be the least likely to support the voucher plan because they would continue to pay taxes, yet they would have no prospect of receiving direct benefits.[5] For the Colorado voucher proposal, we lack measures of school enrollment. Here we must test these hypotheses less directly by using the respondent's age as a surrogate for having a direct interest in education and in possibly receiving vouchers. Younger voters (who are more likely to have children in school) are expected to be more supportive of vouchers.

Changing Rules about Tax Increases

California's Proposition 170 asked voters to change the voting requirements for school funding. In the Proposition 13 "tax revolt" era, Californians used direct democracy to institutionalize a 1 percent property tax limit that required a two-thirds majority referendum vote to sell bonds that would raise local property taxes above the limit. Proposition 170 would have changed these rules to allow school construction bond sales (and associated property tax hikes) to be approved by a simple majority in local referenda. Conversely, Colorado's Amendment 1 proposed a rule designed to make future legislative tax increases more difficult. It required that future taxes be submitted to voters for approval.[6]

In the case of California, the move to a simple majority from a two-thirds requirement would have made future property tax proposals easier to pass (Scott 1993). Thus, if home owners are motivated by private concerns about taxation, we should see them voting against Proposition 170. Moreover, because potential revenue would go to public education, voters with children in public schools would be expected to support this measure. Parents with children in private schools, however, would stand to receive no direct private benefits. If their votes are motivated by private rather than public interests, they would be less support-

---

4. Vouchers present parents of private-school children with an increase in disposable income. They would not necessarily provide an increase in the disposable income of parents with children in public schools.

5. It is important to note that most voters do not have children in school. Therefore, the largest group of voters that decides on a school voucher initiative are those who will not have an opportunity to receive an immediate cash benefit from the policy.

6. Amendment 1 also included limitations on future public spending increases.

ive of Proposition 170. In each of the models estimated subsequently, school enrollment status is represented by unique dummy variables (i.e., 1 = children in
private schools; 0 = all others; 1 = children in public schools; 0 = all others).

Sales Tax Increases

California's 1993 sales tax measure (Proposition 172) directed benefits to a
larger audience than did the voucher initiatives. It proposed permanent adoption of a half-cent addition to the sales tax that would be dedicated broadly to
"public safety" (police and fire) (Starkey 1993). We compare support for this
measure to support for Colorado's 1992 tax measure. Colorado's Amendment
6 proposed an increase in the state sales tax, with revenue specifically directed
to public education. Thus, the Colorado measure had a more narrowly defined
group of beneficiaries: people in the age groups that are likely to have school-
children. That being the case, voters without children in schools (generally, the
elderly) were asked to approve a tax to fund public schools.

The "public-regarding" explanation of referenda voting suggests that there
should be no generational effect in school-funding votes because regard for the
collective good should supersede self-interest (Button 1992). Conversely, private motivations might cause older Colorado voters to oppose a sales tax hike
that they feel provides them with no direct, immediate benefits. Because the
California sales tax distributed benefits more widely, we should not expect a
generational effect there.

We first model vote intentions for voucher programs, tax rule changes, and
sales tax increases, respectively. Because of the celebrated status of Proposition
13, we examine opinions on that measure in greater detail later in the chapter.
To isolate the effects of measures of the private interests we have presented, we
include controls for income, age, and education in our models (see Appendix A
at the back of this book for codings).[7] Because much of the literature on voting
on tax and expenditure referenda emphasizes abstract and "symbolic" motivations, we also include controls for political ideology and concern about state
government taxation (the codings are in Appendix A). If self-interest structures
voter intentions, then the effects of the interest measures should remain significant when ideology and symbolic factors are included in our models.

Self-Interest and Information

In tables 17, 18, and 19 we test for a correlation between presumed measures
of private interest and opinions on these three sets of ballot propositions. These

---

7. Age is considered an indicator of interest in the model of support for the sales tax in Colorado.

tests, however, are based on the assumption that individuals are capable of learning how a policy proposal advances their private interests. Because voters face the fairly difficult task of translating information about policy alternatives into an assessment of how a proposition might affect their interests, this assumption is worth examining. One question central to the issue of self-interested behavior in referenda voting is whether the voter can learn that a proposition is close to the voter's preferred policy position.

In our analysis of the relationship between indicators of self-interest and vote intentions, we examine how the acquisition of relevant information might affect this relationship. We do so by comparing results from two models of vote intentions on the California propositions. We first model intentions with responses to questions in which respondents were offered no information about the proposition. Results from these models are compared with results from models estimated with questions that included information about the nature of the policy proposal. If respondents use information to assess how a policy affects their interest and then form intentions consistent with their interest, we might see stronger self-interest effects in the estimations that use the information-prompted responses.

The information hypothesis is tested with a logistic regression analysis of the Field Institute's California Poll surveys of California voters conducted two weeks before the November 1993 election. Tests for private self-interest motivations are also done with these and additional data from a 1992 Colorado election poll.

In the California sample, voters claiming to have heard of a proposition were asked, "From what you have seen read or heard about proposition _____, are you inclined to vote yes or no?" No information about the subject or content of the proposition was offered to a respondent at this point. Responses to these unaided questions are analyzed here to represent a baseline situation in which voters are asked to make a decision with little information about the issue immediately at hand. Later, a description of the issue several sentences in length is read to respondents. This description (included in Appendix A) prompts the respondent with facts about the ballot issue. The information included as a prompt in the second question is similar to that appearing in the official ballot statement. Respondents are then asked how they would vote.[8] In all estimations, dependent variables are dichotomously coded, with 1 for support of and 0 for opposition to the measure.

Table 17 displays results of models estimating the determinants of vote intentions on school voucher propositions. Only the California survey data allow

---

8. Only those respondents reporting that they had heard of the proposition were asked the unaided question. Responses to aided questions also included individuals who claimed not to have heard of the proposition.

TABLE 17.   Self-Interest and Individual-Level Support for School Voucher Propositions

Measure Variables	California Prop. 174 (no info)	California Prop. 174 (with info)	Colorado Amendment 7
Children in private school	.85*	1.03**	—
	(.46)	(.41)	
Children in public school	.12	.43*	—
	(.26)	(.21)	
Income	−.004	−.01	.02
	(.09)	(.07)	(.08)
Education	.33	−.05	−.65*
	(.26)	(.25)	(.28)
Age	−.01	−.002	−.02
	(.01)	(.006)	(.08)
Home owner	−.001	−.15	—
	(.26)	(.22)	
Liberal	−.79**	−.58*	−.29
	(.33)	(.27)	(.31)
Concerned about taxes	.02	.02	2.25*
	(.26)	(.23)	(1.11)
Constant	−.33	−.97	−.45
	(.75)	(.61)	(.43)
N	430	572	283
Model improvement chi-square	15.02*	15.5*	12.9*
Percentage correctly predicted	71.6	70.1	67.8

Note: Logistic regression estimates. Standard errors in parentheses. Dependent variable = 1 if voter supports, 0 if otherwise.

*Significant at $p < .05$ (two-tail)   **Significant at $p < .01$ (two-tail)

the possibility for using variations in the wording of questions as a test for in-formation effects. Two parameters are of primary interest here: those attached to the indicators for parents with children in public and in private schools. When the model is estimated with data from the unaided question, the coefficient for private-school parents is significant and is in the predicted direction. When re-spondents are prompted with specific information about the voucher proposal (the "aided" estimation), however, the magnitude of the private-school parent coefficient increases significantly and the coefficient for public-school parents attains significance in a direction reflecting support.[9] Liberalism is also asso-ciated with opposition in California, and concern about excessive taxation is as-sociated with support for vouchers in Colorado.

---

9. A t-test comparing coefficients between equations produces a value of 3.41.

$$t = \frac{b_{eq1} - b_{eq2}}{(s.e._{b1}^2) + (s.e._{b2}^2)}$$

We take the findings related to school enrollment as evidence that some voters, when given a minimal amount of information, can assess how a policy affects them personally and then make a decision about the policy in a manner that furthers their personal interests. Differences in results from alternative question wordings suggest that information assists voters in learning how a proposition affects their narrow interest. Parents in California who stand a chance of receiving vouchers (particularly those who would see their existing tuition payments reduced) support the proposition. This support is particularly evident after they are given a summary of the initiative. In Colorado, however, the coefficient for age (our surrogate for interest in Colorado) does not appear to support the self-interest hypothesis. We acknowledge that age is probably a poor proxy for self-interest on voucher measures.[10]

Further evidence of information effects can be found in table 18. The first two columns display the estimations of support for Proposition 170, which would change rules for property tax increases in California. Looking at the un-aided question, support for the simple majority vote rule is not distinguished by indicators of private interests: home ownership (which reflects those bearing the policy costs) and having children enrolled in the public schools (which reflects those enjoying the policy benefits). However, when the question involves prompting with a limited amount of specific information about the proposition (the second column), parents with children in public schools are significantly more supportive and home owners appear less supportive.[11] We take this find-ing to be evidence that is consistent with the argument that some voters can and do recognize and maximize their self-interest when deciding on tax and spend-ing propositions, provided they possess some information about the policy. It is important to note, moreover, that Proposition 170 is a rather difficult test for this process. The proposition did not ask voters whether more money should go to public schools, but instead asked about changing the institutional mechanism for approving taxes.

There is also some logical consistency across estimations from each issue that supports the self-interest thesis. Enrollment measures are significantly as-sociated with support for the voucher program (table 17). The public-school en-rollment coefficient is also significant when we examine support for easing rules about public-school tax hikes, but it is not associated with support for non-school taxes (table 19). The private-schools indicator, moreover, is not associ-

---

10. Nonlinear specifications for age also fail to attain significance.

11. Using the formula shown in note 9, the t values from the public-schools coefficient is 1.62. For home ownership, $t = 0.29$. Responses to the prompted question in table 18 also produce stronger effects for liberalism. Thus, information might trigger ideological voting as well as self-interest effects. In table 18, however, it is difficult to determine if changes in coefficients for vari-ables other than the public-school measure are produced by information effects or by changes in sample size.

ated with support for easing rules for financing public schools (table 18). Furthermore, home ownership structures opposition to the property tax measure (table 18) but not to school vouchers (table 17).

These indicators of narrow self-interest are significant in equations where we control for ideological and "symbolic" factors (concern about taxes). It should be noted that these factors are also important determinants of vote intentions for each issue. Indeed, ideology is the most consistent factor affecting opinions here. Self-identified liberalism, which we assume to reflect a coherent, preexisting set of beliefs about politics and policies, is a significant predictor of attitudes in nearly every estimation. As for contradictory results, table 18 presents our only finding consistent with the public-regarding literature: wealthy Colorado voters opposed placing additional burdens on passing new taxes, despite the assumption that they bear much of the burden of such taxes. In a sense, this makes them more protax than other voters.

TABLE 18.   Self-Interest and Individual-Level Support for Tax Rule Change Propositions

Ballot Measure Variable	California Prop. 170 (no info)[a]	California Prop. 170 (with info)	Colorado Amendment 1[b]
Children in private school	.37	−.18	—
	(.82)	(.50)	
Children in public school	.01	.38[+]	—
	(.56)	(.22)	
Income	.15	.10	−.15*
	(.16)	(.08)	(.07)
Education	.99*	.44	−.58*
	(.45)	(.23)	(.25)
Age	−.01	.01	−.05
	(.01)	(.01)	(.08)
Home owner	−.47	−.63**	—
	(.50)	(.22)	
Liberal	.80[+]	1.11**	−.31
	(.55)	(.25)	(.29)
Concerned about taxes	−.74	−.72**	.31
	(.54)	(.25)	(.89)
Constant	−1.26	−1.85**	1.31**
	(1.37)	(.62)	(.42)
N	125	528	285
Model improvement chi-square	16.30*	46.79**	12.9*
Percentage correctly predicted	72.8	65.3	60.0

Note: Logistic regression estimates. Standard errors in parentheses. Dependent variable = 1 if support, 0 if otherwise.

[a]Coded such that 1 = support the measure aimed at making tax increases easier in future; 0 = oppose.
[b]Coded such that 1 = support the measure aimed at making tax increases more difficult in future; 0 = oppose.
*Significant at $p < .05$ (two-tail)   **Significant at $p < .01$ (two-tail)   [+]Significant at $p < .10$ (one-tail)

Additional evidence of self-interested motivations affecting support for tax referenda is found when we compare results of models estimating support for sales tax propositions across states (table 19). As noted earlier, funds from the California sales tax measure were earmarked for general public safety programs, while the Colorado sales tax would fund K-12 public schools. Assuming private vote motivations, we anticipated that younger voters (who are more likely to have children in school) supported the tax hike in Colorado. Because the Colorado survey did not include questions about parental status and home ownership, we reestimated our model of support for the California sales tax proposition, omitting those questions. Thus, identical models of support for the sales tax are estimated for Colorado and California, as seen on the right side of table 19. Younger voters are clearly more supportive of the sales tax in Colorado (where benefits are directed to schools), but not in California. In other words, generational effects are evident where the distributive consequences of

TABLE 19. Self-Interest and Individual-Level Support for Sales Tax Propositions

Measure Variable	California Prop. 172 (no info)	California Prop. 172 (with info)	California Prop. 172 (with info)	Colorado Amendment 6
Children in private school	−.03	.10	—	—
	(.97)	(.62)		
Children in public school	.24	.05	—	—
	(.45)	(.30)		
Income	−.02	.01	−.08	−.08
	(.14)	(.10)	(.09)	(.08)
Education	−.54	−.25	−.26	.16
	(.42)	(.32)	(.32)	(.28)
Age	−.10	.002	-.003	−.29**
	(.012)	(.008)	(.007)	(.08)
Home owner	−.28	−.65*	—	—
	(.46)	(.30)		
Liberal	1.30*	.53‡	.57‡	1.44**
	(.53)	(.36)	(.35)	(.36)
Concerned about taxes	1.40**	−.32	−.33	−1.35
	(.48)	(.30)	(.30)	(.97)
Constant	.23	−.52	.90*	1.23**
	(1.20)	(.82)	(.49)	(.44)
N	156	288	288	285
Model improvement chi-square	23.3	10.9	6.4	39.5**
Percentage correctly predicted	62.2	63.9	61.9	69.1

Note: Logistic regression estimates. Standard errors in parentheses. Dependent variable = 1 if support, 0 if otherwise.

*Significant at $p < .05$ (two-tail)   **Significant at $p < .01$ (two-tail)   ‡Not significant, but t ratio > 1.48

the tax have a constituency defined by age group. We should also note that, contrary to the public-regarding thesis, wealthy voters are not more supportive of either state's sales tax proposal.

These results demonstrate that voters can and do use instrumental evaluations while reasoning about a number of tax and spending referenda and that their ability to do so is affected by information about the personalized consequences of these measures. It is important to stress that the "prompted" questions cue respondents with the same kinds of information found on ballot statements and in ballot pamphlets. Voters who otherwise know little about a proposition might thus glean enough details from the official ballot summary to make a decision that is consistent with their own self-interest. But *which* voters make their decisions on the basis of self-interest? This is, in itself, an important question that we must address.

Self-Interest and Proposition 13

As noted in earlier chapters, different voters—with different abilities to access, process, and retain political information—might be expected to reason differently about ballot propositions. Unfortunately, the California Poll samples used so far in this chapter are not large enough to subdivide into different education subgroups (as was done in chapters 3 and 4). By focusing again on Proposition 13, we can look more closely at how voters with differing levels of cognitive abilities employ different reasoning processes.

We estimate support for Proposition 13 by using logistic regression models similar to those used in chapter 4. Here, we also include relevant measures of self-interest, including home ownership and local property tax levels.[12] Doing so provides individual-level replication of some of the aggregate tests reported in table 16. Sears and Citrin (1982) note that African-American voters, who are more liberal and more readily exposed to governmental services, could have self-interested reasons for opposing a revenue cut for government. Following this possibility, we also include controls for race and ideology.

It is worth noting that when we pool all respondents together (not reported here), our results appear similar to those found by Sears and Citrin (1982). Home ownership, race, age, partisanship, and ideology are associated with support for Proposition 13. Republicans, home owners, and older voters are more supportive. Self-identified liberals and African-Americans are more opposed. Our basic linear measure of tax rate was not significant

---

12. Property tax rates were attached to the California Poll data by matching respondents' zip codes to their recorded county of residence. In many cases, zip codes were missing. For this reason, we report two sets of models. We also included the nonlinear term for taxes in this model, but it produced no substantive improvement over the linear measure for tax included here.

($p = .22$), nor was a nonlinear representation as used in table 16 (not reported here).[13]

Table 20 reports the results of our models, with the sample once again divided between less-educated (high school graduate or less) and well-educated (at least some college) voters. We assume that these groups are distinguished by their cognitive abilities. When dividing the sample this way, we see that although each set of voters decides whether they are for or against Proposition 13 in ways that "make sense," there are differences between these groups. Once again, we see that well-educated voters' opinions on a proposition are associated with their ideological orientation, but that such is not the case with opinions of the less educated. Conversely, home ownership, perhaps the narrowest and most personal of the self-interest measures employed in analyses of Proposition 13, appears to structure the attitudes of the less educated but not the well educated. Responsiveness to actual tax rates fails to attain significance, but the coefficient is larger (and marginally significant at $p = .11$, two-tail) among the well educated.

We take the results from table 20 and the results from chapter 4 (table 10) as evidence that less-educated voters can and do reason about ballot propositions when casting their votes, but that they do so in what might be seen as a cognitively narrow manner. In assessing the self-interest effects associated with Proposition 13, Sears and Citrin (1982, 212) noted that "the cognitive narrowness of self-interest is . . . illustrated by its failure to produce more schematic thinking, ideologizing or broader belief systems."

We suggest that such narrow self-interested reasoning might be more readily employed by those lacking the cognitive resources for ideological thinking. Indeed, it may be employed in place of the systematic ideological thinking that is demonstrated among those with more education. That does not mean that narrow, self-interested behavior is limited exclusively to the less educated. Rather, we suggest that voters who lack cognitive resources can, at times, employ self-interest to reason about ballot choices when ideology provides no guidance. As illustrated in chapter 4, these same voters, when evaluating other propositions on different topics, can also respond to generalized concerns about state conditions. The point, however, is that those less-educated voters who might be expected to have the most difficulty managing the demands of direct democracy do appear to behave in ways that reflect issue voting. This behavior is something that critics of the process have long assumed was missing, if not impossible.

---

13. In another estimation, we did find that an interaction term representing middle-income property owners residing in higher-tax areas was significantly associated with support. This finding is similar to that reported in table 16, which indicated that support for Proposition 13 associated with responsiveness to property tax burdens was concentrated at the midrange of burden.

Summary

Our findings are consistent with the idea that direct-democracy participants act in a manner reflecting self-interested behavior. That is but one of many ways that voters can sensibly decide what they are for or against in direct democracy. Some appear motivated to support (or oppose) policies based on how the policies affect them directly. Others might make decisions on the basis of their preexisting ideology. It must be stressed that in this chapter, interest was assigned to the voter in the form of assumptions about the private benefits the voter received. Thus, we cannot claim to have definitively proved that voters act instrumentally to further their self-interest in direct democracy. Nevertheless, our evidence appears consistent with assumptions about private concerns affecting decisions on tax and spending referenda. These results are noteworthy because much of the extant literature plays down the role of self-interested motivations.

There are reasons for differences between our findings and those from previous studies of referenda voting. If it is true that private motivations are often related to how policies affect individuals personally, then instruments used here

TABLE 20. Self-Interest and Individual-Level Support for California's Proposition 13 (1978)

	Low Education		High Education	
	Model 1	Model 2	Model 1	Model 2
Home owner	1.06**	.81*	.043	−.38
	(.32)	(.40)	(.30)	(.40)
Income	.074	.018	.008	.038
	(.23)	(.07)	(.069)	(.08)
Age	.014	.009	.026**	.020*
	(.009)	(.011)	(.009)	(.010)
African-American	−1.37*	−1.80*	−1.38	−6.86
	(.62)	(.83)	(1.09)	(17.6)
Liberal	−.037	−.173	−.99**	−.89**
	(.318)	(.40)	(.28)	(.34)
Republican	.62*	.61*	.26	.37
	(.30)	(.37)	(.27)	(.34)
Tax level	—	.03	—	.167
		(.11)		(.106)
Constant	−1.59*	−1.18	−1.13*	−2.66**
	(.67)	(1.15)	(.64)	(1.31)
N	275	172	297	182
Percent correctly predicted	69.1	66.8	63.9	64.8

Source: California Poll 7804.

Note: Logistic regression estimates. Standard errors in parentheses.

*Significant at $p < .05$ (two-tail)   **Significant at $p < .01$ (two-tail)

for measuring self-interest (such as having children in a private school) will not typically be available in standard opinion surveys. This drawback is particularly problematic for research in direct democracy, because most data and measures used in this field are drawn from surveys designed to study candidate elections.

Some of the previous studies of referenda voting that dismiss self-interest motivations have also relied heavily on aggregate data (e.g., Hahn and Kamieniecki 1987; Hall and Piele 1976; J. Mueller 1969; Wilson and Banfield 1963). Using aggregate data presents a double risk. First, the ecological fallacy is a potent problem. Second, the use of aggregate data forces the researcher to impute interests to broad categories of voters generically. Forming categories that are broad might mask the potential effect of narrowly focused self-interested behavior that occurs at the individual level.

We do not mean to suggest that many voters act to advance their self-interest on every initiative. Policy content of the ballot issue is likely to be highly relevant in determining how many voters act that way. Voters are sometimes faced with choices about issues where there are no clear fiscal winners or losers, or where costs and benefits are not readily visible to any category of voters. Furthermore, some voters might find that issues such as school vouchers, abortion rights, or gay rights do not affect them in a direct, material sense. In such a situation, voters might be more likely to be motivated by ideology (if they have the cognitive capacity) or by symbolic themes, or they might draw on what Magleby (1984, 129) refers to as "standing opinions" about these issues.

Furthermore, we do not claim that self-interested motivations supersede symbolic or ideological determinants of the vote. Ideology was consistently important in the estimations provided in this chapter. If these measures of ideology do in fact tap the cognitive aspects of ideology, that might be seen as further evidence of voters having a basis for reasoning about proposition choices. Thus, instrumental evaluations and ideological evaluations are both relevant here.

When we consider these findings in the light of our understanding of voting on the basis of limited information, we begin to see that people can find ways to reason about direct democracy. With propositions such as these tax and spending measures, behavior might begin to resemble traditional definitions of utility-maximizing reasoning. At the very least, this behavior is much more than random voting or Russian roulette. This analysis should demonstrate that we need not assume that direct-democracy voting is primarily a nonrational, idiosyncratic process that produces decisions inconsistent with the voter's desires. The weight of our evidence also supports the idea that private interest, rather than public regard, affects decisions on these referenda.

Thus far, we have established that many voters find and respond to information when evaluating propositions and that many find cues, references, and shortcuts that they might employ to evaluate propositions. In this chapter, we also demonstrated that certain propositions might allow for instrumental evaluations. In chapters 6 and 7, we test for variants of instrumental motivations on measures where costs and benefits are perhaps less clearly identifiable (i.e., term limits, fishing regulations, and park bonds).

To this point, we have paid little attention to questions of how voters might respond to campaigns or to strategies that initiative proponents and opponents might use. We also consider these factors in the next two chapters. Further evidence of voter responsiveness would help establish that voters are competent, at least by the standards set forth in chapter 2.

In chapter 6, we examine the use of instrumental evaluations in another context: voter response to the initiative logroll. Logrolls are used by initiative proponents to generate support, under the assumption that people are more likely to support a measure if they stand to gain some immediate benefits from it. This strategy assumes that voters are sensitive to the content of propositions and that they can make instrumental decisions that are consistent with the pursuit of such benefits. Findings in this chapter suggest that it is possible with tax and spending measures. As we shall see, there is evidence that some voters respond to a distributive logroll.

Voter Response to the Initiative Logroll and the Counterproposition

Having established that there are many readily accessible cues and information sources that voters use when reasoning about direct democracy, in the next three chapters we provide a more detailed examination of how voters respond to various elements of political campaigns associated with ballot initiatives.

We begin in chapter 6 with a look at pre-electioneering elements of the campaign by modeling how voters respond to a proponent's attempts to build support by tailoring the content of an initiative, and how voters respond to initiatives that proponents and opponents have drafted in attempts to counter each other's efforts. In chapter 7, we examine whether voters respond to their party's campaign contacts and partisan interests during a campaign. In chapters 6 and 7 we find further evidence that voters make sense of ballot initiatives—they make decisions on the basis of how initiatives might affect them, their local community's interests, and their political parties' interests.

Finally, in chapter 8 we examine how campaign spending affects opinions on initiatives. Contrary to the critique that "big money" is corrupting direct democracy, we find scant evidence that spending directly affects individual-level opinions. Rather, we suggest that campaign spending increases awareness of issues, and it might create a context in which voters who typically do not reason on the basis of ideology are allowed to do so.

Voter confusion in direct democracy can come from several sources that are independent of the inherent complexity of a given ballot issue. Confusion and vote "manipulation" are often assumed to be products of the way in which proponents and/or ballots frame an issue. Outcomes in proposition elections are thus seen as occasionally being a function of strategies used to frame choices (Magleby 1984; Cronin 1989). In this chapter we test how voters respond to two strategies used by initiative proponents in framing ballot questions: the use of logrolling and the use of counterpropositions.

Both logrolling and counterpropositions represent strategies that combatants can choose when contesting ballot measures. Logrolling—packing a bill with additional items to generate greater support—might be expected to contribute to the building of a winning coalition. Conversely, the use of countermeasures might improve the odds of defeating a measure by increasing voter confusion about a rival's proposal and deflecting campaign resources from the rival's campaign effort. We begin with a discussion of two of these strategies adopted by initiative proponents, and then we use aggregate and individual-level data to test voter responsiveness to these strategies. Next we examine how voters respond to information that is unique to specific geographic areas when they evaluate rival proposals. As we saw in chapter 5, voters can use instrumental evaluations when assessing some tax and spending referenda. Here, we test whether aggregated historical data provide evidence consistent with the idea that voters evaluate propositions in terms of a proposal's potential economic effects even when rival measures appear on the same ballot. Results are consistent with what we might see if voters evaluated the impact of a proposition on themselves or on the local economy on the basis of instrumental evaluations. Such results are noteworthy because they come from the context of competing propositions that are expected to breed voter confusion. While the phenomenon is not limited to contemporary initiative campaigns, some recent elections have been distinguished by the simultaneous appearance of rival propositions on the same topic (Lupia 1994a; Banducci 1992; see also Lowenstein 1983).

In California, an additional innovation is the issuing of public debt with the citizens' initiative. As we will see, the use of the initiative logroll is not new (Lowenstein 1983); however, its use for issuing bond debt for public projects is. The use of such distributive logrolling presents an interesting arena for testing whether voters are responsive to localized public goods enumerated in an initiative. We test whether voter opinions about one such initiative appear responsive to the objective levels of benefits targeted to the area in which the voter resides. One of the more rigorous criteria we can use to assess voters' reasoning about ballot propositions is whether opinions are associated with information about the narrow policy details contained in ballot propositions. In this case, we can see that some people apparently decide whether they are in favor of a proposition on the basis of knowing something about the proposition's content. We see, once again, that well-educated voters might evaluate these measures differently than do less-educated voters. A fairly narrow segment of these well-educated voters appears to be responsive to the distributive logroll.

Multiple Subjects and Pork Barrel Politics

Multiple-Subject Logrolls

Proponents seeking to pass an initiative policy might qualify a measure with multiple subjects (or multiple beneficiaries) in order to generate large electoral coalitions. This form of logrolling can occur when an initiative becomes an omnibus package of additional policy proposals, each added with the intention of bringing more voters on board the supporting coalition. Such strategies are not new. In 1926, for example, there was a push for pari-mutuel betting in California. Proponents of a pro-betting initiative sought to broaden the coalition of supporters by stipulating that revenues were to be split between the State Board of Agriculture and the Veterans Welfare Board (Crouch 1943, 12). A contemporary example of a group of broadly drafted initiatives is California's 1990 "Big Green" environmental package (discussed subsequently).

Key and Crouch (1939) and Crouch (1943, in a subsequent pamphlet written for John Randolph Haynes's progressive organization) suggested that it is difficult for proponents to use the logroll as a strategy for increasing support in direct democracy. They identify the difficulty of keeping together any kind of agreement at the level of the voters. Unlike logrolling in the legislative context, direct-democracy logrolling requires that votes be cast by individuals who are not part of the bargaining process. Elites may agree to a bargain when drafting ballot measures, but voters may balk or may simply remain unaware of how they benefit from a logroll built into an initiative. Legislators are likely to be highly aware of the benefits of supporting a legislative logroll; however, direct-democracy voters are often assumed to be only minimally informed about the narrow, factual content of ballot proposals (Magleby 1984, 142). In addition, as discussed in earlier chapters, the conclusion drawn from much of the previous literature was that voters are unlikely (or unable) to vote on propositions on the basis of their narrow self-interest. If voters typically lack accurate information about the details of the enumerated benefits in a logroll initiative, we might expect that direct-democracy logrolls are doomed to failure.

We might also expect this strategy to fail in some situations in which voters are highly informed about the specific policy-issue content of the logroll. Some observers note that electoral support for Canada's 1992 national referendum on constitutional changes diminished because its proponents included too many items in it (Johnston 1993; Butler and Ranney 1994). Numerous policies were included to gain support inside of Quebec, but in doing so, proponents created what Richard Johnston called an "inverted logroll" that increased opposition in other provinces.[1] Anglophone voters might have supported one or two of the concessions granted to Quebec, but additional concessions increased the odds that a given voter would be opposed to some individual element of the plan and thus vote against the entire package (Johnston 1993; see also Clarke and Kornberg 1994).

If highly competitive elections generate substantial information (as discussed in chapter 3), an expanded referendum proposal can increase the opportunity for voters to be exposed to some salient bit of opposition information, particularly if the referenda includes multiple issues upon which the opposition

---

1. By an inverted logroll, Johnston suggests that too many items were added to the referendum, such that support eventually dissipated.

can focus. That appears to be what happened in the case of the Canadian constitutional referendum of 1992. The logroll allowed the opposition group to seize on various individual items that were unpopular, which mobilized a large opposition coalition and killed the entire package.

In spite of the lack of regard these observers have for the utility of multiple-issue logrolling as a strategy for increasing support on a ballot measure, seventeen states have a single-subject rule (or something similar) to prevent issue logrolling. California's constitution was changed to include a single-subject rule in 1948 after a group of citizens unsuccessfully attempted to place a single measure on the ballot containing an astonishing potpourri of different items involving pensions, taxes, rights to vote for Native Americans, gambling, oleomargarine, health, reapportionment of the state senate, fish and game, repeal of cross-filing for primary elections, and surface mining (California Assembly 1992, 312; see also Lowenstein 1983; *McFadden v. Jordan,* 32 Cal 2d 330 [1948]). Since then the logroll has not been quite the same.

Even with the single-subject rule, proponents continue to build coalitions by increasing the scope of proposals, and the courts (particularly in California) have been reluctant to strike such propositions from the ballot. A contemporary example of the multiple-issue logroll might be California's Proposition 128 of 1990. Also known as "Big Green," the initiative combined strict environmental regulations that covered pesticides, logging, oil drilling, ozone depletion, air pollution, and sewage treatment with the establishment of a new "environmental czar" and the realignment of bureaucratic agencies implementing the policies. The measure was sponsored by a coalition of groups, several of which had individual policy proposals defeated in the state legislature. In the same election, another single omnibus initiative (Proposition 130) proposed the authorization of $742 million in bonds to purchase old-growth forests, banned clear-cutting, changed other forest practices, and restructured the agencies and individuals responsible for forest management in the state.

A New Twist to Initiative Logrolling: Distributive Logrolls

A fairly recent (and rarely used) innovation in the direct-democracy logroll is the initiative proponent's strategy of building statewide coalitions around distributive policies. Distributive, also called *locational,* legislation "is typically an omnibus of divisible benefits" in the form of expenditures where funds for many projects are placed in one piece of legislation (Weingast 1994). Logrolling through a distributive initiative appears similar to attempts at logrolling found in stereotypical river and harbors pork barrel legislation. This strategy presents initiative proponents with an opportunity to build a coalition around distributive politics rather than through multiple-issue logrolls.

This form of locational logrolling is sometimes practiced by local governments seeking to issue bonds through referenda. Archer and Reynolds (1976) note that proponents must overcome a major problem when the electorate is asked to approve bond spending. Costs (taxes on many individuals) are typically more visible than benefits (parks or projects at various locations), even if costs are diffused widely across the electorate. To secure electoral support, proponents must not only distribute benefits widely (universalism), but must also attempt to make voters aware of benefits. Statewide initiatives reflecting this strategy have been used in California twice since 1988.

The first effort took place in 1988 when a coalition of California environmental groups proposed, qualified, and passed Proposition 70. This measure was the first bond issue in the state's history that was generated from the direct citizen initiative process. It authorized $776 million in bonds, primarily for the acquisition of parkland and the protection of wildlife. Of this total, about $415 million was directed to specific projects, with locations of these projects listed in the text of the initiative. Proponents sought pledges of support (in the form of signatures, contributions, and vote mobilization) from local groups in exchange for locating benefits in the group's area (Williams 1994, 47). Unlike previous bond measures that placed revenues in a state fund to be distributed by the legislature, Proposition 70 proponents directed that the money go to specific local agencies and dedicated revenues to specific local projects[2] (Price and Baccioco 1990, 493).

Proponents of Proposition 180 in June 1994 employed a similar logrolling strategy while also including multiple issues in their proposal. The proponents entitled their measure "California Safe Neighborhood Parks, Gang Prevention, Tree Planting, Wildlife, Coastal, Senior Center, Park Wetlands, Rivers, Forest and Agricultural Land Conservation Act of 1994."[3] The act proposed to issue almost $2 billion in bonds. The initiative failed. Had it passed, it might well have been declared invalid under the single-subject provisions. The text of the initiative covered eighteen pages in the ballot pamphlet.

We might also note one or two more subtle attempts at building a demographic—as well as a geographic—constituency for Proposition 180. The proponents' title, for example, included "senior center," and proposed projects included items such as $10,000,000 to build a museum of Latino history, $1,000,000 to build a museum for the Marshall Gold Discoveries Historic Park (a project that was to include "resources relating to mining by the Chinese

---

2. This strategy led a California state senator (Quentin Kopp, Ind., S.F.) to draft a bill (SB 424, 1991) requiring written disclosure of projects that proponents included in the initiative in exchange for campaign contributions. The bill passed but was overturned by California courts. The state of California appealed the decision (Williams 1994, 47).

3. This was the proponents' title. The official title listed on the ballot by the California secretary of state was "Park Lands, Historical Sites and Forest Conservation Bond Act."

community"), $500,000 for a museum on African-American history, plus money to build a museum for African-American explorer James Beckworth.

Table 21 illustrates the attempt at locational logrolling with distributive (parks) expenditure proposed under the first distributive logroll initiative, Proposition 70. The table demonstrates that most of the spending was targeted to areas where voters live (in addition to places where they might hike and

TABLE 21.   Spending Proposed under Proposition 70

Counties with Projects			Counties without Projects	
County	Population[a]	Spending[a]	County	Population
Alameda	1.270	29.000	Amador	0.030
Alpine	0.001	2.500	Butte	0.182
Calaveras	0.031	1.500	Colusa	0.016
Contra Costa	0.790	24.500	Glenn	0.024
Del Norte	0.023	1.900	Imperial	0.109
El Dorado	0.125	2.500	Inyo	0.018
Fresno	0.667	2.500	Kern	0.543
Humboldt	0.119	0.900	Kings	0.101
Lake	0.050	0.400	Lassen	0.027
Los Angeles	8.800	38.000	Mariposa	0.014
Madera	0.088	2.500	Modoc	0.009
Marin	0.230	25.200	Mono	0.009
Mendocino	0.080	5.900	Napa	0.110
Merced	0.178	0.660	Nevada	0.078
Monterey	0.355	33.000	Placer	0.172
Orange	2.400	23.600	Plumas	0.019
Riverside	1.170	32.400	San Benito	0.036
Sacramento	1.040	6.000	Shasta	0.147
San Bernardino	1.418	27.000	Sierra	0.003
San Diego	2.498	39.100	Siskiyou	0.043
San Francisco	0.733	5.400	Sutter	0.064
San Joaquin	0.480	1.000	Tehama	0.049
San Luis Obispo	0.217	5.800	Trinity	0.013
San Mateo	0.649	22.900	Tulare	0.311
Santa Barbara	0.369	18.600	Tuolumne	0.048
Santa Clara	1.490	4.500		
Santa Cruz	0.229	23.800		
Solano	0.340	2.600		
Sonoma	0.388	4.000		
Stanislaus	0.370	2.160		
Ventura	0.669	22.100		
Yolo	0.141	2.000		
Yuba	0.058	2.000		

Source: Population from *County and City Data Book,* Bureau of the Census; Spending listed in California Ballot Pamphlet, 1988 Primary Election.

[a]1990 population in millions; spending in millions of dollars.

camp). The correlation between proposed spending at the county level and county population is .80. This figure should be taken as a partial description only. Coding the county-level location of spending was slightly problematic, because scores of individual local projects were proposed relating to specific towns, cities, and counties, as well as areas that cross city and county lines. Furthermore, a proportion of the bond revenue was allocated statewide and could not be disaggregated into counties. Nevertheless, location-specific spending can be identified for thirty-three of fifty-eight counties (totaling just over $410 million).

To assess how such attempts to target spending at specific locations affect support for these distributive initiatives, we examine whether support for the first distributive logroll initiative (Proposition 70) was associated with the location of proposed benefits. If voters are uninformed about the policy content of initiatives (including the location of expenditure benefits), then we would expect that support for these measures would vary independently of the locations of spending on specific local projects. If some voters do respond to the locational logrolling strategy, we would expect (other things being equal) greater support from individuals living in counties where greater amounts of spending are proposed.

We should stress that these hypotheses are not based on the expectation that all voters wade through pages of fine print in the ballot pamphlet and discover whether the initiative provides a nice park project for their county (although data from chapter 3 indicate that a few might). Rather, we assume that information about the location-specific benefits of the initiative are spread through local media sources, by local environmental groups backing the initiative, and through voters' discussions of local issues. Many of the significant proposals in Proposition 70 involved acquiring land and sites that had long been on the wish list of local governments and citizens' groups. People involved in these issues at the local level are assumed to be primarily responsible for transmitting information about the local benefits involved with the proposition (to media, friends, group mailing lists, etc.). As it stands, however, our data only allow us to test *if* support is a function of levels of spending proposed in the voter's area. We cannot test *how* voters become aware of spending proposals, nor can we test if any voters actually are aware of specific details of the policies proposed in the initiative.

As noted in earlier chapters, different voters are likely to respond to the information demands associated with ballot choices in different ways. Instrumental reasoning on the basis of knowledge of the narrow, distributive impact of a relatively obscure ballot issue such as Proposition 70 might require high levels of factual information and political awareness. Given the low salience of this issue, it is difficult to assume that a large number of voters could have been cognizant of the localized benefits of Proposition 70. Furthermore, data we presented in chapter 3 illustrate that only a small minority of voters actually use the ballot pamphlet to seek out policy-specific details about propositions. That being the case, responsiveness to localized benefits might be limited to more educated voters, or to educated voters having greater knowledge of ballot propositions.

We use a 1988 Field Institute California Poll survey of registered voters to identify the positions of registered voters on Proposition 70. Respondents were informed that approval of the initiative would result in park and wildlife bonds being issued but were not informed of local benefits. Survey results indicated that 73 percent of respondents approved the measure, 20 percent were opposed, and 7 percent were undecided (the measure passed, 65 to 35 percent). We are interested in whether a respondent's likelihood of supporting the proposition occurred uniformly across the state or whether support was conditioned by the level of spending proposed near the respondent's home. To assess the various ways in which different voters might reason about this proposition, we split our sample once again into two groups: the well educated and the less educated.

Because the survey identified the respondent's county of residence, we are able to attach per capita county-level spending measures (as proposed under Proposition 70) to each respondent.[4] Our model of support includes standard demographic variables (age and income) and variables that represent the voter's stock of political information and his or her political orientation (party and ideology). We also include a variable that represents how much the respondent knows about ballot propositions in general. General knowledge of propositions is an index that sums the number of propositions (other than Proposition 70) of which the respondent claims to be aware.[5] This knowledge measure shows a weak but significant ($r = .11$) association with education.

These opinion models also include two interaction terms that allow us to test whether responsiveness to proposed local spending (per capita) is somehow conditioned by education and political awareness (represented here by general knowledge of ballot propositions). We might expect that voters with high levels of knowledge (or education) are more responsive to proposed spending because they are more likely to be cognizant of the actual content of ballot proposals. The first interaction term in table 22 multiplies knowledge by

---

4. Of the $776 million proposed by the initiative, $410 million could be directly attributed to projects having specific locational content. Other funds were directed to projects to be determined later, to administrative expenses, or to funds directed to specific wildlife species, or were to be awarded to localities in the future on a formula basis.

5. These questions were found in a section of the survey that was separate from the question about support for Proposition 70, and the index included no questions relating to knowledge of Proposition 70. That should reduce the chance that responses to questions about knowledge of other propositions were contaminated by questions about Proposition 70.

proposed local spending; the second multiplies education by proposed local spending to test for these effects.

Table 22 reports the results of logistic regression estimations of support for the initiative. The top of the table reports estimates of the model for well-educated voters. Results in the lower half of the table are for less-educated voters. Once again, we see substantial differences between well-educated and less-educated voters in terms of their reliance on party when assessing propositions. Education, which we assume to be a surrogate for cognitive abilities, appears to allow voters to more readily apply their partisan orientations to evaluations of this initiative. The larger coefficient for party among well-educated voters suggests that this is so. Among each group of voters, age displays an inverse association with support. Younger voters in each group tend to support the park bonds initiative. This finding makes sense when we consider that younger voters might be more likely to have been socialized as environmentalists.

When we examine each group of voters, the direct effect of spending proposed in the respondent's area is unrelated to support for Proposition 70. This

TABLE 22. Support for a Distributive Logroll: California's Proposition 70 (1988)

Variable	Low Education	High Education
Republican	−.659**	−1.02**
	(.242)	(.305)
Age	−.029**	−.033**
	(.007)	(.009)
Income	−.122	−.027
	(.128)	(.148)
Per capita county spending	−.010	−.074
	(.015)	(.047)
Knowledge of props.	.003	−.208
	(.206)	(.233)
Education × Spending	−.003	.012+
	(.003)	(.006)
Knowledge × Spending	−.006	−.012
	(.009)	(.011)
Liberal	.191	−.249
	(.497)	(.457)
Constant	3.15**	3.63**
	(.534)	(.680)
N	450	365
Percent correctly predicted	76.2	81.5

Source: California Poll 8803 (1988).

Note: Entries are logistic regression coefficients. Figures in parentheses are standard errors.

**Significant at $p < .01$ (two-tail)   +Significant at $p < .10$ (two-tail)

finding would suggest that the distributive logroll strategy might not have a large direct payoff at the ballot box. The interaction between knowledge and proposed spending also is not significant for either group, but it does appear that well-educated voters in areas with higher proposed spending tend to be more supportive. That is, the interaction between proposed spending and a respondent's education is significant (at $p < .07$, two-tail) in the subset of well-educated voters. Within the well-educated group, those with more education residing in areas with greater per capita spending appear to be responsive to local spending proposals, other things being equal.

Evidence at the aggregate level also suggests that proposed county-level spending was related to county vote. Orange County, for example, is typically known for fiscal conservatism in electoral politics. Proposition 70 directed more than $20 million into the county, one of the largest countywide totals. The measure was approved by 61 percent of the voters there. This rate compares with a 57 percent approval rate in politically moderate San Luis Obispo County, where only $5 million was directed, and 51 percent in favor in conservative Mariposa County, which often votes as Orange County does.[6] That suggests that localized spending in Orange County might have allowed the initiative to win a wider margin there than would otherwise have been the case. Table 23 displays an aggregate-level regression analysis in which county spending is used to predict county vote totals (controlling for county population). The aggregate data demonstrate a strong, positive relationship ($b = .45$, $t = 3.39$) between proposed county park spending and county vote in favor of Proposition 70.

Does this finding mean that initiative proponents can build a winning coalition with a distributive logroll strategy? The magnitude of the individual-level effect is difficult to interpret because the coefficient is for an interactive term. We do know that the individual-level effect is limited to a portion of the best-educated voters. Alone, there are not enough of these voters to win with, but they could provide for larger affirmative vote margins in areas that would otherwise be less sympathetic to spending initiatives (places such as Orange County).

Although there may be more money involved in these contemporary distributive logroll projects than in 1920s-era multiple-issue logrolls, the principle remains the same. Proponents attempt to use the strategy to increase the size of the coalition supporting the initiative. Evidence from California's 1988 parklands initiative indicates that well-educated, knowledgeable voters might respond favorably to proposals for specific localized benefits. Most voters, however, had

6. In candidate races, Orange County is typically one of the stronger Republican regions of the state. San Luis Obispo County votes Republican, but at slightly lower margins than does Orange County. Mariposa County's Republican vote falls between these two.

low awareness of this ballot issue. Fifty-eight percent of survey respondents included in the analysis in table 22 had no awareness of any propositions on the June 1988 ballot prior to being contacted by the survey interviewer. To the extent that the distributive logroll strategy "worked" in 1988 to pass Proposition 70, it might have fostered support among informed voters, who are more likely to complete their ballots and participate in initiative decisions.

Counterpropositions: Competing Proposals

Another strategy that an initiative proponent can use to influence election outcomes is the counterproposition. When one group qualifies an initiative that affects a rival group's interest, that party can attempt to counter the initial proposal with a measure that mutes or voids the first proposal (Banducci 1992). Magleby recognized the increasing importance that this strategy plays in modern initiative politics (1994a, 234). Countermeasures provide an advantage because they can contain "killer clauses" that override the implementation of the initial proposal. These countermeasures might also help defeat the initial proposal by placing voters in the difficult position of having to decide which (if any) proposition should be passed.

The strategy is predicated on the assumption that the additional initiative on the same topic will create so much confusion that voters will be more likely to vote *no* on each initiative. Contemporary use of competing measures might be seen as new (or at least different than in the past) because the rapid qualification of counterproposals is associated with the modern petition management industry and its guarantees of quick qualification for well-funded interests (Magleby 1994a, 235). Banducci (1992, table 1) presents evidence suggesting that, in aggregate, negative voting on initiatives is greater when an initiative appears on a ballot in competition with another measure on the same issue, which might support the assumption that counterproposals breed confusion and thus cause negative voting.

TABLE 23.   County Vote on Proposition 70, by County Spending

Variable	Coefficient	STD Error	t	p (two-tail)
Constant	54.86	1.48	34.955	0.000
Spending[a]	0.47	0.13	3.395	0.001
Population[a]	0.63	1.29	0.488	0.627
$N = 58$				
$R^2 = 0.284$				

Source: See Secretary of State Statement of Result, 1988.
Note: Dependent variable = percentage in favor.
[a]1990 population in millions; spending in millions of dollars.

Opinion data provide contrary evidence, however. In 1990 there were two forestry initiatives on the California ballot after an industry group responded to an environmental initiative by rapidly qualifying their own countermeasure. An examination of opinions about these propositions revealed that individual-level opinions on each measure represented one consistent, underlying attitude (Banducci 1992, 20). This finding implies that the counterproposal strategy of confusing voters might have failed in that instance. In another example, five rival insurance propositions appeared simultaneously on the November 1988 California ballot. Trial lawyers and two separate insurance industry groups qualified their own competing measures in response to an initiative drafted by a consumer group. One study suggests that voters, when given minimal information cues about the sponsor of each initiative, were able to sort out the differences among these measures and vote for their preferred option (Lupia 1994a).

Unlike the distributive logroll, the strategy by which established interests defend their policy preferences via the counterinitiative is not entirely new. According to a 1939 review of twenty-five years of direct democracy in California, "conflicting measures often appear on the same ballot" (Cottrell 1939, 40). Barnett discusses the same phenomenon in the early years of direct democracy in Oregon (1915, 115–17). We now present additional evidence of the ability of voters to sort through competing ballot initiatives as we examine an early example: the Oregon fish initiatives of 1908.

The Fish Initiatives

In chapter 1 we saw that early advocates and critics each pointed to Oregon's fish bills of 1908 as examples to support their positions on the merits (or shortcomings) of direct democracy. Questions concerning salmon and steelhead fishing have appeared on the Oregon ballot fourteen times since the adoption of the initiative in 1902 (Mason 1994). For several years following the turn of the century, two rival groups lobbied the Oregon state legislature in attempts to regulate salmon fishing in the state. Those efforts met with little success. After failing to resolve the issue, the groups resorted to the initiative process in a "spectacular legislative duel" (Cushman 1916, 536).

Two competing proposals to regulate the salmon fisheries of the Columbia River were introduced. Downriver fishermen petitioned to qualify an initiative that would abolish the gear used by upriver fishermen. Their initiative qualified and was adopted by a vote of 56,130 in favor to 30,280 against. Upriver fishermen responded by proposing and qualifying a competing initiative on the same ballot that would limit the length of seines, abolish fishing in the navigable channels of the lower river, and stop fishing at night in all other portions of the river. The competing initiative was also adopted as law by a vote of

46,582 in favor to 40,720 against[7] (Thatcher 1908, 601–5). As a result, the river was supposed to be closed to all fishing.

This election in 1908 provides an opportunity to examine how (or if) voters might be susceptible to confusion when competing initiative proposals appear on the same ballot. Contrary to the aggregate data from California presented by Banducci (1992) that show voters often vote *no* when faced with competing initiatives, many of these voters voted in favor of both initiatives. Counterproposals are assumed to increase negative voting because a negative vote (preserving the status quo) might be a rational response to the high information demands associated with forming decisions on multiple, competing proposals. In other words, the counterinitiative strategy is "based on the assumption that confused voters vote no or not at all" (Banducci 1992, 2; see also Magleby 1984, 1994a; Zisk 1987).

The early supporters of the initiative looked at this duel and pointed out that a nonresponsive legislature had failed to pass relevant legislation for many years and that this neglect threatened the sustainability of the salmon industry. As a result, the voters acted rationally, initiated both measures, and refused to let either the upriver or the downriver fishermen fish. Eventually, this standoff forced the legislature to enact measures that were designed to protect this important industry. Thus, the vote shows what the people will do when the legislature fails to act (this discussion from Eaton 1912). Noted Progressive Charles Beard thought the vote in favor of both rival Oregon fish measures was essentially a conservation measure and was thus another example of rational policymaking by citizens (Beard and Schultz 1912, 51).

Opponents of the system of direct legislation create an entirely different story from the results of the competing fish initiatives. To opponents, the outcome represents the successful use of the initiative to advance narrow interests. As one observer noted, "one class of fishermen endeavored to use the process to put the other class out of business, as a measure of retaliation the other class endeavored to put the first class out of business with another initiative. In their ignorance of the whole situation voters approved both initiatives, thus crippling the great fishing industry of the state" (Eaton 1912).

Rather than simply evaluating the results of this election in terms of the desirability of direct democracy, we shift analytical ground to examine the decision-making process underlying the choices voters made. Specifically, how do these results bear upon the assumption that competing propositions act to confuse voters? How might voters reason when assessing these competing proposals? Why might both Oregon initiatives receive a majority of affirmative votes when the counterinitiative strategy is typically expected to produce negative voting? Was the Oregon electorate voting in a confused or ignorant manner, as suggested by some of the observers at the time?

---

7. This was an electorate composed of white males age 21 and older.

Because of the lack of modern opinion poll techniques in 1908, it is difficult to revisit the election and test such questions directly. Some contemporary observers commenting on the June 1908 election thought that Oregon's voters were acting with clear intention:

> At the last election each party [of upriver and downriver fishermen] had its bill, proposed under the initiative, each legislating the others' method to destruction and preserving its own. The electors, in an access of disgust, tinged with sardonic humor, passed both bills by different but decisive majorities. The law thus passed taken together practically prohibit fishing by either method . . . (Report of the Oregon Conservation Commission to the Governor, November 1908, 119)

A plausible argument can, however, be constructed to the effect that voters were acting somewhat sensibly—at least as far as they relied on the ballot pamphlet.

As is typical of all ballot pamphlets, that of 1908 included arguments for and against the measures. Both arguments in favor of passage laid claim to a need for conservation. Both clearly support the view that there is overfishing and that this is a bad thing, and they both cite relevant authorities to buttress their claims. "In the Columbia the salmon are steadily decreasing, especially our Chinook salmon, the king of all salmon" (see argument in favor of downriver bill, by Orton et al., in Oregon Voter's Pamphlet 1908, 108).

H. A. Webster (writing in favor of the upriver bill) stated more succinctly, "Canned Fish Won't Spawn" (Oregon Voter's Pamphlet 1908, 47). Webster, who was "formerly Deputy Fish Warden, State of Oregon," lists a whole series of reports from the U.S. government, such as the Bureau of Fisheries, and the governments of both Oregon and Washington to the effect that there is overfishing (50–51).

The difficulty comes—of course—in apportioning blame for the overfishing. Each side blamed the other for the problem. Orton and colleagues claimed that the downriver bill would secure employment for between five thousand and fifteen thousand people and would contribute between $5 million and $10 million to the economy. Voting against it would mean "a few rich fish-wheel owners of the upper Columbia will be permitted for a few more years to pile up great wealth at the cost of the destruction of one of Oregon's greatest industries, the salmon fisheries" (Oregon Voter's Pamphlet 1908, 109). Opponents of the downriver bill, meanwhile, mention that the people behind it were "mostly foreigners without fixed residence, and few taxpayers" backed by the International Seamen's Union of America and "allied Astoria interests."

The "affirmative" argument on behalf of both bills thus shared the view that conservation is needed. The arguments filed against each initiative also shared common threads. Both noted the identity of supporters of the "affirmative" campaign. Both give the appearance of being written expressly by those with an interest in the outcome. In response to the statement published in the pamphlet by Orton and colleagues, we see, for example, a "negative" argument being written by

Seuffert Bros, Warren Packing Co
P J McGowan and Sons
For selves and others in interest.

In response to the second (upriver) bill we see a negative opinion signed by H. M. Lornsten, "Secretary Columbia River Salmon Protective Association"— which raises a possible problem of interpretation because this association was also responsible for writing the "affirmative" opinion on the bill favoring downriver fisherman. The CRSPA seems to be a different body from the Columbia River Fisherman's Protective Union headed by Mr. Rosenburg—mentioned, disparagingly, in a letter to the editor of the *Oregonian* from Mr. John Nassa (9 May 1908, 6).

There is in this case the possibility for some simple cue taking because the same endorsee favored one bill and opposed the other. Voters living along the Colombia River could thus know easily which bill favored which interests. So why should voters without any direct stake in the measures vote in favor of both bills? It is possible that, on the basis of the ballot pamphlet evidence, some voters could have voted *yes* on both. To the extent that voters followed ballot pamphlet guidelines, it seems sensible to suppose that voters who did not have a direct stake in the outcome could have been persuaded by each side's affirmative arguments. Some voters might discern, from the evidence in the pamphlet and perhaps supplemented by the information in the *Oregonian,* that the bills were backed by and favored "special" interests of one form or another, interests that were directly opposed to each other both geographically and ideologically. Yet, despite these stark divisions, both parties to the dispute agreed that conservation was necessary. If both of these bitterly opposed sides agreed, then one reasonable inference for voters removed from the conflict along the Columbia was to vote in favor of conservation, which, according to arguments listed in the ballot pamphlet, meant voting for both initiatives.

Analyzing ignorance or confusion in voting without individual-level data is obviously problematic. We have no records of the information sources used by individual voters, nor do we have direct measures of the material attachments to the two fish bills that voters had. However, an analysis of geographical vote data can provide information about the possible extent of electoral confusion and voter responsiveness to interest-based arguments. The geographical distribution of votes illustrates that negative and affirmative votes on each measure occurred in a manner that suggests that voter ignorance and confusion might not have been responsible for the election results.

As noted before, the fish bills had specific constituencies determined by location. One initiative promoted the interests of upriver fishermen on the Columbia, the second promoted the interests of downriver fishermen. If individual-level voting represented informed (or self-interested) choices about the competing initiatives, we might expect that upriver fishermen would vote in favor of the proposal limiting downriver catches because that proposal would have protected their access to fish. By this logic, upriver fishermen would also be more likely to vote against the initiative limiting access to their own upriver fish. Conversely, downriver fishermen would vote in favor of the proposal to limit the fish-wheel gear used by upriver fishers and against the upriver proposal. Downriver fishermen are adversely affected by upriver fishing because it seriously reduces the number of salmon that spawn, thus limiting future runs available to downriver fishermen.[8]

Table 24 displays the geographical distribution of votes on the two fish initiatives of 1908, organized by counties along the Columbia River. The second column ranks each county in order of its distance from the mouth of the river (with 1 = Clatsop, the most coastal county, and 11 = Wallowa, the most interior[9]). The next two columns record the county vote share on the two propositions: "Up Pct." is the percentage of the county's vote in favor of the proposition to close upstream fishing, and "Down Pct." is the percentage of the county's votes in favor of closing downstream fishing. The figures in the "Distance (km)" column represent the linear distance (in kilometers) from the largest city in the county to the Pacific Ocean at the mouth of the Columbia River. We assume that voters who were involved with the fishing economy were aware of their self-interest and that voters who were not fishermen in each county were likely to be exposed to information biased toward the position of the dominant fishing gear group of the county (seine nets or fish wheels). That being the case, we expect a positive correlation between the county's distance from the ocean and its vote in favor of closing the downstream fishery ("Down Pct."). Likewise, we expect an inverse correlation between distance and support for closing the upstream fishery ("Up Pct.").

The Pearson's correlation shown at the bottom of table 24 illustrates the

---

8. Voters with a keen appreciation of fish biology might recognize that the fish wheels were the more destructive and least manageable technology from a sustainable-use perspective. The wheels efficiently harvested (near the spawning grounds) large quantities of the fish that made it past the downriver seiners. Unfortunately, we cannot account for that, given these data. In the contemporary period, commercial upriver fishing for salmon is uniformly prohibited in the western United States and in nearly all of British Columbia.

9. The two easternmost Oregon counties (Union and Wallowa) are not on the Columbia, because the river turns north into Washington at Umatilla County, but Wallowa County's eastern boundary is the Snake River. The Salmon River also joins the Snake in Wallowa County. Snake River salmon migrate up the Columbia to their spawning grounds in the east; thus, upriver fishermen in Wallowa are directly affected by downriver fishing.

TABLE 24. Geography and Vote on the Oregon Fish Initiatives

County	Distance[a]	Up Pct.[b]	Down Pct.[c]	Distance (km)[d]
Clatsop	1	90.486	13.455	30
Columbia	2	74.607	41.453	200
Multnomah	3	62.290	50.123	270
Hood River	4	66.829	53.370	410
Wasco	5	65.756	52.994	470
Sherman	6	73.599	46.503	520
Gilliam	7	59.490	59.639	610
Morrow	8	67.265	55.778	660
Umatilla	9	61.663	55.047	800
Union	10	62.307	52.666	960
Wallowa	11	39.873	60.984	1070

	Correlation Matrix		
	Up Pct.	Down Pct.	Distance (km)
Up Pct.	1.0		
Down Pct.	−.85	1.0	—
Distance (km)	−.81	.73	1.0

Source: Authors' calculations. Statement of Result, Oregon Secretary of State.
[a]Ranking based on distance of county from mouth of Columbia River, with 1 = closest
[b]Percentage of voters in favor of initiative to close upstream fishing
[c]Percentage of voters in favor of initiative to close downstream fishing
[d]Distance from largest town in county to Pacific Ocean at mouth of Columbia River

political geography of this vote. The correlation between "Distance (km)" and "Up Pct." is −.81, and the correlation between "Distance (km)" and "Down Pct." is .73 (the correlation between votes on the two measures themselves is −.85). The upstream counties clearly voted against the downstream ones, and vice versa. The aggregate data suggest that self-interest and perhaps responsiveness to biased information sources (rather than confusion) structured voting on these competing proposals. These same relationships are displayed more clearly when we plot the county votes on a map of Oregon (figures 3 and 4). Support clearly changed in areas farther from the coast.

Another more direct (albeit aggregate) representation of self-interest in voting might be census data on occupation in fishing by county. Unfortunately, the 1910 census does not provide such data, but a 1911 report (employing 1909 data) contains employment and fishing gear investment data for many of the counties listed table 24.[10] The report also includes these data for each coastal county (from north to south; Tillamook, Lincoln, Lane, Douglas, Coos, and Curry) and for Clackamas County. Clackamas is inland (upriver) and south of

---

10. The report is by John Cobb, assistant agent at the Salmon Fisheries of Alaska (Cobb 1911, 751).

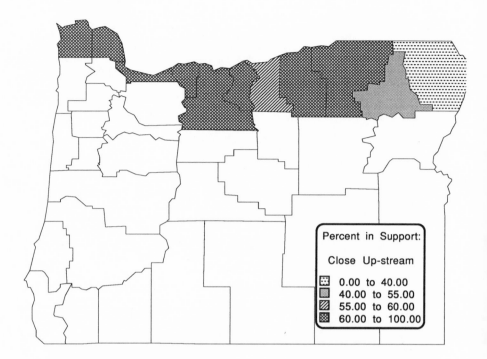

Percent in Support:

Close Up-stream

	0.00 to 40.00
	40.00 to 55.00
	55.00 to 60.00
	60.00 to 100.00

Fig. 3.   County votes on Oregon Fish Initiative (1908) in favor of closing upstream fishing

the Columbia River; it is the first county along the Willamette River after two branches of the Willamette leave the Columbia at Columbia County and Multanomah County.

Table 25 lists these county names and the county vote on each initiative. It also lists three aggregate measures of the economic interests of the county: "Employ." is the number of whites employed in fishing, "Net" is the dollar amount invested in seine nets (coastal gear, the technology of the lower-river fishermen), and "Wheel" is the dollar amount invested in fish wheels by county (the technology used primarily by upriver or inland fishermen).[11]

Table 25 indicates that Clatsop County (at the mouth of the Columbia River and the location of the city of Astoria) was heavily involved in the fishing industry. The 1910 county census gives a population of just over 16,000, more than 3,000 of whom were employed in fishing. The county had an elec-

---

11. Part of the imbalance between employment and investment in table 25 involves the capital-intensive nature of inland fishing. Fish wheels were large, industrial-mechanical devices. Net fishing, on the other hand, was possible from small, individual boats.

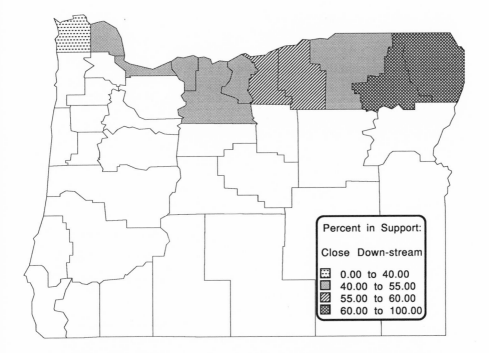

Fig. 4.   County votes on Oregon Fish Initiative (1908) in favor of closing downstream fishing

torate of about 5,000 voters.[12] These data also illustrate an association between objective measures of the economic interests of voters in the county and votes on the two initiatives. When the outlying case of Clatsop County is included, we see a strong positive association ($r = .82$) between investment in net technology and votes in favor of limiting upstream use of fish wheels. Conversely, these data show an inverse relationship ($r = -.88$) between investment in nets and support for closing downstream fishing.[13] Given the skewed nature of these data, they should not be interpreted as confirming the hypothesis that county vote is determined by the dominant mode of fishing in the county. They do illustrate that Clatsop County, housing the greatest investment in coastal net (seine) gear, clearly had the lowest vote in favor of restricting net fishing. Furthermore, the county with the most invested in fish wheels (Multnomah

---

12. The report lists Chinese and Japanese as distinct employment categories, but only white males age 21 and older could vote.

13. It should be noted that these correlations are much less substantial when Clatsop County is removed from the analysis. The data are provided here for the sake of illustration.

TABLE 25. Economic Activity and Voting on the Oregon Fish Initiatives

County	Employ.[a]	Net[b]	Wheel[c]	Up Pct.[d]	Down Pct.[e]
Clackamas	86	4,262	115	57.899	50.431
Clatsop	3,158	479,325	300	90.486	13.455
Columbia	178	2,320	15,825	74.607	41.453
Coos	312	30,246	0	72.918	55.179
Curry	53	3,405	0	63.526	57.061
Douglas	107	6,345	0	63.713	51.542
Hood River	6	360	0	66.829	53.370
Josephine	113	2,884	0	66.604	51.137
Lane	130	7,827	0	73.474	38.848
Lincoln	153	14,890	0	63.374	51.694
Multnomah	119	1,831	74,250	62.290	50.123
Tillamook	169	12,780	0	68.712	56.793
Wasco	69	570	266	65.756	52.994

	Correlation Matrix				
	Employ.	Net	Wheel	Up Pct.	Down Pct.
Employ.	1.0				
Net	.99**	1.0			
Wheel	−.09	−.12	1.0		
Up Pct.	.83**	.82**	−.18	1.0	
Down Pct.	−.89**	−.88**	.01	−.84**	1.0

Source: The Salmon Fisheries of the Pacific Coast, 1911; Bureau of Fisheries Document 751, Dept. of Commerce, Washington, DC; Statement of Vote, Oregon Secretary of State.

[a] Number of whites employed in fishing
[b] Investment (in thousands) in seine nets
[c] Investment (in thousands) in fish wheels
[d] Percentage of voters in favor of initiative to close upstream fishing
[e] Percentage of voters in favor of initiative to close downstream fishing
**Significant at $p < .01$ (two-tail)

County) had the lowest vote in favor of restricting fish wheels (among counties for which we have investment data). This should stand as further evidence that votes on the competing propositions were the result of something other than confusion or ignorance in the mass electorate.

Summary

What can we generalize from an election held in 1908? Negative voting is expected to be an information cost-cutting decision that voters use in response to information demands (see chapter 3). One might ask, compared to contemporary voters, was the 1908 Oregon electorate less likely to use negative voting in response to the potential confusion associated with competing initiatives? It is safe to assume that the contemporary electorate is better educated and at least as well informed as the Oregon electorate of 1908. This assumption might lead us to conclude that the Oregon electorate would be more likely to engage in negative voting to cut information costs. Furthermore, the 1908 ballot was as long as many contemporary ballots, with nineteen separate initiatives and referenda. Lower levels of education, long ballots, and competing initiatives on one topic all seem to be a recipe for negative voting, yet most voters approved these competing initiatives. In spite of these factors that would make us expect negative voting, each measure passed. In this case, the counterproposal failed to preserve the status quo and failed to protect the interests of either "special" group.

We suggest that the Oregon case demonstrates that most voters do not automatically reject competing initiatives out of confusion, nor do they necessarily approve them out of ignorance. An analogous situation in the contemporary era might be found in the competing insurance proposals in California. Many voters appear to have sorted through the options and found the proposal consistent with their preferences (Lupia 1994a). In Oregon, support displays a systematic relationship with a political geography that reflects divergent interests. In the case of these fish initiatives, neither geographical interest was large enough to defeat the other's initiative nor large enough to counter votes from areas less directly affected by the measures.

We propose that the results from this study of the Oregon fish initiatives and the California park logroll tell us something about how the mass electorate responds to strategies that elites adopt when qualifying ballot initiatives. The evidence indicates that location-specific information might cue voter response to propositions. This finding is particularly interesting in the case of counterpropositions, because the counterproposal strategy is often expected to produce confusion and thus cause negative voting. The Oregon data suggest that proposition content can act as an information cue to the voter if policy consequences are localized.

The aggregate data from Oregon cannot directly test whether individuals respond to information about the local effects of a proposal, but the analysis of the California park bond initiative allows us to test for it, at least indirectly. Those results suggest that well-educated voters tend to be more supportive of a bond proposition if they live in an area targeted to receive more benefits from the initiative. That does not mean that loading up a project with pork will necessarily ensure victory: a relatively small proportion of voters appears to make instrumental decisions based on the narrow spending details that are buried in an initiative.

Results from the California initiative raise as many questions as they answer, questions that cannot be addressed with the data that we have available. As earlier chapters illustrate, campaign information or information shortcuts appear to allow voters to determine their positions on many propositions. We know from chapter 3 (and we will see in chapter 7) that voters can find cues easily and that they appear to respond to campaign contacts. But how does a small proportion apparently learn something about the content of a relatively uncontested bond initiative? How do voters living along the Columbia River decide which initiative helps or harms their local economy? How far through the electorate might such information be disseminated?

We speculate that voters hear about these details through local information sources: media, interest groups, and firms involved with the initiatives, or friends and neighbors. Further studies must assess how (or if) voters come to learn such policy-relevant details with different types of propositions. Without a heated campaign or with relatively low stakes and widely diffused costs (as with the park bond initiative), we find it hard to imagine that very many voters would hear about most policy details. In such cases, media coverage will be limited and discussions might be constrained to the highly attentive, so few might vote on the basis of actual details contained in the initiative. In the Oregon case (or in the case of the tax measures discussed in chapter 5), the costs may have been very apparent to many. In the Oregon example, costs involved with the proposals should have been particularly salient in those counties where fishing was the dominant industry. There, many voters could have learned through conversations with family and coworkers—and through campaigns and corresponding press coverage—what stakes were involved with each initiative.

Barring the adoption and enforcement of rules that prohibit these strategies, it is likely that the counterproposal and the logroll initiative will continue to be used by initiative proponents. Our findings suggest that neither strategy has a guaranteed capacity to produce wholesale confusion (in the case of counterproposals) or manipulation (in the case of distributive logrolls) of the electorate. The findings also suggest that parts of the mass electorate, at present and in the past, are somewhat responsive to the location-specific, economic consequences of policy proposals. This result is somewhat surprising given that most studies grant little weight to the ability of direct-democracy voters to make decisions on the basis of any policy-specific information about a proposed initiative.

In chapter 7, we examine how voters might apply instrumental evaluations to propositions on term limits, which have a less clearly defined or less clearly identifiable economic impact. We propose that when costs and benefits associated with a proposition accrue to groups and parties more directly than to individuals, instrumental evaluations might be more group or party based. We again see some evidence of instrumental voting (based on group rather than on private interests) as well as potential responsiveness to campaigns. We illustrate that campaign information might help people evaluate these propositions in partisan terms.

CHAPTER 7

Partisan Interests and Campaign Information: Support for Term Limits

In examining instrumental motivations for choices on tax and spending propositions, we imputed interests to voters on the basis of narrowly defined private (or localized) interests. Interests were defined in terms of how the narrow, economic costs and benefits associated with a proposition might have an immediate effect on a person's income. From this perspective, the decisions of many voters appear to be a way to achieve some sort of tangible economic ends.

The effects of many initiatives, however, are often more intangible. As further evidence that voter behavior in direct democracy reflects an ability to reason, we demonstrated that some voters can also use instrumental motivations when evaluating less tangible, noneconomic initiatives. Instrumental decisions on ballot propositions—voting to advance one's interests—need not be seen as limited to narrowly defined economic self-interest. Voters may view an issue in terms of how it affects the interests of the political parties or social groups with which they identify. This perspective might be particularly relevant with governmental reorganization measures that lack easily identifiable fiscal impacts but nevertheless have consequences on the distribution of political influence.

Unlike a tax or spending proposal, a voter might have a hard time assessing how a reapportionment proposal, campaign finance reform, or legislative term limitation will affect his or her personal finances. But rules proposed by such measures still affect people by changing the ways in which they (or their representatives) interact with government and by changing the ways in which elections are conducted. In such a context, where the costs and benefits of a proposition are diffuse and more abstract—or are political rather than economic—outcomes can affect the political parties and groups that are elected to office, and they can influence government. Rather than deciding on the basis of personal motivations, voters might think instrumentally about such measures in terms of their partisan or group interests.

In this chapter we examine how motivations based on partisan and social-group interests might allow voters to decide whether they are for or against term limitations. We examine, in particular, how partisan voters might "learn" over the course of a campaign and how voters respond to party cues. Some suggest that cues related to party labels and demographic characteristics may be sufficient for voters to act as if they had perfect information (Page and Shapiro 1992, 387–88; McKelvey and Ordeshook 1985). We are not attempting to assess how behavior in direct democracy might compare to a hypothetical, perfectly informed voter. Rather, we seek to learn whether preferences for ballot initiatives appear to "make sense" in terms of underlying values, imputed interests, and available information, and whether changes in opinions reflect sensible adjustments to information.

Term-Limit Initiatives in California

Given the highly visible and contested nature of the 1990 California term-limit conflict, we feel it provides a useful test for group- and party-based instrumental voting. Two term-limit initiatives (Propositions 131 and 140) were on the 1990 California ballot, each supported by distinct political groups. We suggest that as the campaign matured, information about how each initiative might affect partisan representation in California became more clearly defined. In the end, many voters could have had a fairly easy time applying the "Who's behind it?" cue to determine whether their party's interests were served by the proposals.

One proposal, Proposition 140, was drafted by a former Assembly Republican (Pete Schabarum) and was endorsed by many incumbent Assembly Republicans, by Republican Governor Pete Wilson (in a televised debate with Democrat Diane Feinstein), and by Republican President George Bush. A competing initiative (Proposition 131) was drafted by a ranking Democrat (John Van de Kamp) and supported by a handful of elites—notably, Tom McKennery (the Democratic mayor of San Jose) and Ralph Nader. Opposition to both proposals was led by Senate and Assembly Democrats, with Republicans playing a less visible role (Price and Baccioco 1990, 579–80). It is reasonable to expect that many voters could learn some of this information from ballot pamphlets, television news, and general media coverage as the campaign heated up. Each major party also funded efforts to contact voters (direct mail and phone banks).

In this chapter, we test whether support for these initiatives was affected by partisanship and whether the distribution of partisan opinions changed over the course of the campaign in a manner suggesting that voters learned which measure was most consistent with their party's interests. If that were the case, Democrats initially in favor of Proposition 140 would defect, while Republicans would remain supportive. Conversely, Republicans supportive of the measure backed by some Democrats would eventually defect. If we extend this logic, support for term limits might also be expected to be greater among voters who identify with groups most excluded from the legislature in terms of descriptive representation. As we shall see, there is very limited support for this group-based hypothesis, but we find substantial partisan motivations here. Party voting, moreover, is associated with campaign contacts.

The Term-Limits Movement

Voters in at least twenty-four U.S. states have voted on and approved ballot propositions placing limits on the number of terms that legislators may serve. We examine patterns of variation in public support for California's Propositions 131 and 140 of 1990, two of the earliest term-limit initiatives. In November 1990, California voters passed Proposition 140 while rejecting its competitor, Proposition 131. California thus became the third U.S. state to place limitations on the number of terms that members of the state legislature may serve, following precedents set by Colorado and Oklahoma initiative votes. In 1991, voters in the state of Washington rejected a similar initiative that, in addition to limiting terms for members of the state legislature, would have placed limits on statewide offices and the Washington congressional delegation (Olson 1992). In 1992, term-limit initiatives were adopted by voters in fourteen states, including Washington, where a moderate version of the 1991 initiative was approved. Some of these initiatives extended limits to include members of Congress, a maneuver that was later rejected by the federal courts.

By 1996, another eight states approved term-limit propositions. Utah was the only state other than Washington and California to reject a form of limits. In the interim, a great deal has been written about the normative rationale and constitutionality of these measures (see, for example, Fett and Ponder 1993; Benjamin and Malbin 1992; Will 1992), yet little is known about how voters responded to the choices presented by actual initiatives. (For an exception, see Banducci and Karp 1994; Karp 1998; see also Karp 1995. See Soutwell 1995 on opinions about hypothetical term-limitation proposals.)

Some work does exist, however, that forecasts the effect that term limitations would have on the future composition of state legislatures. Moncrief and his colleagues have estimated a model of cohort retention in state legislatures that suggests that limitations will primarily affect a small proportion of members who might otherwise retain their seats in "professional" state legislatures (Moncrief et al. 1992). In another analysis, Moncrief and Thompson (1991) estimate how limitations might restructure group representation in legislative bodies, concluding that if term limits were imposed, long-serving male incumbents would be likely to lose seats (with female representation increasing) and Democrats (as the majority party in most state legislatures) would likely lose more seats than would Republicans (see also Mondak 1995 on consequences).

Partisanship, Representation, and Campaign Information

The actual manner in which these term-limit proposals will alter patterns of representation cannot be known until after the measures have been in force for some time. Nevertheless, we may draw some testable hypotheses about public support for term limitations. We propose that support for limitations might be higher among partisans or groups that tend to be underrepresented in the state legislature.

If we assume that some voters evaluate term-limit proposals with some respect to self-interested expectations about the composition of a "new," post-term-limit body, it is reasonable to expect that members of certain electoral groups might be more inclined to support limitations. That is not to say that all or even most voters are rational, strategic actors seeking to maximize the legislative representation of the respective party or group with which they most strongly identify. Rather, we assume that on one level, the basic argument in favor of limiting terms might have more appeal to those most disenchanted with status quo representative government. Expressed differently, members of underrepresented groups might have less interest in supporting the legislative institution, and thus might be less disposed to defend it against fundamental change (Patterson, Hedlund, and Boynton 1975).

On another level, some individuals might calculate that they would benefit from increased representation if a legislature were to be subjected to rapid membership turnover. In either case, members of the minority party, outgroups, or groups having less attachment to the status quo composition of a legislature are expected to be more supportive of membership turnover and limitations on terms. In California, Republicans were in the minority at the time of Proposition 140. Underrepresented groups might include racial minorities, women, and younger voters.

Partisanship is anticipated to define the constituency that is in favor of term limitations, in part by providing a basis for responding to elite cues about the issue and in part by providing a basis for party-based instrumental evaluations (given the data available, we cannot separate these aspects of party as influences on vote intentions). For example, the upper and lower houses of the California legislature were dominated by Democrats through the 1980s, despite a growing Republican registration and the election of Republican governors in three successive elections (one of these was a reelection). Continued Democratic strength in the legislature has been attributed, in part, to advantages derived from the rancorous 1980 legislative reapportionment process that left Democrats overrepresented in the state legislature and in the state's congressional delegation (C. Bell and C. Price 1984, 206–8). Thus, tenure limitations may be viewed as advantageous to Republicans because most incumbents who lose seats in the state legislature could be Democrats. In other words, Republican voters, as a group, might be better represented if status quo arrangements were changed in 1990.

Voters must sort through multiple issues and choose among competing propositions on the same topic when they make choices about ballot issues, particularly in California (Banducci 1992). When such information demands result in confusion, individuals may abstain or they may voice opposition to a proposal. The decision process in the 1990 California campaign was complicated by the fact that rival term-limit proposals appeared on the ballot. Proposition 131 would have allowed members to serve six two-year terms in the lower house and three four-year terms in the upper house, and then sit out a single term and return again with a "fresh slate." It also included provisions for the public financing of campaigns. The second measure, Proposition 140, was far more restrictive, allowing half as much time in office, with no provision for return. Proposition 140 was also a direct attack on professional legislative careers; if passed, it would reduce the legislature's operating budgets and cut pension benefits and salaries for members (Fiorina 1992, 57; Price and Baccioco 1990, 498).

An alternative to the representation hypothesis would recognize both the information demands and the effects of campaign information on term-limit choices (see, for example, Banducci and Karp 1994; Karp 1994). If issue complexity, confusion, and uncertainty about competing proposals affect choices, the acquisition of information about ballot propositions might also structure opinions. Because so much uncertainty is often associated with ballot propositions, campaign information may be far more important for determining the outcome of ballot propositions than for candidate contests (Magleby 1989). Such information can be received from multiple sources, including targeted mailings from proposition campaigns, contact by political parties, and exposure to media. Thus, we propose that campaign contacts might also affect support for term limitations by providing voters with cues about the partisan consequences of the initiatives.

We also anticipate ideological effects. Conservatives might see limitation proposals as a necessary attack on "legislative professionalism" as well as a means of limiting the power and size of state government (if only in the legislative branch). As such, these measures might find greater support among self-described conservatives if conservative orientations are associated with an outlook on politics that favors less active government.

One potential effect of replacing incumbent legislators with new office-holders is that racial groups "overrepresented" in an unlimited legislature (whites) might be replaced with members of "underrepresented" minority groups under conditions of open-seat elections. In California, for example, Latinos and Asian-Americans might be viewed as underrepresented in the legislature compared with their relative size in the electorate.[1] As such, these groups

---

1. As of 1990, California's population was 69 percent white, 25 percent Latino, 9 percent Asian-American, 7 percent African-American, and 13 percent "other"; it was also 49.9 percent female. In 1990, the California Assembly (lower house) was 16 percent female, 7.5 percent African-American, and 5 percent Latino (with no Asian-American or other nonwhite members). The California Senate was 13 percent female, 5 percent African-American, and 5 percent Latino (with no Asian-American or other nonwhite members).

might see greater representation as a result of the rapid legislative turnover brought about by citizen-mandated limitations (Guerra 1991).

Minority racial groups that are not representationally disadvantaged in a system of unlimited terms, however, are not expected to gain further representation in a body with limited terms. Legislative representation of African-Americans that approaches parity with the proportion of African-Americans in a given population has been attributed to enforcement of the Voting Rights Act (Darcy and Hadley 1988). If limits were imposed on terms, African-American districts would be expected to continue to elect African-American representatives. A simulation of term-limit-induced cohort change in state legislatures finds that limits will not result in substantially increased representation of African-Americans (Moncrief and Thompson 1991).

The Dynamic Context of Support for Limitations

Before assessing the relative merits of hypotheses about support for limitation initiatives, we present data on trends in support of two competing term-limit measures: California's Propositions 131 and 140 of 1990. These early measures of support for term limits are of interest (and are perhaps somewhat unique) because later proposals typically generated less of an opposition campaign. In California, term limits were given wide attention by the press, and via paid campaigning. Thus, these examples provide an opportunity to assess the prospects for voter responsiveness to initiative campaigns. As Magleby (1989) demonstrated, there are often large shifts in opinion over the course of a campaign. Data from California suggest that broad-based support for limitations eroded as election day approached.

We have suggested that support for these issues might be a function of the voter's partisan interest, their exposure to campaign information from the political parties, and dissatisfaction associated with their perceptions of representation. In other words, term-limitation propositions might have a distinctive "constituency" that becomes defined as information about the consequences of the issue is made available during the campaign. The campaign might be viewed as a learning period during which uncertain opinions of various groups are mobilized or converted in favor of or in opposition to limitations. It can also be the mechanism by which individuals acquire information about how a rather complex proposal affects their interests.

To assess these arguments, we draw upon three cross-sectional opinion surveys taken over the course of the 1990 California general election campaign. Data from these surveys are presented in tables 26 and 27. Because we lack panel data, these data are the closest we can come to evaluating the dynamics of an initiative campaign.

We begin with the proposition that Republicans and members of underrepresented groups should, by the end of a campaign, be more likely to support term limits than should members of other groups. Members of underrepresented parties or groups are defined in relation to their share of the state's legislative seats. This concept can be used to assess support for these proposals across state lines, but the operational definition of these groups, to some extent, depends on the composition of each state's legislature. Republicans who are in the minority in one state's legislature (California) might be expected to support changing status quo representation, whereas Republicans who hold the majority in another state (Utah) might be expected to oppose to these measures.

In California, we define underrepresented demographic groups to include Latinos, Asian-Americans, and women. In 1990, these groups were underrepresented in both houses of the California legislature (see footnote 1). We also include younger voters in the analysis. The young have low levels of attachment to political institutions, which is manifest in low levels of voting and political participation (Wolfinger and Rosenstone 1980). We might also expect that weak attachments extend to less support for status quo representation arrangements, if not less support for (or trust of) legislatures as institutions.

Because Proposition 131 included language about campaign finance reform and made provisions for public funds to be used in legislative campaigns, we expect that Proposition 140 provides a clearer test of partisan and group support for limitations. Thus, Republicans and members of underrepresented groups are expected to offer greater support for the more restrictive proposal.

Table 26 reports differences among groups in voting intentions on Proposition 131. The table illustrates that support for the "moderate" term-limit proposal was fairly broad-based in August, prior to the term-limitation campaign. In the early stages, categories of gender and partisanship show little ability to distinguish among those who support Proposition 131. In August, older voters, African-Americans, and whites appear least supportive of the moderate limitation proposal; however, the number of respondents in some categories of race make significance tests difficult here.

Z values in the tables illustrate the probability that there is a significant difference between two reference groups (i.e., Republicans vs. Democrats) by the October 30 survey, and values in the column labeled "% Change" illustrate trends in opinions for each specific group.[2] For Proposition 131, we see little

---

2. The Z values represent significance of differences between the proportion in group 1, supporting, compared with the proportion in group 2, supporting, calculated as:

$$Z_{(p1-p2)} = \frac{p1 - p2}{\dfrac{p1(1-p1)}{N1} + \dfrac{p2(1-p2)}{N2}}$$

TABLE 26. Voting Intentions in California Term-Limit Contests: Proposition 131, August 17–October 30, 1990

		Aug. 17	Oct. 10	Oct. 30	% Change	Nov. 6[a]
All sample						
	Y:	60.3	66.7	44.7	−15.6	38.2
	N:	25.2	18.1	36.3	+11.1	61.8
	U:	14.5	15.3	19.0	+4.5	
		(468)	(249)	(311)		
Party						
Strong Rep.						
(r)	Y:	62.7	62.3	41.2	−21.5	
	N:	20.0	20.8	39.7	+19.7	
	U:	17.3	17.0	19.1	+1.8	
		(75)	(53)	(68)		
Strong Dem.						
(d)	Y:	61.4	59.2	37.9	−23.5	
	N:	25.7	25.9	39.7	+14.0	$Z_{(r-d)} = 0.38$
	U:	12.8	14.8	22.4	+9.6	$(p = .35)$
		(70)	(27)	(58)		
Independent						
(i)	Y:	57.6	70.8	56.6	−1.0	
	N:	25.9	11.1	27.6	+1.7	$Z_{(r-i)} = 1.86$
	U:	16.5	18.1	15.8	−0.7	$(p = .07)$
		(139)	(72)	(76)		
Gender						
Male						
(m)	Y:	58.9	67.5	48.6	−10.3	
	N:	28.1	19.5	32.9	+4.8	
	U:	12.9	13.0	18.6	+5.7	
		(224)	(123)	(140)		
Female						
(f)	Y:	61.5	65.9	41.5	−20.0	
	N:	22.5	16.7	39.2	+16.7	$Z_{(m-f)} = 1.26$
	U:	16.0	17.5	19.3	+3.3	$(p = .10)$
		(244)	(126)	(171)		
Age						
Under 40						
(u)	Y:	62.4	67.7	45.5	−16.9	
	N:	26.6	17.7	34.5	+7.9	
	U:	11.0	14.6	20.0	+9.0	
		(173)	(96)	(110)		
Over 65						
(o)	Y:	55.4	84.4	40.9	−14.5	
	N:	24.1	9.4	30.3	+6.2	$Z_{(u-o)} = 0.60$
	U:	20.5	6.3	28.8	+8.3	$(p = .27)$
		(83)	(32)	(66)		

(continued)

TABLE 26. — *Continued*

		Aug. 17	Oct. 10	Oct. 30	% Change Nov. 6[a]
Race					
White					
(*w*)	Y:	60.9	67.4	44.5	
	N:	24.4	17.4	35.6	
	U:	14.7	15.2	19.6	
		(422)	(224)	(236)	
Latino					
(*l*)	Y:	65.4	64.5	47.4	
	N:	21.2	12.9	42.1	$Z_{(w-l)} = 0.33$
	U:	13.5	22.6	10.5	($p = .37$)
		(52)	(31)	(38)	
African-American					
	Y:	52.2	60.0	45.5	
	N:	30.4	30.0	35.0	
	U:	17.9	10.0	20.0	
		(23)	(10)	(20)	
Asian-American					
	Y:	78.5	55.5	40.0	
	N:	21.2	11.1	40.0	
	U:	7.1	33.3	20.0	
		(14)	(9)	(10)	

Source: Various California Polls, 1990.

Note: Z values compare differences in support between categories within the October 30 sample. Number of cases in parentheses.

Percentage in Favor = Y, Opposed = N, Undecided = U

[a]November 6 general election results

significant difference between groups at the end of the campaign. Independents are significantly more supportive than are Republicans, and men are slightly more supportive than are women. Consistent with Magleby's (1989) findings, the proportion of undecided voters increased over the course of the campaign, while support eroded. The only group showing relatively stable support for Proposition 131 was self-described independents. Thus, as the campaign heated up and as voters were exposed to information about the issue, initially high levels of overall support declined substantially.[3] The measure was soundly defeated.

Table 27 displays patterns of voting intentions for the more restrictive limitation measure, Proposition 140. In general, support did erode as the campaign went on, but not as dramatically as with Proposition 131. Polls show slightly

---

3. A week prior to the election, pro-Proposition 131 forces had raised $300,000, but most of it had been spent qualifying the measure. Pro-Proposition 140 forces raised $1.2 million and spent most of it in the final weeks of the campaign. Anti-term-limit forces raised more than $6 million (Price and Baccioco 1990, 580).

TABLE 27.   Voting Intentions in California Term-Limit Contests: Proposition 140, August 17–October 30, 1990

		Aug. 17	Oct. 10	Oct. 30	Change	Nov. 6[a]
All sample						
	Y:	66.8	68.7	61.6	−5.2	52.2
	N:	19.8	19.3	25.2	+5.4	47.8
	U:	13.3	11.9	13.2	−0.1	
		(428)	(259)	(333)		
Party						
Strong Rep.						
(r)	Y:	72.9	69.8	67.6	−5.3	
	N:	14.1	18.6	17.6	+3.5	
	U:	12.9	11.6	14.9	+2.0	
		(85)	(43)	(74)		
Strong Dem.						
(d)	Y:	62.1	62.5	48.1	−14.0	
	N:	18.2	31.2	38.5	+20.3	$Z_{(r-d)} = 2.21$
	U:	19.7	6.2	13.5	−6.2	$(p = .01)$
		(66)	(48)	(52)		
Independent						
(i)	Y:	63.6	73.8	58.7	−4.9	
	N:	21.8	15.4	28.0	+6.2	$Z_{(r-i)} = 1.27$
	U:	14.5	10.8	13.3	−1.2	$(p = .10)$
		(110)	(65)	(75)		
Gender						
Male						
(m)	Y:	64.7	68.5	59.4	−5.3	
	N:	23.2	20.8	28.4	+1.2	
	U:	12.1	10.8	12.3	−0.2	
		(207)	(130)	(155)		
Female						
(f)	Y:	68.8	69.0	63.5	−5.3	
	N:	16.7	17.8	22.5	+5.8	$Z_{(m-f)} = 0.77$
	U:	14.5	13.2	14.0	−0.5	$(p = .22)$
		(214)	(129)	(178)		
Age						
Under 40						
(u)	Y:	62.4	68.7	68.7	+6.3	
	N:	23.4	20.2	22.9	−0.5	
	U:	14.2	11.1	8.4	−5.8	
		(141)	(99)	(131)		
Over 65						
(o)	Y:	65.9	62.5	49.2	−16.7	
	N:	14.8	22.9	30.8	+16.0	$Z_{(u-o)} = 2.63$
	U:	19.3	14.6	20.0	+0.7	$(p = .004)$
		(88)	(48)	(65)		

(continued)

TABLE 27. — *Continued*

		Aug. 17	Oct. 10	Oct. 30	Change	Nov. 6[a]
Race						
White						
(*w*)	Y:	67.9	68.6	62.1	−5.8	
	N:	19.8	19.7	23.4	+3.6	
	U:	12.2	11.8	14.5	+2.3	
		(393)	(229)	(269)		
Latino						
(*l*)	Y:	69.2	76.9	59.3		
	N:	20.5	15.4	40.0		$Z_{(w-l)} = .22$
	U:	10.3	7.7	.7		($p = .41$)
		(39)	(26)	(35)		
African-American						
	Y:	43.7	64.7	54.5		
	N:	18.7	17.6	45.4		
	U:	37.5	17.6	.0		
		(16)	(17)	(11)		
Asian-American						
	Y:	71.4	70.0	80.0		
	N:	21.4	20.0	10.0		
	U:	7.1	10.0	10.0		
		(14)	(10)	(10)		

Source: Various California Polls, 1990.

Note: Z values compare differences in support between categories within the October 30 sample. Number of cases in parentheses.

Percentage in Favor = Y, Opposed = N, Undecided = U

[a]November 6 General Election results

lower levels of overall support one week prior to the election than are found in the August data. Support continued to erode during the final week of the campaign, with election totals running 8 percent lower than support evident in polls completed October 30. Compared with Proposition 131, we see much less opinion fluidity among voters expected to be supportive of Proposition 140. Table 27 provides evidence that Republicans remained supportive of Proposition 140 throughout the campaign, while Democrats abandoned the measure.

Differences in the vote intentions of Democrats and Republicans for Proposition 140 are most pronounced in the survey when closest to the election date; however, some differences persist throughout the campaign. In early August, support among individuals claiming a strong identification with the Republican party for this "restrictive" limitation measure ran 10 points higher than did support among self-described strong Democrats. Near the end of the campaign, however, this gap widens to 19 points ($p = .01$). By the end of the campaign, a generational difference is also evident: there is a gap of nearly 20 points between older and younger voters, with the young in favor of limitations. These descriptive measures indicate little effect for race. Asian-Americans were most supportive of the restrictive term-limit measure; however, the number of respondents in some racial categories is rather low.

Tables 26 and 27 provide a portrait of shifting opinions over the course of the California ballot proposition campaign. Republicans persisted in supporting restrictive limitations, while general support for it eroded. At the same time, these voters defected from Proposition 131 as the campaign progressed. Overall, these results suggest that opinion change is associated with a process where minority party identifiers—voters defined as less attached to the status quo state legislature—show higher levels of support for the restrictive proposal, and majority-party identifiers come to realize that a proposal they initially embraced was bad for their party. These data suggest a "learning process" whereby some voters determine which initiative is good and which is bad for their party's interests. Findings are weaker for other "underrepresented" social groups that are expected to support Proposition 140.

Opinion data from this campaign suggest strongly that partisan voters "learn" or respond to their party's interest over the course of an initiative campaign. In the next section, a multivariate analysis is used to assess whether party remains significant when other factors are controlled for, and to test where voters might find cues about their party's interests.

Multivariate Analysis of Support for Term Limitations in California

The data presented in the foregoing section provide information about the dynamics of opinion change in these contests, but they fail to provide a rigorous test of our original hypotheses. In this section, we model voter opinions on the California initiative that passed, Proposition 140.

One hypothesis associated with the party interest—the underrepresentation hypothesis—proposed that exposure to campaign information might also affect choices. Logistic regression is used to disentangle the overlapping factors that operate to structure individual opinions aggregated in tables 26 and 27 and to assess the impact that exposure to campaign information has on support. Table 28 reports the results of estimations of support for Proposition 140 one week prior to the election. The dependent variable is coded as 1 = support, 0 = do not support.

Three models were estimated, with a baseline model (Model 1) composed of demographic traits similar to those presented in tables 26 and 27. A second model (Model 2) adds an indicator of conservative ideology and an interaction term designed to represent young voters with weak party attachments in order to test whether generational effects are associated with weak party attachments. The third model (Model 3) adds three indicators of campaign exposure to the baseline demographic model. "Info" is a four-item index that measures whether the respondent uses mail, newspaper, radio, or television campaign advertisements, or possibly a combination, as a source of information when deciding on ballot issues. "Dem. Contact" indicates that the respondent was contacted by the Democratic party during the campaign, while "Rep. Contact" indicates the respondent was contacted by the Republican party. Independent variables in the baseline estimation include indicators of age (measured in years) and dummy variables representing women, Republican identifiers, African-Americans, and Latinos.

The logistic regression results in table 28 illustrate that when we control for multiple independent variables, the independent effect of gender and age structure support for term limits. When we control for partisanship, young vot-

TABLE 28. Estimations of Support for California's Term-Limitation Initiative Proposition 140

Variable	Model 1	Model 2	Model 3
Intercept	.640$^+$	.541	.780$^+$
	(.499)	(.508)	(.513)
Age	−.018**	−.018**	−.019**
	(.007)	(.007)	(.007)
Female	.346$^+$	.356$^+$	.390$^+$
	(.236)	(.237)	(.241)
African-American	−.123	−.001	−.185
	(.675)	(.689)	(.681)
Latino	−.316	−.306	−.338
	(.377)	(.377)	(.381)
Republican	.504*	.646**	.397$^+$
	(.243)	(.272)	(.252)
Conservative		−.225	
		(.311)	
Age × Strength of party attachment		.007	
		(.007)	
Info		−.149	
			(.141)
Dem. Contact		−1.154$^+$	
			(.760)
Rep. Contact		.871*	
			(.488)
N	324	324	324
Model Chi-Square Improv.	12.7*	14.2*	19.5*

Source: California Poll, October 30, 1990.

Note: Logistic regression estimates. Values in parentheses are standard errors. Dependent variable = 1 if respondent intends to vote in favor, 0 if otherwise.

*Significant at $p < .05$ (one-tail)

**Significant at $p < .01$ (one-tail)

$^+$Significant at $p < .10$ (one-tail)

ers and women were more likely to indicate that they intended to vote for Proposition 140. The underrepresentation hypothesis for Latinos, however, is not supported by the coefficient for Latino voters. The insignificant coefficient for the age–party attachment interaction in Model 2 also suggests that generational differences in support are not simply a function of younger voters having weaker attachments to the party system. Indeed, the unique effect of age remains significant when this interaction is included in the model. Young voters thus support term limits regardless of the strength of their party attachments. Alternative interaction terms that utilized indicators of independent identification were not significant. The independent effect of Republican partisanship also displays a significant, positive relationship with support in each model. That is, when we control for conservative ideology and other factors, Republicans remain more supportive of term limits.

Table 28 suggests that exposure to partisan contacts plays some role in cuing voters to realize how an initiative affects their party's interest. Those voters who rely on information from campaign advertisements are no more likely to support Proposition 140. However, voters who have been contacted by the Democratic party are far less likely to support Proposition 140, while voters contacted by the Republicans are far more likely to support it. The magnitude of each party contact coefficient is larger than those for any other variable. All of this suggests that even on an initiative that does not affect their personal finances, many voters may nevertheless determine how to make instrumental decisions that further their party's political interests.

Summary

Our analysis indicates that supporters of the minority legislative party tend to be more likely to support term limitations on legislative officials. These data cannot establish definitively that these voters support limits because they expect greater representation in a post-term-limit legislature. Many results are nevertheless consistent with what we would expect if that were the case. When we control for ideology, for example, Republicans are clearly more supportive of term limits. At the time of the election, Republicans held a minority of seats in each house of the California legislature. We interpret our results as evidence that partisans supported (or opposed) Proposition 140 on the basis of expected partisan advantages (or disadvantages) rather than on the exclusive basis of symbolic appeals or their ideological orientation. Karp (1995) uses National Election Study data concerning a hypothetical national term-limits proposal and also identifies self-interest effects associated with partisanship.

Although journalistic discourse suggested that the term-limit movement may have arrived from a broad-based antiparty, anti-incumbency mood (Clymer 1992), these results illustrate a substantial gap between the opinions of strong Republican and strong Democratic identifiers. Moreover, self-described independents are less supportive of Proposition 140 than are strong Republicans (see table 27), and young voters with weak partisan attachments are not strong supporters (see table 28). Support is not idiosyncratic, and the effects of campaigns and campaign contacts appear to be that of moving voters toward a position (or reinforcing a position) that is consistent with our narrow definition of their group or partisan interest.

It is difficult to say how these findings from California are representative of term-limit conflicts in other states. The California initiatives were associated with a high-intensity campaign, unlike those in many other states. Three million dollars was spent by proponents of the two California term-limit initiatives, and nearly $5 million was spent by opponents (Karp 1996). In this context, we might expect that there is more information available that could produce the conversion of opinions formed before the representational consequences became apparent to voters. In a high-intensity campaign that provides voters with the perspectives of term-limit proponents *and* critics (i.e., the majority party), a majority-party voter who is initially hostile to legislators and is disposed to simply "throw the bums out" can later recognize that such actions are counter to his or her party's interests. That would cause the majority party voter's opinions to move toward opposition by the end of the campaign.

This research does not establish that widespread, early support for a popular ballot measure such as term limits can be defeated by any active campaign. It does clearly suggest that campaigns help some voters form decisions that are consistent with their party's (or perhaps their group's) interests. Other than California's Proposition 131, only two of twenty-four term-limit initiatives have actually been associated with campaigns that changed opinions enough to defeat the measures: Washington's first initiative in 1991 and Utah's in 1994. Some of our results from California are consistent with data from these and other states. A study that used opinion data from Washington (Donovan 1993) found that Republicans were more supportive of limits in that state, where the legislature is controlled by Democrats.

Findings from other states also suggest a partisan learning process similar to that found in California. In Washington and Utah, initial overwhelming support for limits was eventually changed into defeat as majority-party voters moved toward opposition. Karp found this pattern with Washington's 1991 I-553 term-limit initiative. Washington's first campaign was highly contested, with proponents outspending opponents and expenditures exceeding $1 million (Karp 1994, 1996, 1998; Olson 1992). Karp's models of opinion on I-553 (1998) show that the key to defeating that state's first term-limit proposal was that voters learned through editorials and campaign ads that Congress's Representative (and U.S. House Speaker) Tom Foley was against the initiative.

People were more likely to vote against limits when they learned that Speaker Foley did not support them.

Opinion changes of this nature, moreover, are not limited to Democratic voters living in states with majority Democratic delegations and senior Democratic representatives. Magleby and Patterson (1996) demonstrate that politically aware Republicans in a Republican-dominated state (Utah) were most likely to change their opinions from support for limits to opposition over the course of the campaign. They attributed this shift to voter responsiveness to appeals from elite Republicans such as Orrin Hatch, who argued that limits would cost the state by removing senior GOP officials from Congress. Reversing the process seen in California and Washington (where Democratic voter support eroded more heavily than did Republican voter support), the opinion of Utah Democrats shifted less than did that of Republicans, with Republican opinions shifting toward greater opposition as the campaign progressed. In Utah, the campaign may not have been as costly (only $165,000 was spent, with proponents widely outspending opponents), but the opinion reversal among majority-party identifiers was nevertheless striking. As in California, Washington, and other states, early polls showed that limits were approved by a wide majority. A poll conducted just before the November 1994 election placed support at 70 percent among Utah respondents, yet the measure received only 34 percent of the vote (Magleby and Patterson 1996). Republicans, it appears, learned at the very end of the campaign that the initiative would have an adverse effect on their party's legislative influence.

This finding conforms to what we find in California, where the partisan gap in opinions doubled over the course of the campaign. Near the end of the campaign, those voters contacted by the Republicans were likely to voice a favorable opinion of Proposition 140. This finding is consistent with the advantages the initiative could bring in terms of increased Republican strength in the legislature (Moncrief and Thompson 1991). Conversely, those contacted by Democrats were likely to voice an opinion consistent with the disadvantages the initiative might bring to Democrats in the legislature. Given that millions of dollars were spent on the campaign, and that California's political parties (particularly the Republicans) have developed sophisticated means of contacting supporters and facilitating targeted absentee ballot voting, the finding that party contacts are associated with opinions is not entirely surprising. This analysis demonstrates, however, that the partisan consequences of Proposition 140 were perhaps more apparent to individuals toward the end of the campaign as information about the issue was made available.

The analysis of support for term limits illustrates how important campaigns can be in transmitting information about propositions to voters. Data from the 1992 state elections suggest further that differentiation of attitudes by partisanship is triggered by the information context associated with actual state term-limit initiative campaigns. In early 1992, for example, when no visible term-limit campaigns were under way, the Gallup organization measured national public opinion regarding limitations on congressional terms. Gallup found widespread support for term limits distributed equally among Democrats, Republicans, and Independents.[4]

Surveys produced far different results when conducted during actual campaign periods in those states with term-limit initiatives on the ballot. In thirteen of fourteen such states, Republicans were more supportive of limits than were Democrats (there was no difference in Wyoming). The magnitude by which statewide Republican support exceeded Democratic support ranged from a low of 7 percent (Oregon) to a high of 34 percent (North Dakota), with an average of 18 percent (Roper Center 1993, 97). Karp (1995) also found that the probability of an individual supporting term limits was lower if the respondent lived in a state in which there was a competitive campaign. We suggest that this finding is evidence of how campaigns allow people who are evaluating term-limit initiatives to find out "Who's behind it," or in this case, which party is behind it. This process appears to have occurred in California through party contact of voters, and (although our data cannot let us create a model for this directly) through voters learning the positions of members of the party elite through other campaign information.

Thus, where campaigns occur, support for these measures is differentiated by partisanship. This differentiation also appears to "make sense," and it suggests that voters reason about the choices they make because opinions change or correspond according to information that is available to voters. We suggest that these data and those from other studies demonstrate that when campaigns provide information, voters can reason instrumentally on ballot measures, at least on the basis of group or partisan interests. We do not expect that similar claims could be made about voter decisions on these issues if active campaigns were lacking, however.

We speculated that active campaigns might not be such an important prerequisite for allowing voters to apply instrumental evaluations to the tax and spending propositions examined in the previous chapter. With tax and spending choices, a quick assessment of the proposal, subject, or title might reveal narrow costs and benefits to voters. Uncertainty about governmental reorganization propositions such as term limitations might be greater, however. With such choices, voters might have a harder time deciding who benefits and who loses. Term-limit proposals carry qualifications about eligibility for runoff, provisions that may or may not allow members to serve after retiring, variations in

4. In a national sample, Gallup asked voters whether they supported a twelve-year limit on congressional terms. In April 1992, 66 percent of Democrats, 67 percent of Republicans, and 68 percent of Independents said *yes* (Roper Center 1993, 97). These figures are similar to support levels measured at the same stage of the California campaign (see tables 26 and 27).

lengths of terms, applicability to different levels of government, and provisions about whether limits begin immediately, retroactively, or with an allowance for the "clock" to start fresh for influential senior members. The same proposal, moreover, can adversely affect the fortunes of different parties in different places.

Without contested campaigns, we expect that many, if not most, voters are unaware of these details. Voters, however, need not be aware of each detail of the proposition to form an opinion consistent with their party's interest. Campaigns can provide a large number of voters with elite or partisan cues regarding the provisions in the initiatives that the party deems salient. This cue or party contact, rather than detailed knowledge of the issue, can be enough information for a voter to make group- or party-based instrumental evaluations. When there is no campaign with its associated low-cost cues and information, many voters might not be aware of the partisan consequences of term limits. Thus, in places without active opposition campaigns, we might not see the group- and party-based differences in support for initiatives that we see in California (and that others find in Washington and Utah). Campaigns appear to allow voters to see that an apparently simple and appealing proposal ("throwing the bums out") might have effects that are detrimental to their party.

Finally, we acknowledge that other, noninstrumental explanations could also be consistent with our results. It is highly plausible that women and young voters support limitations due to some underlying dissatisfaction with status quo politics that cannot be measured directly with these data. Clearly, political cynicism also affects opinions on term limitations, yet these data are poorly suited to test for such effects. Additional attitudinal measures are needed to assess whether dissatisfaction with status quo legislative policies might mediate the opinions of members of different groups. But results here suggest that researchers interested in identifying the constituency supporting political reforms such as term limits will need to consider how opinions are affected by campaigns that illuminate the partisan consequences of these measures.

CHAPTER 8

How Campaign Spending Affects Voter Awareness and Opinions of Initiatives

As noted in the introductory chapters, one of the persistent critiques of direct democracy is that well-financed interests might use the process to purchase policy. "Big money" can fund petition drives and finance manipulative campaigns that are designed to fool voters into passing policies that are inconsistent with their interests (see, for example, Scott and Nathan 1970; Price 1975; Lowenstein 1982; Zisk 1987; Hadwiger 1992). But while the critique of "success through spending" may be quite common, it is less common to see the distinction made between successful opposition and successful advocacy.

Money can affect outcomes in many ways. There is a distinction to be made between well-financed interests spending lavishly to defeat initiatives and wealthy groups spending heavily to pass initiatives. If the former is more typical, new proposals that threaten well-heeled interests—originating from the grass roots or otherwise—would have difficulty becoming law. Those that pass would have to survive vigorous opposition campaigns. If the latter is more typical, the process would allow wealthy groups to circumvent the legislature and "purchase" policies that might be inconsistent with the majority's underlying preferences. In either case, spending would be expected to affect outcomes. Negative campaign spending would be associated with *no* voting on propositions, while spending on the *yes* side would be associated with *yes* voting. It is also possible that spending affects opinions in other, less direct ways.

In this chapter we examine how spending might affect opinions and proposition outcomes, bearing in mind the distinction—and possible asymmetry—between heavy spending on behalf of an initiative and heavy spending in opposition. We also explore the indirect effects of large-scale spending—especially spending in favor of propositions. Such spending, we suggest, may occasionally have the paradoxical effect of raising opposition to a given proposal. Our broad conclusion is that, contrary to the fears of some of direct democracy's critics, well-financed groups are able to affect outcomes, but their influence appears to be largely defensive. One major, although less direct, impact of spending may trigger the kinds of decision processes and cues that we have examined throughout our discussion.

147

Research on Campaign Expenditure
and Direct Democracy

Thus far, we have largely sidestepped a direct look at how campaign spending affects opinions and voting in direct democracy. Along the way, however, we have indirectly established a number of points relevant to this issue.

First, the analysis in chapter 3 (table 5) indicates that spending against a proposition is associated with greater negative voting. When estimating these same models with affirmative spending, we find no relationship between campaign expenditure and voting. These findings are consistent with much of the existing literature. Similar patterns have been identified by Lowenstein (1982) and Magleby (1994b). Banducci (n.d.) finds a stronger relationship between negative spending and the *no* vote, yet her two-stage model also finds a smaller yet significant relationship between *yes* voting and spending by the *yes* side. In contrast, Owens and Wade (1986) concluded that there is no substantive relationship between campaign spending and outcomes, and Hadwiger (1992) found *yes* spending to be influential in elections on local ballot measures. Thus, at least at the state level, spending against propositions appears to generate more negative voting than spending in favor generates support.

Second, we have also noted the asymmetry in spending effects anecdotally: heavy spending in favor of several major initiatives failed to produce victory. As discussed in chapter 3, there are several examples of initiatives where tens of millions of dollars were spent by proponents, yet these measures were resoundingly defeated. Lowenstein (1982) has identified similar unsuccessful, well-financed *yes* campaigns in California: a 1972 effort by state employees to pass a law affecting state workers' salaries; a 1972 attempt by farmers to pass a law regulating farm labor relations; and a 1980 effort by landlords to pass a law restricting local rent controls. In each case, proponents spent heavily in real terms, outspending opponents 37 to 1, 3.5 to 1, and 26 to 1, respectively. Just as the pro-tort-reform groups (noted in chapter 3) attempted to make their initiatives appear "proconsumer," these earlier *yes* campaigns also tried to make their initiatives sound beneficial to the groups organized in opposition. Despite the potential that might create for voter confusion, these initiatives were soundly defeated. Of these measures, the proposed regulations of farm workers received the widest support—and it garnered only 42 percent in favor.

Magleby (1994b, 4) notes another example of record *yes* spending from Maryland: the National Rifle Association (NRA) spent nearly $7 million dollars in an unsuccessful attempt to pass a measure that would repeal a state law requiring handgun registration. He demonstrates that in ten of the top eleven cases where the *yes* side widely outspent the *no* side, ballot measures failed. Magleby also notes that there has been substantial growth since 1990 in proposition contests where high total spending (more than fifty cents per voter) and proponent spending advantages are associated with *no* voting (21). Of the sixty-five cases he identifies, thirty have been on state ballots since 1990.

Why, then, are such efforts not successful? If spending fails to secure victory, can it nevertheless affect opinions and decisions? We have attributed the failure of some big-money campaigns to the voter's ability to reason on the basis of information that is readily available independently of the campaign. For example, in chapter 3 we demonstrated that few direct-democracy voters claim to be influenced by paid ads and paid mailings provided by campaigns and that voters instead seek out and use additional, neutral sources of information (see table 6). Perhaps the most important piece of information they use is knowledge of who supports and opposes the initiatives.

We suggest that the use of "free" cues (free in the sense of being independent of the paid campaign) can explain why heavy, one-sided spending is frequently unsuccessful in direct democracy. One reason may be the presence of an indirect relationship between campaign spending and initiative outcomes. Rather than simply manipulating or converting opinions (which we grant can occur on occasion), highly contested campaigns should increase voter awareness of initiatives and thus increase the voter's ability to answer questions such as, "Who's behind it?" or "What's in it for me?" Furthermore, if we assume that spending focuses more media and interpersonal discussion on a particular initiative, it might also increase the chance that a voter will be able to evaluate the proposal within one of the standing conceptual frameworks we have already discussed (either ideological or self-interested motivations, or through cues and shortcuts).

There are no easy, nonexperimental ways to test for the effects of exposure to paid media. Given the potential stigma associated with admitting that one is influenced by paid advertising, it is likely that the self-reported survey data used in chapter 3 may underestimate the impact of paid ads. Although the kinds of aggregate-level data used in chapter 3 help us address some of these issues, it is often a less satisfactory approach than individual-level data. Subsequently, we use opinion data to model potential individual-level exposure to television advertising (by media market) in initiative campaigns. We do so by combining aggregate and individual-level data, which provides a variety of overlapping and analytically consistent evidence on the impact of campaign spending.

Overall Spending: The Mobilization of Mass Awareness

We first consider one way that spending can affect opinions indirectly. Large sums of money spent on an initiative are a reflection that a proposal is contentious enough to mobilize interested groups, firms, or individuals to participate in funding a campaign. We assume that as more groups mobilize in support or in opposition, some voters who support or identify with those groups will become aware of their group's position on the initiative. If we assume—as pluralist theory suggests—that groups mobilize to protect their interests when they are threatened, a credible *yes* campaign can lead to the mobilization of many opposition groups. Substantial spending by these groups can increase overall voter awareness of a ballot measure.

Compared to uncontested propositions, we can assume that heavy spending means that there will be more groups and elites taking positions and, hence, more attention given to who supports or opposes an initiative. If a well-funded initiative threatens status quo policy arrangements, it will likely increase the number of groups mobilized in opposition and increase the odds that voters will hear about an initiative and its proponents prior to arriving at the voting booth.

The evidence presented in chapter 3, for example, demonstrated that, other things being equal, overall campaign spending is associated with more participation by voters on a proposition. We anticipate that this propensity to participate is related to voters seeking out those measures they know of and have heard the most about or that they have the easiest time understanding. We assume further that greater information and awareness covary with voters knowing who is for and who is against an initiative. Campaign spending can possibly lower information barriers for many voters by generating information about initiatives. We therefore expect to find increased overall awareness of propositions when spending is greater.

If affirmative spending stimulates sufficient mobilization of groups who disseminate opposition endorsements, *yes* spending could even be associated with voting *no*. At the very least, large sums of campaign funding can reveal that a small number of clearly identifiable groups or firms are involved in a campaign. When a group such as the Philip Morris Company, trial lawyers, or a public employees' union finances a *yes* campaign and media attention emphasizes the source of the funds, many voters are given a cue about "Who's behind it" without having to review the ballot pamphlet. If a large, unknown group bankrolls a campaign, however, the contributors to the group and the group's agenda would have to become the focus of media attention and opposition campaign messages for voters to use the funding source as a cue.

David Olson's study (1992) of the 1991 Washington state term limit initiative (I-553) campaign illustrates how spending brings attention to an initiative and to the group backing the initiative. At the early stages of the I-553 campaign, heavy *yes* spending came from contributions from the unknown and innocuously labeled Citizens for Congressional Reform (CCR). By mid-September, the pro-I-553 side had spent $360,000—outspending opponents 7.5 to 1 at the time. More than 90 percent of the money on the *yes* side had come from CCR, yet proponents claimed "grassroots" status. By October, the state media brought attention to the initiative by reporting that CCR was located outside the state and was largely funded by the owners of the second-largest privately held corporation in the United States, Koch Industries (72). This revelation provided an opening for Democratic officeholders to critique the proposal and raise funds for the campaign against it. Widespread support for the initiative evaporated, and the measure was defeated 46 to 54 percent in a record-turnout election (82). In the end, proponents lost despite having had a proposal that was initially popular and having outspent opponents by a 2-to-1 margin.

Unfortunately, we lack data that allow us to directly estimate how spending might increase voter knowledge of who is backing an initiative, but we can test whether spending is associated with greater awareness of initiatives. If general media attention and information about issues increase in high-spending contests, voters should be more aware of those ballot measures with the greatest amount of campaign spending.

We test for this hypothesis by examining voter awareness of all thirty California initiatives measured in Field Institute California Polls conducted from 1984 through 1990. We use polls taken immediately before each November election. Interviewers asked respondents if they had heard, read, or seen anything about these propositions prior to probing them for their opinions. The California Polls are largely concerned with major ballot initiatives, so they do not offer us the ability to assess voter awareness of propositions across the full range of campaign spending. Our sample is limited to the most visible ballot initiatives—those likely to have campaign spending and free media attention. Tests of the relationship between campaign spending and the percentage of voters claiming awareness of each proposition thus are limited to initiatives, and they omit the pro forma referenda measures that the California Polls ignore.

Our analysis includes propositions listed in general elections (to hold turnout relatively constant). In each case at least $500,000 (in 1986 dollars) was spent on the proposition campaign (for and against). All but three of the thirty ballot measures involved more than $1 million in campaign spending, with median spending at $4.7 million. Because the selection of cases limits the variance in spending across contests, we probably underestimate the relationship between spending and awareness for all propositions.

Given that the less educated are less likely to refer to the ballot pamphlet and are slightly more likely to report using ads as sources of information when deciding on propositions (see table 6), we once again divide the opinion data into high- and low-education groups. We anticipated that, lacking cognitive sophistication and information, less-educated voters' awareness of propositions might be more likely to be affected by paid media.

We estimated two models of the relationship for each group of voters. One includes all thirty propositions. Because the insurance propositions appearing on the 1988 ballot represented a unique situation in which five proposals competed on the same issue, for purposes of comparison we also estimate models that exclude the insurance propositions.

The results presented in table 29 support the idea that voters are more aware of those propositions in which campaign spending is greater. Both groups of voters are more likely to be aware of propositions when more money was spent contesting the measure. If we omit the insurance measures, we see that for every $1 million spent, roughly an additional 1 percent of the voters becomes aware of a proposition. This finding suggests that $5 million in spending (the median here; not an extraordinary amount by California standards) could increase voter awareness of propositions by 5 percent. That is not a trivial effect: in the 1990 California general election, 7.3 million people voted; 5 percent of that is 364,000 voters. If we assume that voters are more likely to make choices on measures they are aware of, then campaign spending not only can facilitate greater awareness of initiatives, but also can conceivably lead to significantly greater participation.

The data offer little support for the idea that the effects of spending are more pronounced among less-educated voters. Models including or omitting the insurance propositions actually fit slightly better when we estimate awareness among the well educated and provide slightly larger (but not substantively different) coefficients. Although this result is not what we expected to find, there is a reason that a stronger relationship might exist among the well educated. If voters become aware of propositions through general attentiveness to

TABLE 29. Relationship between Campaign Spending and Awareness of Ballot Initiatives: California, 1984–90

| | Well Educated | | Less Educated | |
	With Insur. Props.	Without Insur. Props.	With Insur. Props.	Without Insur. Props.
Campaign spending (in millions	.494	1.008+	.395	.928+
of 1986 dollars)	(.332)	(.585)	(.320)	(.557)
Constant	61.20**	60.24**	53.03**	51.79**
	(4.32)	(4.94)	(4.16)	(4.71)
N	30	25	30	25
R^2	0.073	0.114	0.052	0.108

Source: Opinion data, various California Polls, 1984–90; spending data, California Fair Political Practices Commission.

Note: OLS regression estimates. Standard errors in parentheses. Dependent variable = percentage reporting hearing of named initiative in opinion surveys.

**Significant at $p < .01$ (two-tail)   +Significant at $p < .10$ (two-tail)

media, we can expect that the well educated are more attentive to all forms of media and are exposed to more information overall.[1]

We cannot directly establish how this sort of awareness might mediate the link between spending and negative voting found where there is heavy spending *in favor* of propositions. We can, however, offer some possible explanations. Magleby (1994b, 20) suggests that the high volume of information associated with big-spending proposition campaigns can create so much noise that voter doubt about the proposal is increased. This suggestion implies that an information overload causes confusion, leading voters to simply say *no*. Given our findings in chapter 3 and elsewhere, we propose that voters might often say *no* where information is scarce, and not when it is plentiful (unless the information reveals reasons for saying *no*).

Magleby also offers insight into what we see as a more plausible way in which affirmative spending can trigger negative voting (1994b). He suggests that upon hearing information predominately from the *yes* side, voters might somehow become skeptical and reject the proposition. We suggest that this skepticism, if it exists, comes from learning something about the narrowly interested groups or firms that are backing the proposal. In other words, it can be linked to voter responsiveness to elite cues, as we demonstrated in chapter 3. In tables 7, 8, and 9 we saw that elite cues can have both a positive and a negative impact on evaluations of propositions. If a voter (particularly an educated and partisan voter) learns that a group she or he does not like or does not trust is backing an initiative, the information will have a negative influence on that voter's evaluation of the initiative. For example, knowing that farm owners are behind a measure to regulate farm labor conditions might cause the voter to be skeptical about how the initiative could be consistent with her or his interests (or her or his conception of the public interest). When more is spent, voters are more likely to hear of (and about) a proposition. Rather than indicating much about the direct impact of campaign spending on election results, the negative (or null) relationship that many find between spending in favor of a proposition and votes for a proposition might indicate something about voter awareness of the groups and issues that generate high levels of spending on the *yes* side.

Consider how some examples could be perceived by voters: insurers and lawyers trying to change insurance regulations to the advantage of insurers or trial lawyers; the tobacco industry attempting to draft a standard for local smoking ordinances; the NRA trying to repeal gun registration rules; a multibillion-dollar corporation initiating congressional reform. These propositions are "hard sells" by groups that lack widespread popularity (or credibility), to say the least.

---

1. We speculate that identical results for well-educated and less-educated voters also suggest that, contrary to conventional wisdom, the less educated are no more likely to be influenced by political ads on television. See also table 6.

The difficulty of passing the legislation initiates the need for spending, and the spending—if high enough—raises awareness and reveals the group's identity.

Most of the literature to date and the research reported here do show a relationship between campaign expenditure on the *no* side and outcomes on propositions. Here, we also note a relationship between overall spending and awareness of initiatives. When we consider the fears many have of the influence of money in direct democracy, these effects do not seem overwhelmingly invidious—especially given the conventional expectation that campaign spending manipulates opinions, particularly those of the less informed and less educated.

Our assessment is similar to the argument developed by Gerber and Lupia (1995). They demonstrate formally how active campaigns, by enhancing voter competence and the information available to voters, can increase the likelihood that direct democracy produces outcomes that are consistent with voters' preferences. Spending can reveal campaigners' incentives, thereby increasing a voter's ability to evaluate proposals. These authors note the important role that campaign finance disclosure laws could play in facilitating informed choices in direct-democracy elections. News media or opposition campaigns are a partial form of expenditure disclosure. To test how spending actually informs voters of proponent and opponent incentives is beyond the scope of our study. Our findings do suggest, however, that spending could facilitate greater awareness (table 29) of initiatives and greater mass participation on proposition choices (again, see table 5). These are two requirements of any election system that is expected to adequately translate mass preferences into public policy.

Television Spending and Mass Opinions

We now examine how campaign spending might be more directly related to opinions. Spending on television and on petition efforts are probably the two costliest aspects of a major initiative campaign. Television, moreover, is the vehicle that might be best suited to influencing the opinions of the less-educated voters—voters who we know are exposed to fewer sources of information and who are particularly less likely to utilize print information (see table 6).

Distinguishing between the effects of media spending and other sources of campaign information can quickly become quite complicated. Indeed, many previous studies failed to disaggregate media spending from spending on petition efforts. The period of qualification (the petition phase) can involve huge amounts of campaign money and effort. For example, $14 million was spent on signature gathering alone on the November 1988 "no fault" California insurance initiative (Proposition 104). Some $2.2 million was spent gathering enough signatures for qualification of another insurance initiative, Proposition 100, on that same ballot (Price 1988, 484). We are concerned with the effect of information disseminated by campaign organizations during the campaign period—when electronic advertising purchases are made. Information transmitted via electronic media expenditure is only one part of the proposition campaign process, but it is often the largest single campaign expenditure (Price 1988). The aggregated spending totals shown in table 29 and in most other studies make it difficult to distinguish between these very different types of spending.

One way to broaden our understanding of the impact of money in proposition elections is to examine the relationship between opinions and expenditure on electronic media. The examination of spending on one set of hotly contested ballot propositions presented later in this chapter reveals a relatively complicated process by which media spending is seen to have no direct impact on opinions on ballot issues. In short, the fact that it proves relatively difficult to find evidence of a process that conventional wisdom suggests should be strong (if not self-evident) provides indirect support for our idea that other sources of readily available information and cues affect voting in direct democracy.

One way to address the impact of media spending on individual opinion is to examine one election in particular for which money might have been expected to matter. Several propositions from the 1988 California general election present an ideal opportunity because such large amounts of money were spent by organizations backing initiatives. In particular, tens of millions of dollars were spent contesting a cigarette tax and insurance regulation issues. Given the volume of media expenditure, one might expect to see fairly substantial effects of advertising.

The 1988 election also provides a rare opportunity to test for effects of spending because data are available that detail the location of electronic advertising aired during this election. The California Fair Political Practices Commission reported money spent by the various campaigns to purchase airtime on individual television and radio stations. These data provide at least some means of examining variation in opinions in response to spending across California's twelve media markets. With only one or two exceptions, media markets embrace entire counties, allowing us to merge local spending measures onto California Poll survey data from November 1 of that year.[2] Because the California Poll records each respondent's county of residence, we can determine the amount spent on television advertising in each respondent's home area. Thus, we can test whether respondents residing in an environment of heavy advertising hold different opinions than do respondents residing in low-advertising environments. (For a similar approach in candidate contests, see Stewart and Reynolds 1990.)

---

2. *Broadcasting Yearbook* 1988; *California Yearbook* 1988, lists TV and radio station call letters.

Once again, we divide our sample to account for the distinct reasoning processes associated with distinct groups in the electorate. We assume that the well educated have more cognitive abilities and a greater ability to evaluate propositions in terms of their preexisting stock of information (party identification). Well-educated voters are also expected to have more constrained belief systems, allowing ideology to guide the evaluation of various propositions. Findings from earlier chapters demonstrate that less-educated voters with limited cognitive abilities and limited use of party and ideology as an established store of information and beliefs should respond to different information when evaluating propositions. In that case, our theory had us expecting that the less-educated voters would be more likely to have their opinions affected by campaign spending. In earlier chapters we also saw that voters with limited cognitive resources rely on readily available cues rather than on party or ideology when making a decision on a proposition. These cues include evaluations of state conditions or their own narrow self-interest. Here we test whether various media provide a similar alternative source of information that structures opinions on propositions.

In table 30 we model vote intentions on four initiatives using the measures of spending that are most relevant to each contest. Vote intentions are estimated for two insurance propositions (Proposition 100, a trial lawyer group's proposal to discount fees for "good drivers," and Proposition 103, a consumer group's proposal). We also include estimates of opinions on a cigarette tax proposition designed to raise funds for public health (Proposition 99) and an initiative to provide constitutional guarantees for K-12 school funding (Proposition 98).

Different spending variables are used because the initiatives had different balances of spending advantages for proponents and opponents in each contest. On two of the propositions (Propositions 99 and 103), the *no* side widely outspent the *yes* side. Tobacco and insurance groups, respectively, spent heavily against them. The spending variable for these campaigns is thus measured as television spending against each proposition, in dollars per capita in the respondent's media market. This pattern reflects the potential effect that well-funded *no* campaign might have in an area. In the Proposition 100 campaign, there was heavy spending on each side. Insurance groups spent more than $50 million against Proposition 100 (and Proposition 103), and trial lawyers spent roughly $13 million in favor of Proposition 100.[3] For this contest, we represent spending by the per capita advantage that one side had over the other in a media market. In contrast, Proposition 98 is a case where the *yes* side, backed by the California Teachers' Association, widely outspent the *no* side, particularly in television spending. For this initiative, we use per capita spending in favor

---

3. Three committees spent jointly on media to defeat Propositions 100 and 103. One of these groups, the Citizens for No Fault, also spent in favor of two other insurance propositions. Yes on 103 forces spent little on media.

TABLE 30. Campaign Spending on Television Media and Support for Contested Ballot Initiatives

	Prop. 98		Prop. 99		Prop. 100		Prop. 103	
	Lo Ed	Hi Ed	Lo Ed	Hi Ed	Lo Ed	Hi Ed	Lo Ed	Hi Ed
Republican	-.24	-.52*	-.018	.03	-.61+	-.24	-.54*	-.68*
	(.23)	(.24)	(.23)	(.22)	(.36)	(.32)	(.32)	(.30)
Liberal	-.13	.77*	.51+	.53*	1.19+	.88*	.73+	.92*
	(.37)	(.27)	(.38)	(.27)	(.67)	(.43)	(.56)	(.46)
Spending[a]	-.006	.0004	-.0006	-.0034	-.023	.031	.0043	.001
	(.02)	(.02)	(.005)	(.005)	(.04)	(.050)	(.006)	(.006)
Age	-.016*	-.014*	-.004	-.007	-.019*	-.015	-.020*	-.009
	(.006)	(.006)	(.006)	(.006)	(.009)	(.010)	(.008)	(.01)
Income	-.063+	-.046	.066	-.027	-.158*	-.010	.026	.052
	(.041)	(.040)	(.044)	(.033)	(.070)	(.05)	(.06)	(.05)
Constant	1.12*	1.52*	-.355	.65+	2.09*	.78	1.08*	.51
	(.46)	(.43)	(.41)	(.42)	(.69)	(.69)	(.57)	(.69)
N	331	466	331	466	178	212	178	212
Percent correctly predicted	58.0	60.0	57.7	65.6	68.3	58.0	59.5	60.4

Source: California Poll, October 1988.

Note: Logistic regression estimates. Figures in parentheses are standard errors. Dependent variable = 1 if intends to vote for, 0 if intends to vote against named proposition (after given summary).

*Significant at $p < .05$ (two tail)   +Significant at $p < .10$ (two-tail)

[a]For Prop. 98, spending is market per capita spending in favor; for Prop. 99 and Prop. 103, market per capita spending against; for Prop. 100, the market per capita difference between spending in favor and spending against (see text).

of the initiative in each media market. Regardless of the measures of media market television spending used (including specifications not reported here), we find no relationship between spending on television ads and opinion.[4]

If spending affects opinions, we would expect that, other things being equal, voters residing in markets with greater per capita negative spending would be more opposed to each measure. Our tests do not identify such a correlation. What is striking about these data is that over this wide variety of ballot contests where different amounts of money were spent, television expenditure does not appear to affect opinion.

Yet these results still might tell us something about how spending indirectly affects voting and opinions. We see once again that for the well educated, it is ideology that structures vote intentions. Self-identified liberals favored both insurance reform proposals—these initiatives each explicitly proposed lower rates and greater regulation of the insurance industry. Well-educated liberal identifiers also supported the initiative that guaranteed a minimal level of funding for K-12 education and supported the cigarette tax that earmarked funds for public health projects. On two of the initiatives, partisanship once again structured the opinions of well-educated voters. Republicans were opposed to the school funding proposal and the consumer-group initiative to roll back insurance rates. All of this "makes sense" because these opinions appear consistent with what we might expect from liberals and Republicans if they were to evaluate policies in a manner consistent with standard definitions of ideology and party.

In contrast, on the measure with the least overall spending and the least opposition spending (Proposition 98), party and ideology again produce no guidance for less-educated voters. As we demonstrated in chapter 5, we again see what might be cognitively narrow voting among the less educated on an expenditure measure for education. Older voters in the less-educated group are more likely to oppose guaranteed funds for K-12 education, as are wealthier voters in this group.

But there are some interesting departures in table 30 from our previous findings. On the three other initiatives where substantial amounts of money were spent in the campaign phase (Propositions 99, 100, and 103), opinions of less-educated voters appear to be structured by the same factors affecting the opinions of well-educated voters. Less-educated liberal identifiers were supportive of liberal initiatives. Less-educated Republicans were opposed to the measures that propose regulation of automobile insurance.

These results, especially when compared with those discussed in earlier chapters that show a divergence between the determinants of opinions held by well-educated and less-educated voters, suggest that heavy campaign spending

---

4. Absolute spending in the respondent's media market is also insignificant.

might somehow allow the reasoning processes of less-educated voters to emulate those of voters with greater cognitive abilities.

We suggest that campaign spending, rather than simply converting voters' opinions, can change the context of decisions in direct democracy. Spending brings more attention and more awareness to an issue (see table 29), which somehow allows voters with different cognitive abilities to see an initiative in partisan or ideological terms. Lupia (1994a), using different data, has identified what we believe is the key here: when voters know who supports a proposal, even those who know little about a measure can make decisions that emulate the well informed. High amounts of spending over these insurance measures and the cigarette tax measure could possibly blur the differences between well-educated and less-educated voters by revealing more cues about proponents and opponents and by revealing more general information about who benefits from the initiatives. In the end, even less-educated voters could then be able to apply partisan or ideological referents to evaluating the measures.

Our analysis provides very little support for the idea that variation in media market expenditure had a direct impact on opinions across markets with different rates of expenditure or that media spending shapes the opinions of less-educated voters—which does not establish that spending has no direct effect on voting and opinion. Given that California has only twelve media markets and that many respondents to the California Polls are concentrated in relatively few markets, there might not be enough variance in our individual-level measures of spending to capture how spending directly affects individual opinions in direct democracy. Before dismissing the relationship between spending and opinions in direct democracy, we employ aggregate data in an attempt to address the problem of limited variance in our measure of spending.

Media Spending in Aggregate

One way to address the problem of limited variation in spending within media markets is to examine county vote results rather than survey data. Even when we do so, we still find limited (or odd) effects of media spending. Table 31 displays the relationship between county-level campaign spending on television and radio for three of these propositions, and the county vote in favor of each proposition. (Because there was no significant spending on behalf of Proposition 103, we omit it from this stage of the analysis.) Where more money is spent in favor of each, the county vote in favor is significantly greater. This finding is consistent with the conventional wisdom. There are also counterintuitive results, however. On two measures (Propositions 99 and 100), spending against is associated with a greater vote share in favor of the propositions. At least part of the reason for these counterintuitive aggregate-level results is the multicollinearity between spending for and spending against a given proposition in each county.

TABLE 31. Correlation of County Vote Share with Local Media Spending

	Spending in Favor	Spending Against	Colinearity (for−against)	Spending Differential (for −against)
Prop. 98	.31*	.07	.72	.32*
Prop. 99	.27*	.27*	.88	−.27*
Prop. 100	.78*	.65*	.98	.12

$N = 58$

Source: Spending data, California Fair Political Practices Commission; voting results, California Office of Secretary of State.

Note: Pearson's correlation coefficients.

*Significant at $p < .05$

We can sort through this multicollinearity by looking at the difference between pro and con spending in each county (spending in favor of each initiative and spending against). Doing so provides an indicator of the relative advantage one side has over the other. Correlations between spending differentials and county vote share produce a slight positive correlation for the trial lawyers' insurance initiative (Proposition 100, $r = .12$), a contest in which each side spent substantially. That is, this proposition received slightly greater support in those counties where a greater proportion of spending was made in favor of the proposition.[5] For Proposition 98 (the school funding measure), most money was spent in favor of the initiative. This measure also received more support where the *yes* side outspent the *no* side. For this one case, we have some evidence that county-level *yes* media spending (coupled with the absence of a well-funded *no* campaign) was associated with a greater county vote share for the *yes* side.

For the cigarette tax (Proposition 99) there is a −.27 differential, which is perverse given conventional expectations about the effects of spending. In this case, large spending advantages for the *no* side, which the literature and our

5. Aggregate-level spending effects can also be identified by examining Proposition 100. When we look at spending by radio and television separately, partial correlations for spending and county vote share are:

TV in favor: .16
Radio in favor: .08
TV against: .14
Radio against: −.39

Spending effects are visible here, in part, because there is low collinearity between spending on radio ads against Prop. 100 and spending on radio ads in favor of Prop. 100. Opponents of Prop. 100 placed radio ads in marketing areas not covered by supporters. For most propositions examined here, that is not the case.

own aggregate results in chapter 3 indicate should typically have the greatest chance of affecting outcomes, failed to produce negative voting. Where most money was spent in opposition (or where money in favor minus money against has a low or negative value), the vote for Proposition 99 was actually higher. It might be that opponents directed money to areas where they had the hardest time moving opinions. The lack of impact would thus reflect money spent where opinion was strongly mobilized in favor of the cigarette tax. There is an alternative interpretation that is more consistent with our basic argument, however. As with the example of the Washington term-limit initiative, spending could have "backfired" by revealing the campaigner's (tobacco companies) interests. Either way, this case illustrates that although spending to defeat a measure can often be effective, there are limits to it.

Summary

What do these aggregate results and individual-level opinion models tell us about the capacity for well-financed campaigns to use media spending to "manipulate" or move public opinion in direct democracy? We do find some effects of spending in aggregate data. When more is spent contesting an initiative, more voters become aware of the initiative. Furthermore, county-level data from 1988 illustrate that media spending is associated with voting, but the *yes* side gained an advantage only in a case in which there was no television spending by the *no* side (Proposition 98). In another example where the *no* side widely outspent the *yes* side (Proposition 99), voters appear not to have responded. Overall, we find here (and in our aggregate model in chapter 3) that spending leads to more awareness and participation and that spending against leads to more negative voting. At the level of individual opinion, local measures of spending on television in California appear to have no direct effect on opinions about propositions.

In other words, effects of spending on awareness, participation, and outcomes are evident if we move away from individual-level data. It required much effort to achieve results that conventional wisdom suggests should have been quite direct and apparent, however. These affects presumably should have been fairly strong, because standard information cues such as party identification and incumbency are typically assumed to be of little or no guidance for vote choice on ballot propositions.

There are a number of reasons that electronic media spending effects are so difficult to document here, particularly at the individual level.[6] It could be

---

6. Many additional individual-level null results are not reported here. For example, an attempt to separate the impact of television from radio spending for all the propositions noted earlier also failed to detect spending effects across media markets. Using measures of spending that reflect absolute spending in a market, or absolute differentials between spending in favor and spending against, also failed to demonstrate spending effects at the individual level.

that these data have such serious problems of collinearity and limited variance that we need to take additional steps to interpret them. Following Kramer (1983), the objection might be raised that we can only see spending effects at an aggregate level and that the individual level is not the appropriate place to model such effects. It might also be noted that this election was peculiar because vast amounts of money were spent by industry. Even if that were the case, 1988 should be an outlier in a direction that is favorable to the "spending matters" hypothesis because so much was spent and so much spending was one-sided. If it is to be argued that this is an inappropriate case because so much money was spent, the argument must be tied to claims about how we expect spending effects to be felt if "too much" spending produces no results or counterintuitive results. At present, the literature offers limited guidance here.

A somewhat different response is to note that these aggregate findings and individual-level nonresults of spending have a substantive interpretation: spending matters, but the effect is complex and possibly indirect. Surely some voters decide directly on the basis of advertising (as noted in chapter 3, it might be a small group). If we can generalize from the opinion data examined here, spending on ads transmits a campaign's information, and it is possible that it mobilizes additional information in the form of claims countering the ads. This information might allow a broad group of voters to make decisions on the basis of their ideology.

We speculate that when media spending on an initiative is high, more people become aware of details about who is behind a measure, what the proponent's intentions are, and who will benefit from the measure. With Proposition 99, for example, many voters became aware of sensational television ads about the proposal. In one ad, opponents of the cigarette tax stated that murders would increase because law enforcement efforts would be redirected toward enforcing the tax and intercepting cigarette smugglers. The substance, credibility, and source of such claims became the subject of media coverage, providing additional cues about the initiative.

The sheer volume of such advertisements in big-spending contests is likely to increase the odds that the news media will run stories that mention the initiative, and it will increase the odds that elites will publicize their positions. If there are more (or any) stories, the chances increase that attention will be directed at the benefits associated with the proposal (in this case, public health spending), if it is not directed at the credibility of the ads. At a minimum, the volume of advertising might lead more voters to perceive that the initiative is important enough to vote on (if only to vote a defensive *no*), or it might cause voters to find out who is listed as a supporter or an opponent in the ballot pamphlet. With the additional information created by the context of a sensational, high-spending campaign, a less-educated voter might then make a decision about the specific proposal or about the opposition (in this case, the tobacco industry), and the voter might even see the issue in terms of ideology.

We are not so sanguine as to conclude that there is nothing to fear from heavy spending on media campaigns in direct democracy. Given the data presented here and in earlier research, however, we suggest that spending, while affecting opinions directly or indirectly, plays a fairly conservative role in direct democracy. Well-financed interests are typically unable to "buy" public policy via the initiative process. Spending by the *no* side can often protect the status quo, but it is difficult to spend in favor of a measure and win. If the *yes* side is relatively unopposed, then *yes* spending might matter on some rare occasions—if the Proposition 98 analysis presented earlier provides a basis for generalization.

Perhaps the most interesting finding here relates to the prospect that spending can facilitate broader cognitive reasoning in direct democracy. We suggest that campaign spending and contested campaigns have the potential for enhancing voter competence in direct democracy. If competence is defined as voting on the basis of a preexisting ideology or party attachment (or as being evident when the opinions of less-educated voters have a structure that is similar to those of the well educated), then our results can be interpreted as supporting the idea that campaign spending in direct democracy—even one-sided spending—can contribute to the voter's ability to reason on the basis of party and ideology.

CHAPTER 9

Conclusions about Voter Reasoning
in Direct Democracy

What do the findings in this book tell us about voters' ability to deal with the demanding choice context of direct democracy? What do our results say about how voters might reason when making decisions about propositions? We find that voters can and do think about and decide upon propositions in ways that make sense and in ways that take advantage of readily available information. Although our impression of direct-democracy voters might be more sanguine than those formed by previous scholars who have examined this arena, we do not intend to imply that the behavior we have examined reflects something approaching classical models of the ideal voter. The mass electorate engaged in direct democracy is not likely to be fully informed, nor do they deliberate long, nor do they always evaluate policy from an objective, public-regarding perspective, but many have an ability to respond to the steep information demands presented to them. They are likely to reason in ways that conserve cognitive resources, time, and energy, and they often vote on the basis of subjective, instrumental concerns.

More interesting, perhaps, is that many voters, particularly the well educated, decide across a wide range of issues on the basis of their partisan and ideological orientations. Moreover, we have identified instances when opinions of less-educated voters are also structured by these "cognitively broad" factors. With these basic findings in mind, we can draw two broad sets of substantive conclusions from the findings in this study. The first relate specifically to direct democracy, the second relate more generally to our understanding of voting behavior.

Implications for Our Understanding
of Direct Democracy

We should restate that at the outset, we sought to avoid evaluating the merits of direct democracy in terms of the actual policy outcomes that result from the process. We feel that for too long, scholars have dismissed voter competence in direct democracy in part because of some of the distasteful policies that this majoritarian system can occasionally produce. From this view, we are reduced to using logic that suggests that if a majority of voters reject a "good thing," it must be because they were duped, alienated, uninformed—or lacking some appropriate political ethos. The same assumption holds if the majority passes a "bad thing."

Many previous studies of proposition voting have simply been unable to separate normative evaluations of policy content from theoretical and empirical explanations of decision making. As some studies of legislative decision making have advanced our understanding of choice by examining behavior, rather than focusing on occasionally "inappropriate" policy outcomes (Kingdom 1989; Kozak 1987; Matthews and Stimson 1975), we have attempted to evaluate the process of choice through which the mass electorate produces policy outcomes in direct democracy. Rather than assess the fundamental desirability of direct democracy, we have attempted to examine how voters behave when making decisions. Just as studies of legislative decision making avoid wholesale condemnation of the legislative process on the basis of outcomes (and representative government), we avoid damning the process of direct democracy here on the basis of outcomes.

When, for example, legislatures produce antiminority policies or laws that, from a few years in retrospect, appear unwise (or unconstitutional), we rarely question the merits of representative democracy and the legislative process. We assume that the basic process of is sound, in part because we assume that most of the time, legislators are able to make decisions that are based on information (if only cues) and that their decisions are consistent with their preferences and interests as politicians representing their constituents (Miller and Stokes 1963). In part, some might also approach legislators with the "civics class" perspective that assumes they occasionally make decisions that set aside partisanship and ideology—indeed, populists such as Pat Buchanan and Ross Perot seek to gain favor by attacking Congress for its failure to live up to this expectation.

Thus, when the Tennessee state legislature approved a resolution on posting the Ten Commandments in public places and moved to fire teachers who taught evolution as fact in 1996, we were unlikely to see the blame placed upon the process of representative government. The fundamental process was not at issue when Utah's legislature risked losing hundreds of millions of federal aid dollars after voting to keep gay clubs out of its public schools that same year (after watching a political-religious group's antigay propaganda film in closed session that detailed homosexuals' "needs" to "recruit" through school since they could not reproduce). When the state legislature in Washington and several other states began approving legislation to ban the recognition of same-sex marriages that no one recognized (in anticipation of a possible Hawaii law, which if passed and ignored by Washington and other states could be a violation of the U.S. Constitution privileges and immunities clause), voter and legislator competence in representative democracy was not at issue. When popularly elected legislators pass policies that raise eyebrows, we simply do not accuse them of producing such policy stupidly or accidentally. Rather, we seek to understand the electoral, political, ideological, or moral motives for acting in such a way.

In sharp contrast, the process of direct democracy is critiqued for just that reason. Outcomes are questioned in terms of the process by which they are arrived at, and the process is condemned on the basis of bad outcomes. Direct democracy is also feared either for its raw majoritarian threat, for the stigmatization it might bring to groups, if not for its simple incapacity to articulate preferences in any meaningful way that produces outcomes that people actually wanted—let alone understood—when they voted on them. In addition to fears about its treatment of minorities, critics of direct democracy have long advanced a series of arguments that have depended, directly or indirectly, upon the supposed proclivity of voters to be uninformed, uncaring, and, most of all, unthinking. We hope that this book has, at least in part, alleviated some of the criticism and fears associated with these later concerns.

Yet we cannot deny that direct democracy can produce policies that are completely at odds with tolerance of minorities and on occasion produce egregious violations of minority rights. Contemporary examples include the spate of antigay initiatives appearing on state ballots in the 1990s (see, e.g., Donovan and Bowler 1998; Donovan, Wenzel, and Bowler 1996). Bruce Cain (1992, 274) also notes "that referendums and initiatives are essentially forms of at-large elections. As such, they tend to produce outcomes with a majoritarian skew." Cain described the emergence of a "New Populism" that, through the initiative process, expresses the frustrations of the white middle and working classes. The increased use of direct democracy to dictate (or limit) the budget authority of state legislatures "undercuts the power of representative mechanisms" (Cain 1992, 275) where minority groups have made substantial inroads since *Baker v Carr* and the Voting Rights Act of 1965.

Cain's perspective is particularly prescient when we consider two of the major California initiatives to appear since he wrote: the anti-immigrant Proposition 187 of 1994 and the anti-affirmative-action initiative filed as the California Civil Rights Initiative of 1996. Among other things, direct democracy can cause specific taxes to be levied for specific purposes, bypassing the process of legislative allocation of revenues. As Matsusaka (1995) demonstrates empirically, direct-democracy states use broad-based taxes less frequently, causing a decline in redistributive activity that might benefit the poor (see also Dwyer et al. 1994; Donovan and Bowler 1995).

We are not in a position to assess which process—representative or direct democracy—is more abusive of minorities and the poor. Obviously, each process can work against these groups. The point of this book is simply to demonstrate that, regardless of outcomes, the process of direct democracy is by no means a random, incoherent exercise in choice for voters. While not being fully informed, voters nevertheless make successful attempts to reason by "soft" criteria. In that they seek out available information (chapter 3) and vote on the basis of ideology, party, cues, and instrumental concerns, we might say that they exercise their choices fairly competently over a very wide range of different ballot propositions.

Many of these voters thus appear able to figure out what they are for and against in ways that make sense in terms of their underlying values and interests. Failing that, others appear to use a strategy of voting *no* when information is lacking or when worries about general state conditions are greatest. Just as legislators do, these voters make choices purposefully, using available information. We might infer, then, that outcomes in direct democracy—good or bad—represent the preferences of the voters. Just as legislators are, voters are prone to occasionally produce outcomes that are abhorrent on normative (or fiscal) grounds. Just as legislators do, we suggest they do so intentionally.

Much of this discussion begs a question, however, about whether cue taking works or does not work in terms of democratic theory. As noted in the introduction, the mass electorate cannot be expected to be as informed as legislators. Our direct-democracy voters admit they lack factual, detailed information about the ballot measures upon which they decide. We cannot suggest that the cues they find in ballot pamphlets, from parties, from their own self-interest, or from concerns about state conditions effectively emulate the information a legislator gets from lobbyists or a committee hearing. A citizenry making policy decisions on the basis of cues, shortcuts, and instrumental concerns is hardly the portrait of a well-informed, deliberative electorate familiar from many to the normative classical theorists.

Indeed, Bartels (1996) and Kuklinski and Hurley (1994) note that voting decisions structured by cues and shortcuts might fall far short from emulating the behavior of well-informed voters. The qualitative value of these shortcuts might be questionable. As Sniderman, Brody, and Tetlock (1991) demonstrated, well-educated and less-educated voters alike, using cues and shortcuts, often reason on the basis of feelings and dislikes rather than on the basis of a command of the facts associated with policies.

The implications of these and other studies is that when we identify direct-democracy voters responding to the elite cues found from intense campaigns (chapter 8) or in voter's pamphlets (chapter 3) or from parties (chapter 7), it might very well be the messenger that is important, not the content message. That being the case, when we suggest that voters deal with the demands of direct democracy by using cues and shortcuts, we must acknowledge that the reasoning we claim to demonstrate is, for the most part, crude compared to standards of deliberation found in classic democratic theory. As Kuklinski and Hurley (1994, 747) note, when cue taking is examined in a context that allows for much greater dissection of voter responsiveness to information, "affect apparently drove much of the cue-taking we identified." Karp (n.d.) found something very similar when evaluating voter responsiveness to then House Speaker Thomas Foley's appeal to vote against Washington state's 1991 term-limit initiative. Karp's models of opinions on the issue, drawing upon Zaller (1992, 1990) show that although Foley told voters they risked "losing clout" in Washington, D.C., if the tenure of their congressional delegation was limited, voters responded not to this argument, but on the basis of their feelings for Foley.

So voters might indeed figure out what they are for or against, but many probably do so on the basis of affect, feelings, and "visceral reactions" (Kuklinski and Hurley 1994, 747; Kuklinski et al. 1991) to the individuals or groups they use as cues. Yet we do not mean to suggest that the mass electorate's reasoning about voting in direct democracy is so crude as to be meaningless. Voters do figure out what they are for or against. They do so facing steep information demands, and they do so in way that might be seen as impressive as the reasoning process that structures choices in candidate races. Furthermore, not all decision making in direct democracy is purely affect driven. We have demonstrated that over certain types of initiatives (chapters 5 and 6), voters can and do employ instrumental concerns when making decisions. And where information shortcuts are used, Bartels (1996) notes that—while failing to produce behavior that perfectly emulates the a well-informed voter—shortcuts improve things when compared to voting on the basis of no information.

Thus, although many voters might not be well informed and most do not appear very interested in consuming the details of propositions, this does not mean that when looking at complicated ballot issues, they fail to decide in a manner consistent with their interests or ideology. Consider the example of a modestly complicated term-limit proposal. While the proposal might be initially appealing to many voters on the basis of their visceral feelings about "politicians," voters might not know which "bums" will be kicked out if they approve the measure, or for how long. They also might not know if members can return after sitting out for a period, how much their pensions will be cut, and so forth.

But if campaigns are active, they can know who is backing an initiative. This information can provide some voters with as much as they need to make a choice that is informed—at least indirectly—about consequences. If members of your party or key individuals you identify with are in favor of something, as a voter you might assume—credibly—that they are aware of the consequences and that their motives for promoting the initiative are centered upon their awareness of consequences. If you like them, you accept the cue. In the end, if campaigns provide cues and minimal amounts of information, outcomes can represent voter preferences.

One troubling implication of our view of voter behavior in direct democracy is that citizens with preferences for antiminority policies (not to mention racists, homophobes, nativists, etc.) might thus be equally competent in obtaining the minimal amounts of information they need to determine that a particular initiative is to their liking. They need only figure out who is backing it or who is opposing it (or who is targeted) and then decide on the basis of their evaluations of this information—or on their feelings about the group or individuals. Our model of the direct-democracy voter does not mean that "good" or "bad" things are inevitable from the process; it means only that the decisions and the outcomes resulting from the aggregation of voter decisions are purposeful. If only a minority of voters hold preferences for an antiminority policy, and elites are unified against the policy, then it probably will not pass. We illustrate this principle elsewhere in the case of antigay initiatives (Donovan and Bowler 1998). If a majority are in favor of such a policy, and a large number of elites are endorsing the policy (as with California's Proposition 187 and the California Civil Rights Initiative), then institutions of direct democracy should be effective in translating majority preferences into policy.

Implications for the Study of Voting Behavior in General

Since voters cast their ballots on issues in direct democracy, we suggest that, from some perspectives, the mass electorate's response to the decision context of direct democracy might actually look closer to ideals of democratic theory than voting in candidate contests. An "ideal" voter would be fully informed, or at the least would deliberate prospectively and make choices on the basis of issues of the day. Much of the voting literature (reviewed in chapter 2) suggests that "hard" issue voting of this sort is not the norm in candidate races (Carmines and Stimson 1980) and that voting on the basis of something other than "gut" issues that evoke visceral responses is often lacking in presidential elections. When found, issue voting might typically be retrospective rather than prospective, as voters opt for the cognitive simplicity of looking backward at performance rather than thinking forward about how some proposals might affect them in the future. A sophisticated voter, from the perspective of studies such as the *American Voter,* furthermore, is expected to vote on the basis of ideology or issues. Debate continues about the prospects for such behavior in the American electorate (Nie, Verba, and Petrocik 1976; Smith 1989, Sniderman, Brody, and Tetlock 1991; Popkin 1991; Page and Shapiro 1992).

Direct-democracy choices, however, are fundamentally decisions about issues. The context of choice, while associated with substantial information demands, is inherently and explicitly issue based. Elections to select candidates— particularly presidents—are fundamentally different, highlighting nonissue (or at least nonpolicy) factors such as a candidate's competence, honesty, integrity,

and so on. As such, voters decisions are shaped in no small part by these factors (Miller, Wattenberg, and Malanchuk 1986). We suggest that voters respond
to the decision context they face. The sense that the behavior of the American
electorate reflects only limited attention to issues might stem in part from the
heightened attention directed at candidate races that are by their nature less issue dominated than direct-democracy elections. By turning more attention to
direct democracy in the future, voting studies might discover a context that provides a rich opportunity for studies of issue voting in the mass public.

Candidate races, we suggest, often create a context that emphasizes personality over issue substance. When presented with choices about people who
will represent them or lead them, even in the context of a partisan election, voters may be less likely to reason on the basis of policy and more likely to think
about personality, since they are, after all, electing people as representatives.
When personalities are placed more in the background and become cues about
policies, rather than the central focus of the decision, and policies are in the
foreground as with ballot propositions, people can be expected to reason differently. In other words, candidate races might simply be the wrong place to
look for ready examples of instrumental policy voting, prospective voting, or
ideological reasoning about policies. When issues are placed in the foreground,
decisions could be shaped more by issue-based reasoning.

As we have demonstrated, people make decisions on these ballot issues on
the basis of elite and party and elite positions on issues (chapters 3 and 7), on
the basis of how proposals might affect themselves narrowly (chapters 5 and
8), and on the basis of how proposals affect their community generally (chapter 6). In a crude way, some might even be making decisions in terms of an (economic) analysis of the risk associated with changing status quo policies (chapter 4). Information used to assess issues (i.e., who supports what position, who's
behind what) are easily available in public pamphlets and often available from
campaigns. If a proposition is going to have substantial impact on groups in a
state, the odds are increased that an active campaign will be disseminating information about the issue and voters will then be able to decide on the basis of
issues, even if relying upon affect-driven cues.

Take, for example, the California initiative to tax cigarettes and raise dollars for health care (Proposition 99 of 1988). Tens of millions of dollars were
spent in a heavily one-sided campaign to defeat the measure. Information provided directly from the tobacco industry's campaign might not have been accurate (voters were told, for example, that the tax would lead to more murders
since police would be fighting cigarette smuggling). But as millions were spent,
the spending and the ads became such an event in themselves that voters could
learn—through editorial responses to the ads, through news reporters covering
the race, and other media attention—that the tobacco industry was the primary
group fighting the proposition (as opposed to law enforcement officials).

Knowing that, knowing something about the other side, and knowing how they feel about each group, we can expect that many voters were able to figure out how to vote for what they really wanted in terms of this policy. Still other voters, being smokers or lacking health care, could decide on instrumental concerns. As deceptive as any advertisements might have been, they are ultimately forced to focus on issues and give cues about issues since that is all that is essentially what is being contested.

Candidate races, on the other hand, are about people and issues simultaneously, with the fundamental choice centering upon a person who will fill an office. As Douglas Amy notes (1993, 55–67), American-style, winner-take-all plurality candidate races force contestants to centrist vote-maximizing positions (also Downs 1957). To win a broad base of support, candidates must often avoid issues in this context. Amy contrasts this context with proportional representation systems that allow electoral success without a plurality requirement, suggesting that under proportional representation, the electoral system will produce more emphasis on issues and policy and less on personality.

The point is that electoral contexts themselves might largely determine the possible factors that affect choices. Under the context of plurality elections, issues take a backseat in the campaign and hence perhaps in the voter's decision process. Candidates "avoid any meaningful engagement of the issues . . . [they] neglect policy issues in favor of creating a pleasing and appealing image of the candidate" (Amy 1993, 59). As empirical evidence of this contention, Amy cites Benjamin Page's examination of American presidential candidates' speeches. Page identified "extreme vagueness" as the most striking feature of candidate speech and noted that "speeches say virtually nothing about specific policy alternatives" (Page 1978, 153). Raymond's study (1987) of congressional campaign literature (mail pieces) also found that if issues were in fact mentioned, actual programs and policies were not mentioned. Further, if ever specifics were offered (and such was rarely the case), they were uniformly banal and noncontroversial. Joslyn's study (1987) of TV spots run by U.S. House and Senate candidates in 1984 produced similar results: half had no policy or ideological content, and only 16 percent provided information that would lead to an accurate assessment of the candidate's policy preferences.

Thus, in a presidential election, voters might learn, for example, that they are "better off than you were four years ago" or that it is "morning again in America." More likely, they will vote on the basis of party attachments and the stock of information and history associated with those attachments. But can it be said that retrospective voting on the basis of these themes, or voting on the basis of party identification, is a normatively better approximation of the democratic ideal than opposing a smoking regulations initiative on the basis of knowing that the tobacco industry was funding the proposal? Is voting in candidate races done in a normatively "better" fashion than voting to support or oppose an initiative due to instrumental, prospective evaluations about how the policy affects the voter?

Again, we are not in a position to make such comparisons effectively. We will suggest, in closing this book, that much could be said in defense of the direct-democracy voter. Just as proportional representation systems might be expected to produce more issue or ideological voting than winner-take-all plurality rules, direct democracy may also be a context that forces voters to think prospectively about specific issue proposals. Obviously, not all voters behave this way when evaluating all propositions. But when faced with explicit choices about issues, they find ways to make decisions on these issues that not only make sense, but also reflect "issue voting" more clearly than might be evident in candidate races. Considering much of what has been written in the past about a citizen's ability to deal with direct democracy, this finding might be a bit surprising. Considering the fundamental position of issues in the direct-democracy decision context, however, perhaps it should not be.

Appendix A: Coding of Variables on Private Interests and Voting Behavior

Coding

Independent variables for California data were coded as follows:

Age in years
Liberal, where 1 = liberal if self-described liberal, 0 = otherwise
Income as five categories, where 1 = lowest, 6 = highest
Home ownership as a dummy, where 1 = own, 0 = rent
Education a dummy, where 1 = college graduate, 0 = otherwise
Tax concerns, where 1 = respondent is "extremely concerned" about taxes
    as a California issue (California Poll question 14G), 0 = otherwise
Parental school-status indicators as dummies (created from California Poll
    question Q108), where 1 = lowest, 6 = highest

Independent variables for Colorado data were coded as follows:

Age as six categories, where 1 = youngest, 6 = oldest
Liberal, where 1 = liberal if self-described, 0 = otherwise
Income as six categories, where 1 = lowest, 6 = highest
Education as a dummy, where 1 = college graduate, 0 = otherwise
Tax concerns, where 1 = taxes given as response to the open-ended
    question, "What is the most important problem facing Colorado?" and
    0 = otherwise

Undecided Voters

Models in Tables 17, 18, and 19 were estimated with responses to questions drawn from the 9304 California Poll (1993). Models were estimated such that 1 = support for the proposal, 0 = opposition. This coding omits a nontrivial number of undecided voters. These models were also reestimated with "not sure" respondents included in the opposition category. The substantive results are not changed with the alternate estimation.

Wording of Questions for Table 17: School Vouchers

Unaided:

From what you have seen, read or heard about Proposition 174, are you inclined to vote *yes* or *no* on Proposition 174?

N	Label
136	Yes
323	No
79	Not Sure

Aided:

Proposition 174 is entitled, "Education. Vouchers." It permits conversion of public schools to independent voucher-redeeming schools. It also requires state-funded vouchers for children enrolled in qualifying private schools and restricts regulation of such schools. If you were voting today, would you vote *yes* or *no* on Proposition 174?

N	Label
182	Yes
421	No
105	Not Sure

Wording of Questions for Table 18: Tax Rule Changes

Unaided:

From what you have seen, read or heard about Proposition 170, are you inclined to vote *yes* or *no* on Proposition 170?

N	Label
48	Yes
84	No
133	Not Sure

Aided:

Proposition 170 is entitled "Property Taxes. Schools. Majority Vote." This measure would permit property taxes to exceed the 1 percent limit to pay for school construction bonds when approved by a simple majority, rather than the current two-thirds vote. If you were voting today, would you vote *yes* or *no* on Proposition 170?

N	Label
210	Yes
343	No
155	Not Sure

Wording of Questions for Table 19: Sales Tax

Unaided:

From what you have seen, read or heard about Proposition 172, are you inclined to vote *yes* or *no* on Proposition 172?

N	Label
77	Yes
88	No
58	Not Sure

Aided:

Proposition 172 is entitled, "Local Public Safety Protection and Improvement Act of 1993." It would make permanent a temporary half-cent sales tax increase enacted in 1991. It would provide a dedicated revenue source for public safety purposes such as police, sheriffs, fire, criminal prosecutions and corrections with moneys distributed to cities and counties. If approved, the tax would be collected in all counties. However, a county could receive revenues only if approved by the board of supervisors or by a majority of voters within the county. If you were voting today, would you vote *yes* or *no* on Proposition 172?

N	Label
188	Yes
123	No
70	Not Sure

References

Achen, C. 1975. "Mass Political Attitudes and the Survey Response." *American Political Science Review* 69:1218–31.

Agger, Robert, and Marshall Goldstein. 1971. *Who Will Rule the Schools: A Cultural Class Crisis.* Belmont, CA: Wadsworth.

Alexander, A., and G. Bass. 1974. *Schools, Taxes, and Voter Behavior: An Analysis of School District Property Tax Elections.* Santa Monica, CA: Rand Corporation.

Amy, Douglas. 1993. *Real Choices New Voices: The Case for Proportional Representation Elections in the United States.* New York: Columbia University Press.

Ansolabehere, S., and S. Iyengar. 1993. "Information and Electoral Attitudes: A Case of Judgment under Uncertainty." In S. Iyengar and W. McGuire, eds., *Explorations in Political Psychology.* Durham, NC: Duke University Press.

Archer, J. Clark, and David R. Reynolds. 1976. "Locational Logrolling and Citizen Support of Municipal Bonds: The Example of St. Louis." *Public Choice* 18:21–39.

Atkeson, Lonna, and Randal Partin. 1995. "Economic and Referendum Voting: A Comparison of Gubernatorial and Senate Elections." *American Political Science Review* 89:99–107.

Bain, H. M., and D. Hecock. 1957. *Ballot Position and Voter's Choice.* Westport, CT: Greenwood.

Baldassare, Mark. 1985. "The Suburban Movement to Limit Growth: Reasons for Support in Orange County." *Policy Studies Review* 4:613–25.

Baldassare, Mark. 1989. "Citizen Support for Regional Government in the New Suburbs." *Urban Affairs Quarterly* 24:460–69.

Balmer, Donald G. 1972. *State Election Services in Oregon.* Princeton, NJ: Citizens' Research Foundation.

Banducci, Susan. 1992. "Voter Confusion and Voter Rationality: The Use of Counter-Initiatives in the Direct-Democracy Process." Paper presented at the annual meeting of the American Political Science Association, Chicago, 29 Aug.–2 Sept.

Banducci, Susan. 1998. "Frequency and Use of Counter Propositions and Outcomes in Direct Democracy. In S. Bowler, T. Donovan, and C. Tolbert, eds., *Citizens as Legislators: Direct Democracy in the American States.* Columbus: Ohio State University Press.

Banducci, Susan, and Jeffrey Karp. 1994. "Campaigns, Information, and Public Support for Term Limits." Paper presented at the annual meeting of the Western Political Science Association, Albuquerque, NM, 10–12 March.

Barber, Benjamin. 1984. *Strong Democracy: Participatory Politics for a New Age.* Berkeley and Los Angeles: University of California Press.

Barnett, J. 1915. *The Operation of the Initiative and Referendum in Oregon.* New York: Macmillan.

Bartels, Larry. 1988. *Presidential Primaries and the Dynamics of Public Choice.* Princeton, NJ: Princeton University Press.

Bartels, Larry. 1996. "Uninformed Voters: Information Effects in Presidential Elections." *American Journal of Political Science* 40:194–230.

Beard, Charles, and Birl E. Schultz. 1912. *Documents on the State-wide Initiative, Referendum and Recall.* New York: Macmillan.

Beck, Paul Allen, and Frank J. Sorauf. 1992. *Party Politics in America.* 7th ed. New York: HarperCollins.

Bell, Charles, and Charles Price. 1984. *California Government: The Politics of Reform.* Homewood, IL: Dorsey Press.

Bell, Derrick Jr. 1978. "The Referendum: Democracy's Barrier to Racial Equality." *Washington Law Review* 54:1–29.

Benedict, Robert. 1975. "Some Aspects of the Direct Legislation Process in Washington State: Theory and Practice." Ph.D. diss., University of Washington.

Benedict, Robert, Hugh Bone, Willard Leavel, and Ross Rice. 1980. "The Voters and Attitudes toward Nuclear Power: A Comparative Study of 'Nuclear Moratorium' Initiatives." *Western Political Quarterly* 33:7–23.

Benjamin, Gerald, and Michael Malbin. 1992. *Limiting Legislative Terms.* Washington, DC: Congressional Quarterly Press.

Bennett, W. Lance. 1980. *Public Opinion in American Politics.* New York: Harcourt Brace Jovanovich.

Berelson, Bernard. 1952. "Democratic Theory and Public Opinion." *Public Opinion Quarterly* 16:313–30.

Berelson, Bernard, Paul Lazarsfeld, and William McPhee. 1954. *Voting.* Chicago: University of Chicago Press.

Blair, G. S. 1967. *American Legislatures: Structure and Process.* New York: Harper and Row.

Bogart, L. 1957. "Opinion Research and Marketing." *Public Opinion Quarterly* 21, no. 1: 129–40.

Boix, C., and J. Alt. 1991. "Partisan Voting in the Spanish 1986 NATO Referendum." *Electoral Studies* 10:18–32.

Bollens, Scott A. 1990. "Constituencies for Limitation and Regionalism: Approaches to Growth Management." *Urban Affairs Quarterly* 26:46–67.

Bone, Hugh. 1974. *The Initiative in Washington: 1914–1974.* Washington Public Policy Notes, vol. 2. Seattle: Institute of Governmental Research, University of Washington.

Bone, Hugh, and Robert Benedict. 1975. "Perspectives on Direct Legislation." *Western Political Quarterly* 28:330–51.

Boskoff, Alvin, and Harmon Zeigler. 1964. *Voting Patterns in a Local Election.* New York: J. B. Lippincott.

Bowler, Shaun, and Todd Donovan. 1994a. "Opinion Change on Ballot Propositions." *Political Behavior* 16:411–35.

Bowler, Shaun, and Todd Donovan. 1994b. "Is Direct Democracy Good for Public Budgets? The Constitution of State Indebtedness." Paper presented at the annual meeting of the Western Political Science Association Albuquerque, NM, 10–12 March.

Bowler, Shaun, and Todd Donovan. 1995. "Popular Responsiveness to Taxation." *Political Research Quarterly* 48:79–100.

Bowler, Shaun, Todd Donovan, Dave Broughton, and Joe Snipp. 1992. "The Informed Electorate? Voter Responsiveness to Campaigns in Britain and Germany." In Shaun Bowler and David Farrell, eds., *Electoral Strategies and Political Marketing*. New York: St. Martin's.

Bowler, Shaun, Todd Donovan, and Trudy Happ. 1992. "Ballot Propositions and Information Costs: Direct Democracy and the Fatigued Voter." *Western Political Quarterly* 45:599–68.

Bowler, Shaun, Todd Donovan, and Joe Snipp. 1993. "Local Sources of Information and Voter Choice in State Elections." *American Politics Quarterly* 21:473–89.

Bowler, Shaun, Todd Donovan, and Caroline Tolbert. 1998. *Citizens as Legislators: Direct Democracy in the American States*. Columbus: Ohio State University Press.

Brady, Henry, and Stephen Ansolabehere. 1989. "The Nature of Utility Functions in Mass Publics." *American Political Science Review* 83:142–63.

Broadcasting Yearbook. 1988. Washington, DC: Broadcasting Publications.

Butler, David, and Austen Ranney. 1978. *Referendums: A Comparative Study of Practice and Theory*. Washington, DC: American Enterprise Institute Press.

Butler, David, and Austen Ranney. 1994. *Referendums around the World: The Growing Use of Direct Democracy*. Washington, DC: American Enterprise Institute Press.

Butler, David, and Uwe Kitzinger. 1976. *The 1975 Referendum*. New York: St. Martin's.

Button, James W. 1992. "A Sign of Generational Conflict: The Impact of Florida's Aging Voters on Local School and Tax Referenda." *Social Science Quarterly* 73: 786–97.

Cain, Bruce. 1992. "Voting Rights and Democratic Theory: Toward a Color-Blind Society." In Bernard Grofman and Chandler Davidson, eds., *Controversies in Minority Voting: The Voting Rights Act in Perspective*. Washington, DC: Brookings Institution.

California Assembly. 1992. California Commission on Campaign Financing. *Democracy by Initiative*. Los Angeles.

California Assembly. 1972. Committee on Elections and Reapportionment. *Public Hearings on the Initiative Process*, October. Los Angeles.

California Green Book. 1990. Sacramento, CA: Dutra Communications.

California Yearbook. 1988. La Verne, CA: California Almanac Co.

Campbell, Angus. 1960. "Surge and Decline: A Study in Electoral Change." *Public Opinion Quarterly* 24:397–418.

Campbell, Angus, Phillip Converse, Warren Miller, and Donald Stokes. 1960. *The American Voter*. New York: John Wiley and Sons.

Campbell, Henry. 1911. "The Initiative and Referendum." *Michigan Law Review* 10, no 6: 427–36.

Carmines, Edward, and James Stimson. 1980. "The Two Faces of Issue Voting." *American Political Science Review* 74:78–91.

Chappel, Henry, and William Keech. 1990. "Citizen Information, Rationality and the Politics of Macroeconomic Policy." In John Ferejohn and James Kuklinski, eds., *Information and Democratic Processes*. Urbana: University of Illinois Press.

Chubb, John. 1988. "Institutions, the Economy and the Dynamics of State Elections." *American Political Science Review* 82:133–52.

Citrin, Jack. 1979. "Do People Want Something for Nothing? Public Opinion on Taxes and Spending." *National Tax Journal* 32:113–29.

Citrin, Jack, and Donald Phillip Green. 1990. "The Self-Interest Motive in American Public Opinion." *Research in Micropolitics* 3:1–28.

Clarke, Harold, and Alan Kornberg. 1994. "The Politics and Economics of Constitutional Choice: Voting in Canada's 1992 National Referenda." *Journal of Politics* 56:940–62.

Clingermayer, James, and B. Dan Wood. 1995. "Disentangling Patterns of State Debt Financing." *American Political Science Review* 89:108–20.

Cobb, John. 1911. *The Salmon Fisheries of the Pacific Coast.* A special report prepared for the Bureau of Fisheries, Department of Commerce and Labor. Washington, DC: GPO.

Converse, Philip. 1962. "Information Flow and the Stability of Partisan Attitudes." *Public Opinion Quarterly* 26:578–99.

Converse, Philip. 1964. "The Nature of Belief Systems in Mass Publics." In D. Apter, ed., *Ideology and Discontent.* New York: Free Press.

Converse, Philip, Warren Miller, Jerrold Rusk, and Arthur Wolfe. 1969. "Continuity and Change in American Politics: Parties and Issues in the 1968 Election." *American Political Science Review* 63:1083–1105.

Cottrell, Edwin. 1939. "Twenty Five Years of Direct Legislation in California." *Public Opinion Quarterly* (January): 30–45.

Croly, Herbert. 1912. "State Political Reorganization." In *Proceedings of the 8th Annual American Political Science Association.* February. Washington, DC: APSA.

Cronin, Thomas. 1989. *Direct Democracy: The Politics of Initiative, Referendum and Recall.* Cambridge: Harvard University Press.

Crouch, Winston. 1943. *The Initiative and Referendum in California.* Los Angeles, CA: Haynes Foundation.

Cushman, Robert. 1916. "Recent Experience with the Initiative and Referendum." *American Political Science Review* 10 (August): 532–39.

Dahl, Robert. 1956. *A Preface to Democratic Theory.* Chicago: University of Chicago Press.

Darcy, Robert, and C. Hadley. 1988. "Black Women in Politics: The Puzzle of Success." *Social Science Quarterly* 69:629–45.

Darcy, Robert, and Michael Marsh. 1990. "Ballot Position Effects." *Electoral Studies* 9:5–17.

Dawes, Robyn. 1966. "Memory and Distortion of Meaningful Written Material. *British Journal of Psychology.* 57:77–86.

Dolbare, Kenneth, and Janette Hubbell. 1996. *USA 2012: After the Middle-Class Revolution.* Chatham, NJ: Chatham House.

Donovan, Todd. 1993. "Social and Political Basis of Support for Term Limitation Initiatives in California and Washington." Paper presented at the annual meeting of the Western Political Science Association, Pasadena, Calif., 23–25 March.

Donovan, Todd, and Shaun Bowler. 1995. "State Parties and Direct Democracy: The Distribution of State Tax Burdens." Paper presented at the annual meeting of the Pacific Northwest Political Science Association, Bellingham, WA, 16–18 Oct.

Donovan, Todd, and Shaun Bowler. 1997. "Direct Democracy and Minorities: Opinions on Anti-Gay Initiatives." In S. Witt and S. McCorkel, eds. *Assessing Anti-Gay Voter Initiatives.* Westport, CT: Praeger.

Donovan, Todd, and Joe Snipp. 1994. "Support for Legislative Term Limitations in California: Group Representation, Partisanship and Campaign Information." *Journal of Politics* 56:492–501.

Donovan, Todd, James Wenzel, and Shaun Bowler. 1996. "Changes in Public Attitudes about Minorities Targeted by Ballot Initiatives." Paper presented at the Western Political Science Association meeting, San Francisco, 25–27 March.

Downs, Anthony. 1957. *An Economic Theory of Democracy.* New York: Harper and Row.

Dreyer, Edward. 1971. "Media Use and Electoral Choices: Some Consequences of Information Exposure." *Public Opinion Quarterly* 35:533–44.

Dubois, Philip, and Floyd Feeney. 1991. "Improving the California Initiative Process: Options for Change." Berkeley: California Policy Seminar.

Dubois, Philip, Floyd Feeney, and Edmond Costantini. 1991. *The California Ballot Pamphlet: A Survey of Voters.* Report Prepared for the Office of the Secretary of State of California, March.

Durand, Roger. 1972. "Ethnicity, 'Public Regardingness' and Referenda Voting." *Midwest Journal of Political Science* 16:259–68.

Dwyer, Diane, Michael O'Gorman, John Stonecash, and Robert Young. 1994. "Disorganized Politics and the Have Nots: Politics and Taxes in New York and California." *Polity* 27:25–47.

Eaton, Allen. 1912. *The Oregon System: The Story of Direct Legislation in Oregon.* Chicago: McClurg and Co.

"Government in California: Buckling under the Strain." 1993. *Economist* 326 (Feb. 13): 21–23.

Enelow, James, and Melvyn Hinich. 1984. *The Spatial Theory of Voting: An Introduction.* Cambridge: Cambridge University Press.

Everson, David. 1981. "The Effects of Initiatives on Voter Turnout: A Comparative State Analysis." *Western Political Quarterly* 34:415–25.

Fenno, Richard Jr. 1973. *Congressmen in Committees.* New York: Little and Brown Co.

Ferejohn, John. 1990. "Information and the Electoral Process." In John Ferejohn and James Kuklinski, eds., *Information and Democratic Processes.* Urbana: University of Illinois Press.

Ferejohn, John, and James Kuklinski. 1990. *Information and Democratic Processes.* Urbana: University of Illinois Press.

Fett, Patrick, and Daniel Ponder. 1993. "Congressional Term Limits, State Legislative Term Limits and Congressional Turnover." *PS: Political Science and Politics* 26:211–16.

Fiorina, Morris. 1981. *Retrospective Voting in American National Elections.* New Haven, CT: Yale University Press.

Fiorina, Morris. 1992. *Divided Government.* New York: Macmillan.

Flanigan, William H., and Nancy Zingale. 1994. *Political Behavior of the American Electorate.* 7th ed. Washington, DC: Congressional Quarterly Press.

Fountaine, Lisa. 1988. "Lousy Lawmaking: Questioning the Desirability and Constitutionality of Legislating by Initiative." *Southern California Law Review* 61:733–76.

Franklin, Jimmie. 1971. *Born Sober: Prohibition in Oklahoma, 1907–1959.* Norman: Oklahoma University Press.

Gamson, William. 1961. "The Fluoridation Dialogue." *Public Opinion Quarterly* 25:526–37.

Gardner, C. 1911. "The Workings of the State Wide Referendum in Illinois." *American Political Science Review* 3:394–417.

Gerber, Elizabeth. 1996. "Legislative Responsiveness to the Threat of Popular Initiatives." *American Journal of Political Science* 40:99–128.

Gerber, Elizabeth. 1998. "The Effects of Initiatives on Legislative Behavior and Policy." In Shaun Bowler, Todd Donovan, and Caroline Tolbert, eds., *Citizens as Legislators: Direct Democracy in the American States.* Columbus: Ohio State University Press.

Gerber, Elizabeth, and Arthur Lupia. 1995. "Campaign Competition and Policy Responsiveness in Direct Legislation Elections." *Political Behavior* 17:287–306.

Gilbert, J. 1916. "The Single Tax Movement in Oregon." *Political Science Quarterly* 6:25–52.

Giles, Micheal, Douglas Gatlin, and Everett Cataldo. 1976. "Parental Support of School Referenda." *Journal of Politics* 38:442–51.

Gold, David. 1962. "Independent causation in Multivariate Analysis: The Case of Political Alienation and Attitudes toward School Bond issues." *American Sociological Review* 27:85–87.

Gottinder, Mark, and Max Neiman. 1981. "Characteristics of Support for Local Growth Controls." *Urban Affairs Quarterly* 17:55–73.

Granberg, Donald, and Sören Holmberg. 1986. "Preference, Expectations and Voting in Sweden's Referendum on Nuclear Power." *Social Science Quarterly* 50:379–92.

Granberg, Donald, and Sören Holmberg. 1990. "The Berelson Paradox Reconsidered." *Public Opinion Quarterly* 54:530–50.

Green, D. P., and J. A. Cowden. 1992. "Who Protests: Self-Interest and White Opposition to Busing." *Journal of Politics* 54:471–96.

Green, D. P., and A. E. Gerken. 1989. "Self-Interest and Public Opinion toward Smoking Restrictions and Cigarette Taxes." *Public Opinion Quarterly* 53:1–16.

Guerra, Fernando. 1991. "Term Limits and Minority Representation in California." Paper presented at the annual meeting of the American Political Science Association, Washington, D.C., 30 Aug.–2 Sept.

Hadwiger, David. 1992. "Money, Turnout and Ballot Measure Success in California Cities." *Western Political Quarterly* 45:539–47.

Hahn, Harlan. 1968. "Northern Referenda on Fair Housing: The Response of White Voters." *Western Political Quarterly* 21:483–96.

Hahn, Harlan. 1970. "Correlates of Public Sentiments about War: Local Referenda on the Vietnam Issue." *American Political Science Review* 64:1186–99.

Hahn, Harlan, and Timothy Almy. 1971. "Ethnic Politics and Racial Issues: Voting in Los Angeles." *Western Political Quarterly* 29:440–57.

Hahn, Harlan, and Sheldon Kamieniecki. 1987. *Referenda Voting: Social Status and Policy Preferences.* New York: Greenwood Press.

Hall, John Stuart, and Philip K. Piele. 1976. "Selected Determinants of Precinct Voting Decisions in School Budget Elections." *Western Political Quarterly* 29:440–56.

Hamilton, Howard. 1970a. "Direct Legislation: Some Implications of Open Housing Referenda." *American Political Science Review* 64:124–37.

Hamilton, Howard. 1970b. "Voting Behavior in Open Housing Referenda." *Social Science Quarterly* 51:715–29.

Hamilton, Howard, and Sylvan Cohen. 1974. *Policymaking by Plebiscite: School Referenda.* Lexington, MA: Lexington Books.

Harrop, Martin, and William Miller. 1987. *Elections and Voters: A Comparative Introduction.* New York: New Amsterdam Books.

Haynes, George. 1907. "The Education of Voters." *Political Science Quarterly* 22: 484–97.

Haynes, George. 1913. "Peoples Rule on Trial." *Political Science Quarterly* 28:18–33.

Hendrick, B. J. 1911. *McClure's.*

Hensler, Deborah, and Carl Hensler. 1979. *Evaluating Nuclear Power: Voter Choice on the California Nuclear Initiative.* Santa Monica, CA: Rand Corporation.

Hey, John. 1981. "Are Optimal Search Rules Reasonable? And Vice Versa? (And Does It Matter Anyway?)" *Journal of Economic Behavior and Organization* 2:47–70.

Hey, John. 1982. "Search for Rules of Search." *Journal of Economic Behavior and Organization* 3:65–82.

Hey, John. 1993. "Testing Search Theory." *Manchester School* 61, no. 1: 82–93.

Hicks, Robert. 1972. "Influences on School Referenda in Ohio: Factors Affecting the Voting on Taxes and Bond Issues." *American Journal of Economics and Sociology* 31:105–8.

Holbrook, Thomas. 1991. "Presidential Elections in Time and Space." *American Journal of Political Science* 35:91–109.

Horton, J., and W. Thompson. 1962. "Powerlessness and Political Negativism." *American Journal of Sociology* 67:485–93.

Howe, Frederic. [1904] 1967. *The City; The Hope of Democracy.* Seattle: University of Washington Press.

Howell, Susan, and James Vanderleeuw. 1990. "Economic Effects on State Governors." *American Politics Quarterly* 18:158–68.

Ippolito, Dennis S., and Martin L. Levin. 1970. "Public Regardingness, Race and Social Class: The Case of a Rapid Transit Referendum." *Social Science Quarterly* 51:628–33.

Jackson, John. 1979. "Statistical Estimation of Possible Response Bias in Close Ended Issue Questions." *Political Methodology* 6:393–424.

Jacobson, Gary. 1975. "The Impact of Broadcast Campaigning on Electoral Outcomes." *Journal of Politics* 37:769–95.

Jacoby, William G. 1994. "Public Attitudes toward Government Spending." *American Journal of Political Science* 38:336–61.

Jennings, Robert, and Mike Milstein. 1973. "Citizen's Attitudes in School Tax Voting." *Education and Urban Society* 5:299–319.

Jervis, Robert. 1993. "The Drunkard's Search." In Shanto Iyengar and Mark McGuire, eds., *Explorations in Political Psychology.* Durham, NC: Duke University Press.

Jewell, Malcolm. 1982. *Representation in State Legislatures.* Lexington: University Press of Kentucky.

Johnston, Richard. 1993. "An Inverted Logroll: The Charlottetown Accord and the Referendum." *PS: Political Science and Politics* 26:43–48.

Joslyn, Richard. 1987. "Liberal Campaign Rhetoric in 1984." In Jan Pons Vermeer, ed. *Campaigns in the News.* New York: Greenwood.

Kahneman, D., and A. Tversky. 1984. "Choices, Values and Frames." *American Psychologist* 39:341–50.

Karp, Jeffrey. 1994. "Political Awareness, Elite Leadership and Mass Opinion in Initiative Campaigns: The Case of Term Limitations in Washington State." Paper presented at the annual meeting of the Pacific Northwest Political Science Association, Portland, OR, 13–15 Oct.

Karp, Jeffrey. 1995. "Explaining Public Support for Term Limits." *Public Opinion Quarterly* 59:373–91.

Karp, Jeffrey. 1996. "Voting on Term Limit Initiatives: A Rational Act or a Symbolic Protest?" Paper delivered at the annual meeting of the Western Political Science Association, San Francisco, 14–16 March.

Karp, Jeffrey. 1998. "The Influence of Elite Endorsements in Initiative Campaigns." In Shaun Bowler, Todd Donovan, and Caroline Tolbert, eds. *Citizens as Legislators: Direct Democracy in the American States.* Columbus: Ohio State University Press.

Kelley, S. 1956. *Professional Public Relations and Political Power.* Baltimore: Johns Hopkins University Press.

Key, V. O. 1936. "Publicity of Campaign Expenditures on Issues in California." *American Political Science Review* 4:713–23.

Key, V. O. 1959. "Secular Realignment and the Party System." *Journal of Politics* 21:198–210.

Key, V. O. 1966. *The Responsible Electorate.* Cambridge: Harvard University Press.

Key, V. O., and Winston Crouch. 1939. *The Initiative and the Referendum in California.* Berkeley and Los Angeles: University of California Press.

Kiewiet, D. Roderick. 1981. "Policy Oriented Voting in Response to Economic Issues." *American Political Science Review* 75:448–59.

Kiewiet, D. Roderick. 1983. *Macroeconomics and Micropolitics.* Chicago: University of Chicago Press.

Kiewiet, D. Roderick, and Douglas Rivers. 1984. "A Retrospective on Retrospective Voting." *Political Behavior* 6:369–93.

Kinder, Donald R., Gordon Adams, and P. Gronke. 1989. "Economics and Politics in the 1984 American Presidential Election." *American Journal of Political Science* 33:419–515.

Kinder, Donald, and D. Roderick Kiewiet. 1981. "Sociotropic Politics." *British Journal of Political Science* 11:129–61.

Kingdon, John W. 1989. *Congressmen's Voting Decisions.* 3d ed. Ann Arbor: University of Michigan Press.

Kozak, David C. 1987. "Decision Settings in Congress." In D. Kozak and J. Macartney, eds., *Congress and Public Policy.* Chicago: Dorsey Press.

Kramer, G. 1971. "Short-term Fluctuations in U.S. Voting Behavior: 1896–1964." *American Political Science Review* 65:131–43.

Kramer, G. 1983. "The Ecological Fallacy Revisited: Aggregate versus Individual Level Findings on Economics and Elections and Socio-tropic Voting." *American Political Science Review* 77:92–111.

Kuklinski, James H., and Norman Hurley. 1994. "On Hearing and Interpreting Political Messages: A Cautionary Tale of Citizen Cue-Taking." *Journal of Politics* 56:729–51.

Kuklinski, James H., Daniel Metlay, and W. D. Kay. 1982. "Citizen Knowledge and Choices on the Complex Issue of Nuclear Energy." *American Journal of Political Science* 26:615–42.

Kuklinski, James H., Ellen Riggle, Victor Ottati, Norbert Schwartz, and Robert Wyer Jr. 1991. "Cognitive and Affective Bases of Political Tolerance Judgments." *American Journal of Political Science* 35:1–27.

LaPalombara, Joseph. 1950. *The Initiative and Referendum in Oregon, 1938–1948.* Corvallis: Oregon State College Press.

Lau, Richard. 1982. "Negativity in Political Perceptions." *Political Behavior* 4:353–78.

Lau, Richard. 1985. "Two Explanations for Negativity Effects in Political Behavior." *American Journal of Political Science* 29:119–38.

Lau, Richard, T. A. Brown, and D. O. Sears. 1978. "Self-Interest and Civilian's Attitudes toward the Vietnam War." *Public Opinion Quarterly* 42:464–83.

Lawrence, David. 1995. *California: The Politics of Diversity.* Minneapolis: West Publishing.

Lazarsfeld, Paul, Bertram Berelson, and Hazel Gaudet. 1944. *The People's Choice.* New York: Duell, Sloan and Pearce.

LeDuc, Lawrence. 1993. "Canada's Constitutional Referendum of 1992: A Great Big NO." *Electoral Studies* 12:257–63.

Lee, Eugene C. 1978. "California." In David Butler and Austen Ranney, eds., *Referendums: A Comparative Study.* Washington, DC: American Enterprise Institute Press.

Lee, Eugene C. 1989. "Power to the People? A Scholar of Government Looks at the Initiative System." *Government Finance Review* (October): 26–27.

Levine, Steven, and Nigel Roberts. 1994. "The New Zealand Electoral Referendum of 1993." *Electoral Studies* 12:138–67.

Lewis-Beck, Michael. 1988. *Economics and Elections: The Major Western Democracies.* Ann Arbor: University of Michigan Press.

Lindblom, Charles. 1959. "The Science of Muddling Through." *Public Administration Review* 19:79–88.

Lippmann, Walter. 1922. *Public Opinion.* New York: Basic Books.

Lippmann, Walter. 1925. *The Phantom Public.* New York: Macmillan.

Locke, L. A. 1993. "The Voucher Initiative: Breakthrough or Break-up for California Schools." *California Journal* 24 (October): 8–14.

Lockley, L. 1950. "Notes on the History of Marketing." *Research Journal of Marketing* 16:733–36.

Lowenstein, Daniel. 1982. "Campaign Spending and Ballot Propositions: Recent Experience, Public Choice and the First Amendment. *UCLA Law Review* 29: 505–641.

Lowenstein, Daniel. 1983. "California and the Single-Subject Rule." *UCLA Law Review* 30:936–75.

Lowenstein, Daniel. 1995. *Election Law: Cases and Materials.* Durham, NC: Carolina Academic Press.

Lowenstein, Daniel, and Robert Stern. 1989. "The First Amendment and Paid Initiative Petition Circulators: A Dissenting View and a Proposal." *Hastings Constitutional Law Quarterly* 17:175–224.

Lowery, David, and Lee Sigelman. 1981. "Understanding the Tax Revolt: Eight Explanations." *American Political Science Review* 75:963–74.

Lowrie, S. Gale. 1911. "New Forms of Initiative and Referendum." *American Political Science Review* 5 (August):566–72.

Lupia, Arthur. 1992. "Busy Voters, Agenda Control, and the Power of Information." *American Political Science Review* 86:390–403.

Lupia, Arthur. 1994a. "Shortcuts Versus Encyclopedias: Information and Voting Behavior in California Insurance Reform Elections." *American Political Science Review* 88:63–76.

Lupia, Arthur. 1994b. "The Effect of Information on Voting Behavior and Electoral Outcomes: An Experimental Study of Direct Legislation." *Public Choice* 78:65–86.

Luskin, Robert. 1987. "Measuring Political Sophistication." *American Journal of Political Science* 31:856–99.

Lutrin, Carl, and Allen Settle. 1975. "The Public and Ecology: The Role of Initiatives in California's Environmental Policies." *Western Political Quarterly* 28:352–71.

Magleby, David B. 1984. *Direct Legislation: Voting on Ballot Propositions in the United States.* Baltimore: Johns Hopkins University Press.

Magleby, David B. 1989. "Opinion Formation and Opinion Change in Ballot Proposition Campaigns." In M. Margolis and G. A. Mauser, eds., *Manipulating Public Opinion.* Pacific Grove, CA: Brooks/Cole.

Magleby, David B. 1994a. "Direct Legislation in the American States." In *Referendums Around the World: The Growing use of Democracy?* (eds.) David Butler and Austin Ranney. Washington, DC: AEI Press.

Magleby, David B. 1994b. "Campaign Spending and Referendum Voting." Paper presented at the annual meeting of the Western Political Science Association, Albuquerque, NM, 10–12 March.

Magleby, David B., and Kelly D. Patterson. 1996. "Political Knowledge and Term Limits: Can Angry Citizens be Educated." Paper presented at the annual meeting of the Western Political Science Association, San Francisco, 14–16 March.

Maisel, L. Sandy. 1981. "Congressional Information Sources." In J. Cooper and G. C. Mackenzie, eds., *The House at Work.* Austin: University of Texas Press.

Marando, V. 1972. "Life Style Distances and Suburban Support for Urban Political Integration." *Social Science Quarterly* 53:155–60.

Markus, Gregory. 1988. "The Impact of Personal and National Economic Conditions on the Presidential Vote: A Pooled Crosssectional Analysis." *American Journal of Political Science* 23:137–54.

Mason, Thomas. 1994. *Governing Oregon: An Inside Look at Politics in One American State.* Dubuque, IA: Kendal Hunt.

Matasuka, John G. 1995. "Fiscal Effects of the Voter Initiative: Evidence from the Last 30 Years." *Journal of Political Economy* 103:587–623.

Matthews, Donald R., and James Stimson. 1975. *Yeas and Neas: Normal Decision-Making in the U.S. House of Representatives.* New York: Wiley and Sons.

Mayhew, David. 1974. *Congress: The Electoral Connection.* New Haven, CT: Yale University Press.

McDill, Edward, and Jeanne Ridley. 1962. "Status, Anomie, Political Alienation, and Political Participation." *American Journal of Sociology* 68:176–87.

McKelvey, Richard D., and Peter C. Ordeshook. 1985. "Information, Electoral Equilibria and the Democratic Ideal." *Journal of Politics* 48:909–512.

McWilliams, C. 1951. "Government by Whitaker and Baxter." *Nation,* 14 and 21 April, 5 May.

Mill, John Stuart. [1859] 1947. *On Liberty.* New York: Appleton Century Crofts.

Miller, Warren, and Donald Stokes. 1963. "Constituency Influence in Congress." *American Political Science Review* 57:45–56.

Miller, Arthur H., Martin P. Wattenberg, and Oksana Malanchuk. 1986. "Schematic Assessments of Presidential Candidates." *American Political Science Review* 80(2): 521–40.

Minar, David. 1966. "Community Basis of Conflict in School System Politics." *American Sociological Review* 31:822–35.

Moncreif, Gary F., and Joel A. Thompson. 1991. "The Term Limitation Movement: Assessing the Consequences for Female (and Other) State Legislators." Paper delivered at the annual meeting of the Western Political Science Association, Seattle, 23–25 March.

Moncreif, Gary F., Joel A. Thompson, Michael Haddon, and Robert Hoyer. 1992. "For Whom the Bell Tolls: Term Limits and State Legislatures." *Legislative Studies Quarterly* 17 (February): 37–47.

Mondak, Jeff. 1995. "Elections as Filters: Term Limits and the Composition of the U.S. House." *Political Research Quarterly* 48:701–27.

Morgan, David, and Kenneth J. Meier. 1980. "Politics and Morality: The Effect of Religion on Referenda Voting." *Social Science Quarterly* 61(1): 144–48.

Mueller, Dennis. 1989. *Public Choice II.* Cambridge: Cambridge University Press.

Mueller, John E. 1965. *Reason and Caprice: Ballot Patterns in California.* Ph.D. diss., University of California at Los Angeles.

Mueller, John E. 1969. "Voting on the Propositions: Ballot Patterns and Historical Trends in California." *American Political Science Review* 63:1197–1212.

Neal, Tommy. 1993. "The Voter Initiative." National Conference of State Legislatures, *Legisbrief* 1(38). Denver.

Neiman, Max, and Ronald Loveridge. 1981. "Environmentalism and Local Growth Control: A Probe into the Class Bias Thesis." *Environment and Behavior* 13. 759–72.

Neiman, Max, and Gerry Riposa. 1986. "Tax Rebels and Tax Rebellion." *Western Political Quarterly* 39:435–45.

Nie, N., S. Verba, and J. Petrocik. 1976. *The Changing American Voter.* Cambridge: Harvard University Press.

Nordhaus, W. 1975. "The Political Business Cycle." *Review of Economic Studies* 42:169–90.

Oleszek, Walter. 1989. *Congressional Procedures and the Policy Process.* Washington, DC: Congressional Quarterly Press.

Olson, David J. 1992. "Term Limits Fail in Washington: The 1991 Battleground." In G. Benjamin and M. Malbin, eds. *Limiting Legislative Terms*. Washington, DC: Congressional Quarterly Press.

Oregon Voter's Pamphlet. 1908. Oregon Secretary of State. Salem, OR.

Ostrum, Charles. 1990. *Time Series Analysis: Regression Techniques*. Newbury Park, CA: Sage.

Owens, John R., and Larry L. Wade. 1986. "Campaign Spending on California Ballot Propositions, Trends and Effects, 1924–1984." *Western Political Quarterly* 39:675–89.

Page, Benjamin I. 1978. *Choices and Echoes in Presidential Elections: Rational Man and Electoral Democracy*. Chicago: University of Chicago Press.

Page, Benjamin I., and Richard Brody. 1972. "Policy Voting and the Electoral Process." *American Political Science Review* 66:979–95.

Page, Benjamin I., and Robert Y. Shapiro. 1992. *The Rational Public: Fifty Years of Trend in American's Policy Preferences*. Chicago: University of Chicago Press.

Partin, Randal. 1995. "Economic Conditions and Gubernatorial Elections: Is the State Executive Held Accountable?" *American Politics Quarterly* 23:81–95.

Patterson, Samuel, Ronald Hedlund, and G. R. Boynton. 1975. *Representatives and Represented*. New York: Wiley and Sons.

Peabody, W. Rodman. 1905. "Direct Legislation." *Political Science Quarterly* 20:443–55.

Pease, L. 1907. "Initiative and Referendum." *Pacific Monthly* 17:563.

Piele, Philip, and John Stuart Hall. 1973. *Budgets, Bonds and Ballots: Voting Behavior in School Finance Elections*. Lexington, MA: D. C. Heath.

Peltzman, Sam. 1987. "Economic Conditions and Gubernatorial Elections." *American Economic Review* 77:293–97.

Peterson, L. 1986. "Call These Political Persuaders: The Wizards of Cause." *Golden State Report* (July): 16–23.

Pindyck, Robert, and Daniel Rubinfeld. 1981. *Economic Models and Economic Forecasts*. New York: McGraw Hill.

Popkin, Samuel L. 1991. *The Reasoning Voter: Communication and Persuasion in Presidential Campaigns*. Chicago: University of Chicago Press.

Price, Charles. 1975. "The Initiative: A Comparative State Analysis and a Reassessment of a Western Phenomena." *Western Political Quarterly* 28(2): 243–62.

Price, Charles. 1988. "Initiative Campaigns: Afloat on a Sea of Cash." *California Journal* 19:481–86.

Price, Charles. 1992. "Signing for Fun and Profit." *California Journal* 23:545–49.

Price, Charles, and Ed Baccioco. 1990. "Term Limits: Is This a Far, Far Better Thing than We Have Ever Done Before?" *California Journal* 21:497–99.

Pritchell, R. 1958. "The Influence of Professional Campaign Management Firms in Partisan Elections in California." *Western Political Quarterly* 11(2): 278–300.

Quattrone, G., and A. Tversky. 1988. "Contrasting Rational and Psychological Analyses of Political Choice." *American Political Science Review* 82:719–36.

Rapaport, Richard. 1989. "In the beginning . . . A History of California Political Consulting." *California Journal* 20:418–24.

Raymond, Paul B. 1987. "Shaping the News: An Analysis of House Candidates' Campaign Communications." In Jan Pons Vermeer, ed., *Campaigns in the News.* New York: Greenwood.

Reed, Robert, and D. Eric Schansberg. 1995. "The House Under Term Limits: What Would It Look Like?" *Social Science Quarterly* 76:699–716.

Renisch, P. 1912. "The Initiative and Referendum." *Political Science Quarterly* 27:155–61.

Roper Center Review of Public Opinion and Polling. 1993. "Term Limits." *Public Perspective* 4, no. 2: 97.

Rosenbaum, W. A., and J. W. Button. 1989. "Is There a Gray Peril?: Retirement Politics in Florida." *Gerontologist* 29:300–306.

Rubinfeld, D. L. 1977. "Voting in a Local School Election: A Micro-level Analysis." *Review of Economics and Statistics* 59:30–42.

Samish, A., and B. Thomas. 1971. *The Secret Boss of California.* New York: Crown.

Sanborn, J. B. 1908. "Popular Legislation in the U.S." *Political Science Quarterly* 12:587–603.

Schmidt, David. 1983. "INR Campaign Spending Study." *Initiative News Report* 2:1–5.

Schmidt, David. 1989. *Citizen Lawmakers: The Ballot Initiative Revolution.* Philadelphia: Temple University Press.

Schneider, Edward, and Bertram Gross. 1993. *Congress Today.* New York: St. Martin's.

Schrag, Peter. 1994. "California's Elected Anarchy: A Government Destroyed by Popular Referendum." *Harpers,* November, pp. 50–59.

Schroeder, Larry D., and David Sjoquist. 1978. "The Rational Voter: An Analysis of Two Atlanta Referenda on Rapid Transit." *Public Choice* 33:27–44.

Schumacher, Waldo. 1932. "Thirty Years of the People's Rule in Oregon." *Political Science Quarterly* 46:242–58.

Schuman, David. 1994. "The Origin of State Constitutional Direct Democracy: William Simon U'Ren and 'The Oregon System.'" *Temple Law Review* 67:947–63.

Schumpeter, Joseph. 1942. *Capitalism, Socialism and Democracy.* New York: Harper and Row.

Scott Stanley, and Harriet Nathan. 1970. "Public Referenda: A Critical Reappraisal." *Urban Affairs Quarterly* 5(3): 313–28.

Scott, Steve. 1993. "Proposition 170: Swamped by the Lingering Tax Revolt." *California Journal* 24 (December): 20.

Sears, David O. 1993. "Symbolic Politics: A Socio-Psychological Theory." In S. Iyengar and W. McGuire, eds., *Explorations in Political Psychology,* 113–49. Durham, NC: Duke University Press.

Sears, David O., and Jack Citrin. 1982. *Tax Revolt: Something for Nothing in California.* Cambridge: Harvard University Press.

Sears, David O., and C. Funk. 1990. "Self-Interest in Americans' Political Opinions." In J. J. Mansbridge, ed., *Beyond Self-Interest.* Chicago: University of Chicago Press.

Sears, David O., and C. Funk. 1991. "The Role of Self Interest in Social and Political Attitudes. In M. Zanna, ed., *Advances in Experimental Social Psychology.* Vol. 24. Orlando, FL: Academic Press.

Sears, David O., C. Hensler, and L. Speer. 1979. "White Opposition to Busing: Self-Interest or Symbolic Politics?" *American Political Science Review* 73:369–84.

Sears, David O., Richard Lau, Tom Tyler, and Harris Allen. 1980. "Self-Interest Versus Symbolic Politics in Policy Attitudes and Presidential Voting." *American Political Science Review* 74:670–84.

Selten, R. 1990. "Bounded Rationality." *Journal of Institutional and Theoretical Economics* 146:649–58.

Shockely, John. 1980. "The Initiative Process in Colorado Politics: An Assessment." Boulder: Bureau of Governmental Research, University of Colorado.

Simon, Herbert. 1955. "A Behavioral Model of Rational Choice." *Quarterly Journal of Economics* 69:99–118.

Simon, Herbert. 1959. *Models of Man.* New York: Wiley.

Simon, Herbert. 1985. "Human Nature in Politics: The Dialogue of Psychology with Political Science." *American Political Science Review* 79, no. 2: 293–304.

Smith, Eric R. A. N. 1989. *The Unchanging American Voter.* Berkeley and Los Angeles: University of California Press.

Sniderman, Paul. 1993. "The New Look in Public Opinion Research." In A. Finifter, ed., *Political Science: The State of the Discipline II.* Washington, DC: American Political Science Association.

Sniderman, Paul, Richard Brody, and Philip Tetlock. 1991. *Reasoning and Choice: Explorations in Political Psychology.* Cambridge: Cambridge University Press.

Soutwell, Priscilla. 1995. "Throwing the Rascals Out versus Throwing in the Towel: Alienation, Support for Term Limits and Congressional Voting. *Social Science Quarterly* 76:741–48.

Squire, Peverill. 1993. "Professionalization and Public Opinion of State Legislatures." *Journal of Politics* 55:479–91.

Stanley, John. 1969. "Majority Tyranny in Tocqueville's America: The Failure of Negro Suffrage in 1846." *Political Science Quarterly* 84(3): 412–35.

Starkey, D. 1993. "Proposition 172: Voters Approve Sales Tax Extension." *California Journal* 24 (December): 20–21.

Steel, B. S., and N. P. Lovrich. 1993. "Causes and Consequences of Public Knowledge Concerning State and Local Taxes: An Oregon and Washington Case Study." Paper presented at the annual meeting of the Western Political Science Association meeting, Pasadena, CA, 25–27 March.

Stein, Robert. 1990. "Economic Voting for Governor and U.S. Senator." *Journal of Politics* 51:29–53.

Stewart, Charles III, and Mark Reynolds. 1990. "Television Markets and U.S. Senate Elections." *Legislative Studies Quarterly* 15:495–524.

Stone, C. 1965. "Local Referendums: An Alternative to the Alienated Voter Model." *Public Opinion Quarterly* 29:213–22.

Sutro, Stephen. 1994. "Interpretations of Initiatives" *Santa Clara Law Review* 34:945–76.

Taebel, Delbert A. 1975. "The Effects of Ballot Position on Electoral Success." *American Journal of Political Science* 19:519–26.

Tedin, Kent. 1994. "Self-Interest, Symbolic Values and the Financial Equalization of the Public Schools." *Journal of Politics* 56:601–27.

Tedin, Kent, and Richard Murray. 1981. "Dynamics of Candidate Choice in a State Election." *Journal of Politics* 43:435–55.

Tempelton, Frederic. 1966. "Alienation and Political Participation: Some Research Findings." *Public Opinion Quarterly* 30:249–61.

Thatcher, G. 1908. "The Initiative, Referendum and Popular Election of Senators in Oregon." *American Political Science Review* 4:601–4.

Tietz, R. 1990. "On Bounded Rationality: Experimental Work at the University of Frankfurt/Main." *Journal of Institutional and Theoretical Economics* 146:659–72.

Tolbert, Caroline. 1994. "Direct Democracy and State Governance Policies." Paper presented at the American Political Science Association Meetings New York, 31 Aug.–3 Sept.

Tolbert, Caroline. 1998. "Direct Democracy and State Governance Policies." In Shaun Bowler, Todd Donovan, and Caroline Tolbert, eds., *Citizens as Legislators: Direct Democracy in the American States.* Columbus: Ohio State University Press.

Tufte, Edward. 1978. *Political Control of the Economy.* Princeton, NJ: Princeton University Press.

Tversky, A., S. Sattah, and P. Slovic. 1988. "Contingent Weighting in Judgment and Choice." *Psychological Review* 95:364–74.

Wall, Kent D. 1993. "A Model of Decision Making under Bounded Rationality." *Journal of Economic Behavior and Organization* 20, no. 3 (April): 331–52.

Warner, Daniel M. 1995. "Direct Democracy: The Right of the People to Make Fools of Themselves." *Seattle University Law Review* 19:47–100.

Weingast, Barry. 1994. "Reflections on Distributive Politics and Universalism." *Political Research Quarterly* 47:319–28.

Will, G. 1992. *Restoration: Congress, Term Limits and the Recovery of Deliberative Democracy.* New York: Free Press.

Williams, Liv. 1994. "The June Ballot Propositions." *California Journal* 35:43–47.

Wilson, James Q., and Edward C. Banfield. 1963. *City Politics.* Cambridge: Harvard University Press.

Wilson, James Q., and Edward C. Banfield. 1964. "Public Regardingness as a Value Premise in Voting Behavior." *American Political Science Review* 58:876–87.

Wilson, James Q., and Edward C. Banfield. 1971. "Political Ethos Revisited." *American Political Science Review* 65:1048–63.

Wolfinger, Raymond, and Fred Greenstein. 1968. "The Repeal of Fair Housing in California: An Analysis of Referendum Voting." *American Political Science Review* 2:753–69.

Wolfinger, Raymond, and Steven Rosenstone. 1980. *Who Votes?* New Haven, CT: Yale University Press.

Zaller, John. 1989. "Bringing Converse Back In: Information Flow in Political Campaigns." *Political Analysis* 1:181–234.

Zaller, John. 1990. "Political Awareness: Elite Opinion Leadership and the Mass Survey." *Social Cognition* 8:125–53.

Zaller, John. 1992. *The Nature and Origins of Mass Opinion.* Cambridge: Cambridge University Press.

Zax, Jeffrey. 1989. "Initiatives and Government Expenditures." *Public Choice* 63:267–77.

Zisk, Betty. 1987. *Money, Media and the Grassroots: State Ballot Issues and the Electoral Process.* Newbury Park, CA: Sage Publications.

Index